PRACTICAL CAT MANAGEMENT

PRACTICAL CAT MANAGEMENT

G. N. Officer

Pelham Books

To Elmsworth

First published in Great Britain by
Pelham Books Ltd
27 Wrights Lane
Kensington
London W8 5TZ

Copyright © G. N. Officer 1987

British Library Cataloguing in Publication Data
Officer, Grace N.
    Practical cat management.
    1. Cats
    I. Title
    636.8′083   SF447

ISBN 0 7207 1739 6

Printed and bound in Great Britain by
Butler and Tanner, Frome, Somerset

Contents

ACKNOWLEDGMENTS

My sincere thanks to the following, who have helped me write this
book: my vets, without whose knowledge, expertise and infinite
patience, it would not have been written; the Cats Protection League;
the Cornell Feline Health Center, USA; VetHealth; Lever Industrial;
Andrew Macvean, ARICS, for diagrams of units and planning
considerations for catteries; Dave Smith for photographic advice; all
my cat-loving friends who have, knowingly or unknowingly, provided
invaluable information; my cats.

Foreword

A wealth of contradictory advice on cat care appears regularly in books and other media. This confusion arises because the average or typical cat is a non-existent animal. A method of restraining, treating, feeding or managing one cat may be totally unacceptable to ninety-nine others! A piece of equipment or a lifestyle may prove idyllic for one cat, but anathema to another. Cats respond in different ways to each other, to situations, to stress and to illness, and, to complicate the issue further, they do not think, behave or react to events as we do. Many writers have grappled with feline psychology, but I have not even tried! In my opinion, mere humans cannot hope to understand what goes on in the mind of a cat. No explanation of feline behaviour, based on human experience and values and expressed in human language, is possible. We must simply accept our cats' eccentricities and recognize and respect those differences between individual cats, and between them and us. This is the essence of their fascination and mystery which has intrigued humans for centuries.

Practical Cat Management, therefore, is about alternatives – grass-roots cat care based on the fact that cats have a wide range of vocal and body language which can be learnt by humans, like any other language. Owners have to be guided by the cat regarding equipment, routine, accommodation, diet, and so on. Cats quickly indicate what is best for them. Many one-cat owners soon acquire a second cat, and possibly many more. It is important to accept that, whilst a first cat may be a quiet, home-loving, non-hunting lap animal, a second may be an out-in-all-weathers, independent, roaming, hunting cat!

It is generally accepted that cats are the most difficult animals to restrain and treat – some can even be dangerous. Unless we can handle our cats firmly, confidently and without fear of them, even the simplest treatments mean a visit to the vet and there will be little we can do when faced with a life-threatening emergency.

Vets are the only reliable sources of up-to-date information. Although their opinions and treatments differ in some respects, their knowledge, expertise and experience vastly exceed that of any lay person. But educating cat owners takes time, and cannot be regarded as part of a vet's function. It is up to us to acquire background knowledge, so that we know what questions to ask and stand some chance of understanding the answers. This book, I hope, will provide some background information, acquired over nearly twenty years of cat ownership. I have tried to answer 'How?' and 'Why?', and to help cat owners recognize dangers and anticipate problems so that, if they cannot be avoided, at least they can be met halfway.

A glance through the detailed Contents list will, I hope, prove that this book contains many items of interest to all cat owners, whether they own one cat or 100! Many chapters are complete in themselves and useful for the odd few minutes' browse. In general, however, this is not a book to be skimmed through over a cup of tea: it is intended for long-term reading and reference.

Many cat lovers may wish to run a boarding/breeding or rescue cattery at some later date, or, at least, want to know how a good cattery should be run and what questions to ask when choosing a boarding cattery for their own animals. Chapter 8 contains information on planning, construction and management of catteries.

Cat care is an on-going, constantly changing subject, as research workers probe deeper and deeper into the mysteries of disease and its prevention. Your vet will be aware of most recent developments in this field.

Grey areas in cat care still remain, however. The theories and opinions expressed in this book are my own and do not necessarily conform to any of those held by persons or organizations listed in the Acknowledgments.

G. N. Officer
August 1986

1 Introducing Cats

Under feral (wild) conditions cats live in small, loosely knit communities, each animal owning a personal territory of 1–5 acres (about ½–2 hectares), some of which may contain, or overlap, the personal territory of another cat. A tom's territory is larger than a queen's, and he will visit territories of neighbouring toms (resulting in many fights over territory and queens) in order to sire as many kittens as possible. Thus each community may consist of a sexually-active tom, several queens, kittens and often non-sexually-active young cats of both sexes, born the previous year. Young males will eventually leave their community to set up their own domains, often driving off other, less successful, young males. Throughout his lifetime, a tom is constantly threatened by younger toms, trying to gain ascendancy and effect a takeover of his queens. Eventually, as a tom ages, he will lose his battles and be replaced. Here the natural law of the survival of the fittest operates. The strongest and most successful tom sires the most kittens, many of whom will inherit his strength and fighting prowess.

Far fewer kittens are born to feral cats as a result of the restraints of a limited food supply and lack of veterinary attention. Those that survive common infectious diseases may be killed by predators of kittens like farm dogs, foxes with cubs to feed, or owls. Cats enjoying human welfare in domestic houses, and those living in colonies and fed by humans in towns and in the country, on farms, in the grounds of hospitals and in warehouses, usually become sexually mature earlier and breed faster.

The normally de-sexed domestic cat travels in a radius of about 220 yards (200 metres), generally eschewing busy through-roads, but this cannot be assumed. Some de-sexed domestic cats travel up to 1¼ miles (2 kilometres), and if they have no fear of main roads, cars or hostile humans, their life expectancy may be short. It should be remembered that, in the case of cats, domestication is only a thin veneer, and if domestic conditions become untenable for them, or they are moved away from their beloved environments, anti-social behaviour towards humans, unacceptable habits or a departure back to the wild may be their only options.

The average one- or two-cat domestic households can be considered normal low-density environments, comparable to that of the feral cat. But when the cat density is artificially high, as occurs in multicat households, in boarding and breeding catteries, among communally housed rescued cats and those living permanently in sanctuaries, the animals will suffer from symptoms of stress (called 'the stress syndrome') because they are living in what are, to them, overcrowded conditions. Most cats are only too glad to accept warmth, shelter and regular food, but there will be a few who simply will not integrate because of their natural aggression towards or undue fear of domiciled cats, and these may have to be housed separately or taken back to the wild and fed. Stress has various symptoms: it may cause territorial fighting (even in de-sexed cats), spraying (possibly in a human house), diminished appetite, diarrhoea, vomiting or unacceptable aggression towards other felines or humans.

Far greater dangers operate in the case of holiday-boarded cats or those exhibited at shows. Their lifestyle changes completely; their normal routine is disrupted; they are plunged into unfamiliar environments, among unknown and potentially hostile cats, humans and, in some boarding establishments, dogs. Whilst the usual multicat household progresses gradually from one to many, giving domiciled cats time to adjust to increased numbers, a boarded or exhibited animal is plunged in at the deep end. When subjected to stress, a cat is more liable to infection, particularly one to which he has not previously been exposed. This risk is especially high in the case of boarded or exhibited cats brought together from many parts of the country.

Healthy, well-fed, unstressed animals have a natural resistance to all infections, but once they have been exposed to a particular one it is rarely shed completely. Inactive forms remain in the cat which, again, tend to activate under stress. This is a very important consideration when a domestic cat goes missing from home, and when you take in such an ex-domestic cat after rescue. (Such a cat, which is often simply lost and unable to find its way back home, is called a 'stray'.) All cattery owners, or friends looking after cats while their owner is on holiday, will be aware that animals apparently healthy on admission can rapidly develop symptoms of, for example, cat flu or ear mites. This is due to a lowering of immunity caused by stress. Animal rescue organizations, and individuals who adopt local strays, know that cats living rough on unsuitable waste food will probably be weakened by heavy parasitization and liable to suffer from previously contracted infections which normally they could combat.

Why is it that a seemingly healthy cat can spend a wet day watching a molehill, or a night out in bad weather, and next day succumb to cystitis? It is because the chill has depressed the cat's immunity. This happens to humans too, of course: fatigue and chill may cause a depression of the immune system and soon they are in the throes of a streaming cold!

To contract an infection a cat does not *have* to come into contact with another actively infected feline, although this greatly increases the risk. Infections are in the air, on soil, on garden plants used as sleeping areas; they may already be dormant in the cat. This book is concerned with helping the cat owner to recognize and so minimize the risk of infection whether his or her house contains one cat or many. Disinfection is the key to success wherever more than one cat is present. This does not mean total elimination of all infections from the environment – such an aim would be totally unrealistic – but a reduction of the concentration of infections; avoiding prolonged close contact with infected cats; keeping your cat apart from neighbours' if it is infected; and, in the case of a rescue centre or cattery, housing

FIGURE 1   Cats prefer to roam free when it is safe for them to do so.

cats in hygienic, well-spaced, separate accommodation units. It means reducing, or eliminating from an indoor environment, travelling insects – for example, flies, lice, fleas, wasps, moths, mites and ticks – which can carry infections from cat to cat.

Our well-loved domestic cats can be protected from many infections by the provision of a safe, warm environment, with as high-quality food as we can afford, and prompt veterinary attention when needed. Cats prefer to roam free and should be allowed to where it is safe for them to do so, or they should be confined in large, enclosed gardens. They prefer a stable, routined environment with no moves to unfamiliar territory. They need familiar humans forever on red-alert standby to provide food and entertainment when required. Fresh air, free from smoke or factory fumes, and exposure to *direct* sunlight, are vital.

Domestic cats expect from humans what my vet calls 'TLC' – tender, loving care! Humans have to learn to expect *nothing* in return from their cats: these animals will not put themselves out to please any human, although some give a little of themselves – when it suits them!

2 Nutrition

Good food is an investment. By feeding the best possible food you can afford, you will not only save on vets' bills, but save yourself endless work clearing up vomit and replacing toilet-tray filler because of diarrhoea. Whilst some cats can exist solely on artificial canned catfoods, to others these are anathema. For most cat owners a mixture of both types of cat food is probably the most convenient.

Before any consideration can be given to feline diets, it is essential to dispel any ideas concerning what is good or bad food from a human point of view. A cat is a carnivore (meat eater); his natural

FIGURE 2   A feline food consultancy panel.

food is the raw carcase of a prey animal, consisting of muscle, fat, offal, gristle, skin, bone, vitamins, minerals and water. A cat is adapted to catching, killing, tearing up, tenderizing and digesting *raw* prey. Humans by contrast are primarily vegetable, fruit and nut eaters: their bodies and teeth are in no way adapted to catching and eating meat. Only the intelligent use of weaponry brought about the inclusion of meat in human diets.

Many kinds of bacteria, harmless and potentially harmful, are present in raw meat. *E. coli* and *Salmonella* bacteria are far more dangerous to humans than to cats. Carnivores have short guts relative to their size and digest food rapidly – conditions in which bacteria have little chance to multiply and thus enter puncture wounds in the gut in large numbers. Carbohydrate (plant-derived food) used in many artificial catfoods and human canned meats requires slow digestion and is not an efficient energy source for most cats.

Research has shown that cats thrive on a diet consisting of raw meat, with an approximate analysis of 15 per cent fat, 25 per cent protein and 60 per cent water, but active young cats, thin cats, pregnant and lactating queens and kittens need extra fat – as much as 20 per cent. A normal human diet consists of about 6 per cent fat, 8 per cent protein, 11 per cent carbohydrate and 75 per cent water. All animal fat contains a substance called cholesterol, derivatives of which deposit in human arteries, causing 'hardening'. But cats do not suffer from hardening of the arteries and high blood pressure due to cholesterol! They thrive on fat, in moderation. Thus the fat that humans cut from their chops and joints of meat will increase the food value *and* palatability of catfood. It is a mistake to feed cats only lean cuts of meat.

Kittens and young cats can exist on unsuitable foods if they are strays and unable to hunt. But by the time they are about two or three years old, strays are usually in a very poor condition; if they are lucky, at this point they are rescued. An old stray is a rarity. In kittens a mild respiratory or gut infection can reduce the appetite and arrest growth. Kittens who can carry on eating regardless are most likely to survive.

If a queen's diet is inadequate, this has an effect on the quality of her milk, and in such a case milk production will result in withdrawal of body fat, protein, bone, vitamins and minerals from the queen's body. The effect of this can be seen in the often appalling condition of stray queens with kittens. Persistent production of one or two kittens (instead of three to six) may occur in the wild as an indication of dietary deficiencies, and may also be witnessed in breeding catteries with the same cause, or as a result of underlying virus infections in the queens.

Every animal must receive his natural food in order to thrive, in contrast to merely existing. We do not know what 'wild' man eats, but we do know what wild cats – large and small – eat. Our aim is to provide food for our domestic cats as near as possible to that preferred by their wild relatives from the point of view of composition, texture, odour, flavour and temperature. The right temperature is blood heat (as when prey is freshly killed) or room temperature. Research has indicated that growth and reproduction of cats fed on raw meat is higher than that of cats fed on cooked meat or artificial catfood. Cats fed exclusively on low-quality canned foods have been known to leave home to live in the wild on prey and to have gained weight; and the cat who has left home to live with another human offering fresh rabbit is certainly not unknown!

As already explained, raw meat presents problems. First, because we are neither able nor would wish to catch voles, mice and birds in sufficient numbers to supply our cats with the quantity of raw meat they require, we give them instead the meat of *human* prey animals (pigs, horses, sheep, cows, fish, poultry) which are readily available. Second, only meat sold for *human* consumption is safe to serve raw to cats, with the exception of rabbit, poultry and fish, which should normally be cooked.

The 'typical' cat does not exist, particularly where food preferences are concerned. An ideal diet for one cat may be anathema to another. Symptoms of a deficient diet include: thin, dry coat, constant moulting, vomiting and diarrhoea. Some cats cannot use *any* carbohydrate food and must have only fresh white meat (rabbit, chicken and fish). It cannot be assumed that an ideal diet for a young cat will remain ideal all his life. A pregnant queen will need increasing quantities of food, plus a vitamin/mineral supplement, but she should not be allowed to grow too fat for difficult births may occur in an obese queen. A lactating queen feeding three to six kittens needs three or four times her normal food quota. Kittens require extra fat, and up to twice the amount of food an adult needs when they are over about four months old. At over six months old a kitten may suddenly become intolerant to cow's milk and suffer diarrhoea. A middle-aged cat (about seven years old) may eat less because of inactivity. De-sexed cats become obese only if they are overfed. In cases of chronic nephritis, the commonest cause of natural death in old cats, a change to white meats may be advisable. An old cat may need again the small, frequent, easily digested meals of kittenhood.

Domestic cats may enjoy hunting, but may not consume their prey: because humans have removed the spectre of hunger, hunting for pleasure is possible. Big cats hunt antelopes, deer, sheep, zebras – and humans if available! Small cats hunt mice, voles, rats, rabbits, pigeons, smaller birds, frogs, slow-worms, lizards, beetles, grasshoppers, flies and worms. Squirrels, moles and shrews are killed, but rarely consumed. Cats are predators, carrion eaters and scavengers. Free-roamers will enjoy fighting over the privilege of consuming rotting meat and bones from refuse bags, or mouldy bread and currant cake from birdtables, however well fed they are. In natural foods the animal-derived protein, fat, vitamins, minerals, water and animal roughage (skin, bone, fur, feathers) are all there, in the correct proportions. No one knows exactly what a cat's dietary requirements are – we can only simulate a natural diet by providing food of the right kind and in large variety. In this way a cat cannot avoid obtaining all his body needs.

THE COMPOSITION OF FOOD

FATS

Sometimes called 'lipids', these are broken down on digestion into fine particles consisting of glycerol and fatty acids. The most important fatty acids are: linoleic acid (sometimes called vitamin F), linolenic acid and arachidonic acid. Fat is a constituent of all animal cells. It is stored as reserve fat under the skin and surrounding and protecting some internal organs (for example, kidneys and heart).

Fat is a high-energy food, providing over twice the calories of protein or carbohydrate. In addition it provides a transport system, in the blood, for vital fat-soluble substances: the fat-soluble hormones (for instance, the sex hormones); vitamins A, D, E, K, choline and inositol.

Only fresh, raw, animal fat contains the above-named vitamins. Vitamin content is considerably reduced by ageing, canning and cooking. Fish oil becomes rancid on storage and interacts with other constituents of food. Vitamin E, a fat preservative, is added to artificial canned catfoods high in oily fish. Rancid oils can cause a serious disease in cats, in which the fat in the abdomen and around the shoulder blades turns hard and yellow: this is called steatitis, or yellow-fat disease. Because of this storage difficulty, and because animal fat is expensive and tends to make food look unappetizing (to humans), all artificial catfoods (particularly dry catfoods) are far too low in fat, and, if used for kittens, must be supplemented by chopped fat. Cats do not mind what a food looks like!

The fat-soluble carotene, from plants, which many animals use to manufacture vitamin A, cannot be utilized by cats, who must obtain vitamin A from milk fat, liver fat and other animal fats.

PROTEIN

This is the main constituent of all animal cells. Proteins are complex chemical compounds of nitrogen, carbon, oxygen and hydrogen, combined with various metals and non-metals: for example, the oxygen-carrying blood protein called haemoglobin contains iron. The sub-units of digested protein are called amino acids. These are sometimes referred to as the body's 'building bricks' because amino acids from meat protein are used to build up the right kind of proteins required by cats. There are about twenty-five known amino acids, but only about ten, present in meat-derived protein, can be utilized by cats. Examples of meat-derived amino acids are: tryptophan, taurine, glycine, phenylalanine and lysine. A deficiency of taurine will cause gradual loss of vision.

All cats need some meat protein as an energy source, in addition to dietary animal fat, although some can utilize carbohydrate for part of their energy requirement. Since protein is the main constituent of *all* types of body cells, it follows that kittens need even more protein than adults for growth. All cats, therefore, require amino acids: to make skin, muscle, internal organs, protein antibody, blood cells, enzymes (aids to food digestion), hormones, fur, bone, claws, blood vessels; to provide energy and to replace damaged tissue – in fact for everything! Protein, unlike fat, cannot be stored. A daily supply is essential. Excess protein is converted into urea by the liver and excreted by the kidneys as urine. In cases of starvation, the use of body protein is a last resort, and self-destruction takes place.

Since the whole of an animal's body consists mainly of protein, it follows that the cat can, theoretically, use the entire prey body as a source of protein. But some protein sources are of lower value to the cat than others. Connective tissue, feathers and hair, although providing amino acids, do not promote growth an efficiently as, say, muscle, liver or kidney. Much of the meat used in artificial catfoods consists of meat not used for human consumption like gristle, connective tissue and blood vessels, and this accounts for the low nutritional value of some of these canned foods.

Fish and poultry are part of a wild cat's diet. Egg protein contains all the amino acids essential to cats, except that it is low in taurine.

Lack of protein from meat, poultry or seafood results in low resistance to infections, slow healing, poor growth, impaired vision, thin coat, heavy moulting, lethargy – in fact all the symptoms of ill health.

CARBOHYDRATES

These are mainly of plant origin. A carbohydrate known as animal starch (or glycogen) is made by the cat from glucose and stored in the liver. Carbohydrates can be grouped under three headings: sugars, starches and cellulose. Cats make glucose from amino acids. A queen's milk contains an animal carbohydrate called lactose (or milk sugar). Lactose can only be considered a natural food for cats up to weaning (at about three weeks in domestic kittens). But in the wild, kittens may not be fully weaned for six months, so young cats up to six months old can use cow's milk. After that age, however, many cats become intolerant to lactose, which results in diarrhoea. Milk may have to be reduced or eliminated from the diet. Cow's milk can cause diarrhoea at *any* age, and is often the main cause. Certain canned catfoods which contain whey, high in lactose, should be avoided if your cat is intolerant of it.

Cellulose is the constituent of cell walls in plants and cannot be digested, raw or cooked, by cats. It is a gut irritant, which is why cats regularly eat couch grass and other grasses, for these act as emetics and laxatives, ridding the stomach or gut of fur or animal roughage by causing vomiting or defecation. All foods which are wholly or partially plant-derived – such as artificial catfoods, breakfast cereals and vegetables – contain cellulose and this could account for vomiting and diarrhoea in some cats. Such foods may have to be withdrawn from the diet.

Cats rarely eat food containing sugar, like cakes and fruit, but manufacture glucose as an energy source. Glucose is used in queen's milk substitutes and given intravenously in cases of starvation, or when solid food cannot be taken. A glucose solution fed a few drops at a time by means of a dropper bottle or Brunswick syringe will keep a non-eating cat going in the short term.

Occasionally cats eat catnip, catmint and leaves of other garden plants, but usually these are simply bitten off and spat out. Their value is unclear, since they do not cause vomiting. Cats cannot digest *any* raw starch in vegetables (green or root) or raw cereals. Even cooked starch (especially in potato) can cause diarrhoea or vomiting. Cats' saliva contains no ptyalin, an enzyme plant eaters produce which begins starch digestion in the mouth. Cats cannot chew: their molars can only spike meat and tenderize it. Carbohydrates take much longer to digest than protein and fat, and since food travels fast along a cat's gut (some unsuitable foods pass through practically unchanged!) not all starch can be digested. A raised amount of fat in the diet will have the effect of slowing down digestion and possibly increasing starch utilization.

Provided vegetables and cereals comprise no more than a quarter of the bulk of a meal, they can be an economic energy source. Any vegetables· (except possibly potato) or cereals can be used, but they must be *cooked*. If whole seeds such as sweet corn or peas are used, they must be chopped or mashed, since cats cannot digest the cellulose seed coat covering them. Some cats are allergic to wheat protein (gluten).

VITAMINS
The healthy cat makes many of his own vitamins. Strictly speaking, they should not be so termed unless obtained from food, but are thus referred to for convenience. Daily supplies are essential, for the body cannot store vitamins. Vitamin supplements can be dangerous to *healthy* cats and should be used only in certain cases (see page 33).

All vitamins are gradually destroyed by heating at temperatures of 212°F (100°C) and over – the amount lost depends on the length of cooking time.

Very high amounts of vitamin pre-mixes are therefore added to artificial foods, to ensure that some remain after sterilization. Because gradual loss of vitamins occurs as a result of ageing (this occurs in fresh food too), vitamin content in canned food is guaranteed for only one year.

Although much research has been done into the vitamin requirements of both cats and dogs, a fair amount of uncertainty still surrounds the subject, and the best way to ensure that a cat receives the right amounts is to feed as many different kinds of raw meat and offals as possible – remember that most essential vitamins are destroyed by cooking. Cow's milk is also an excellent source of most vitamins, but in view of the problems milk can cause, some cat owners may decide to leave it out of the diet.

Vitamins may be assigned letters of the alphabet for identification, but all are chemical compounds, present in raw plant and animal foods. Vitamins from raw plant sources are not available to cats. Cats are unable to synthesise (make up within the body) vitamin A from carotene, nor can they synthesise niacin (a B vitamin) from the animal-derived amino acid called tryptophan. Niacin (and indeed all the B vitamins) are present, already manufactured, in raw, red meats.

Certain foods contain substances which destroy vitamins essential to cats. Raw egg white contains a substance called avidine, which inactivates an essential B vitamin called biotin. Thus egg albumen should nearly always be cooked when served to cats, whereas egg yolk can be served raw. Raw freshwater fish contains a substance called thiaminase, which destroys vitamin B_1 (thiamine) which cats make themselves.

A list is given below of known vitamins, essential to cats only in minute amounts. Cats do not need vitamin C or vitamin K (menaquinone). This list will help you to understand the analyses given on the labels of supplements and artificial foods.

Fat-soluble Vitamins

Vitamin A (retinol)
Vitamin D (cholecalciferol)
Choline

Vitamin E (tocopherol)
Vitamin F (linoleic acid)
Inositol

Water-soluble Vitamins

The B vitamins (some of which have numbers):

Vitamin B_1 (thiamine)
Vitamin B_2 (riboflavin)
Vitamin B_6 (pyridoxine)
Vitamin B_{12} (cyanocobalamin)

niacin (nicotinic acid)
pantothenic acid
folic acid
biotin (also called vitamin H)

Of the fat-soluble vitamins, only vitamin A is needed from a food source. The easiest way to ensure adequate vitamin A is to serve a dessertspoonful of chopped raw lamb's liver twice a week. Vitamin E is made by healthy cats. Liquid paraffin dissolves fat and must never be used routinely as a laxative, otherwise fat and fat-soluble vitamins will be lost via the faeces.

All the water-soluble B vitamins are abundant, and in the correct proportions, in raw meat, offals and blood. The gut flora are believed to manufacture thiamine. B vitamins are destroyed by sulphur dioxide. Marmite and other yeast extracts used as vitamin B supplements must not be cooked.

Vitamin C (ascorbic acid) is not important in cats. It is used medicinally as a urine acidifier and given for respiratory infections, but no beneficial effects in the latter case have been proved.

Indiscriminate use of supplements may result in symptoms of overdosage of vitamins and minerals. The following are a few examples of the dangers of overdosage of vitamins (hypervitaminosis).

Vitamins A and D are often given as halibut liver oil, but adult cats synthesise vitamin D on their skins, in the presence of direct sunlight (that is, *not* through glass). This spreads to the fur, and is licked off. If excess vitamin D is given and the diet also contains too much calcium, then, instead of calcium being voided in the faeces, it may be deposited as calcium salts in the kidneys, heart, lungs or major blood vessels. If there is too much vitamin D, but *too little* calcium, calcium will be withdrawn from the skeleton, resulting in fragile, easily broken, deformed bones, for vitamin D controls the calcium blood levels. Too much vitamin A (caused by serving too much liver, fat or supplement) will result in symptoms of poisoning – death of irreplaceable kidney cells, paralysis, convulsions (fits), unconsciousness and even death. All the symptoms of ill health will be present if there is long-term deficiency or long-term overdosage of any vitamin.

MINERALS

The most important minerals to cats are: sodium, potassium, calcium, phosphorus, magnesium, iron and iodine. Minerals occur naturally in rocks, and therefore soil. They are combined in simple chemical compounds, like sodium chloride (salt) and calcium carbonate (chalk). They dissolve in water, and are absorbed by the roots of plants. Herbivores eat plants, and cats eat herbivores!

Minerals are not destroyed by cooking, canning or ageing. They are present in all plant and animal foods, raw or cooked. Bone is a useful source but, because of their potential danger, bones are not normally given to domestic cats unless they are finely chopped or soft. However, all cats can extract unwanted or dangerous bones from food and leave them neatly on the plate. Approximately 50 per cent of bone consists of a compound of calcium and phosphorus (called calcium phosphate) and 50 per cent of protein. So the much-relished dustin and birdtable bones are eaten mainly as a protein source by adult, non-breeding cats, who need very little calcium phosphate for growing bones and teeth, or to form the skeleton of an unborn foetus, or to provide calcium and phosphorus in queens' milk.

When a canned catfood is burnt, only minerals remain. This is called ash. The ash figure, given on artificial catfoods and supplements is a measure of the kind of food used. Plant-derived foods such as vegetables and cereals are far higher in ash content than animal-derived foods, with the exception of bone. A diet high in plant-derived foods is called a high-ash diet. High-ash diets, such as artificial catfoods (canned, semi-moist, dry), ox-heart and fishbone, are high in magnesium, and these foods have been implicated in the formation of crystals in the urinary system, called struvite (magnesium ammonium phosphate). An all-meat diet with plenty of juices, but *no* supplements, seems the best insurance against the deposition of crystals in the bladder, a condition known as feline urolithiasis (see page 114). An all-meat diet results in an acid urine in which crystals are less likely to form.

All animal milks (cat's, cow's, goat's) are high in minerals, but should not be regarded as normal foods (or drinks) for healthy adult cats.

Minerals are absorbed from food in the gut, according to need, but calcium absorption, and possibly absorption of other minerals, varies. Pregnant and lactating queens and growing kittens may absorb 80 per cent of their calcium requirement from food, whereas an adult male may absorb only 30 per cent of his dietary calcium. Siamese cats are more liable to calcium deficiency due to low gut absorption levels. Minerals absorbed in the gut, excess to needs, are excreted by the kidneys.

Sodium chloride (salt) is a mineral occurring naturally in food. A slight artificial salting of food is used to encourage cats susceptible to feline urolithiasis to drink more water.

All meat contains iron and potassium. Fish is a source of iodine, important to breeding queens.

BONE

In nature, cats eat varying quantities of bone according to need. Discarded bones are an important protein source for stray cats. The fact that most cats will refuse even pilchard bones suggests that adult, domestic, de-sexed felines need very little calcium. All meat, particularly muscle, contains phosphorus but is low in calcium, particularly meat which has been hung and therefore had most of its blood removed. But all pregnant and nursing queens, kittens and young cats need plenty of calcium, and in these cases supplements should be given. In view of the dangers of too much phosphorus, it is preferable to use calcium carbonate (chalk) rather than ground bone (calcium phosphate). Calcium carbonate (BP) is obtainable from chemists and very inexpensive. Cats acquire adult bone structure at about a year old, but bone is not a static organ for, even in adults, it is constantly being absorbed and remodelled.

WATER

Cats are desert-type animals, adapted to water conservation, and have been recorded as surviving for six weeks without water. Loss of water due to perspiration is limited to sweat glands situated on the pads only. The nose of a healthy cat is ice-cold, so that water vapour present in the air breathed out is condensed on the nose, licked by the tongue, and put back into circulation! The kidneys reclaim most of the water filtered into the kidney tubules. Thus urine is normally concentrated, which tends to favour crystal formation, particularly in lazy or housebound cats who do not keep up a good flow by spraying urine every few metres in the garden! The faeces of healthy cats are firm and sectioned, indicating maximum water absorption in the large intestine. A cat with persistent vomiting or diarrhoea, or one who cannot eat or drink, rapidly dehydrates and a vet may have to inject water. The more urea there is the blood, the more toxic it becomes, and any enforced lack of water, for whatever reason, will in the long term cause kidney damage.

It makes sense, in view of the dangers of concentrated urine, to ensure that our cats drink plenty of water. They drink little plain water, so water consumption cannot be left to chance or the water bowl left exposed to the air to gather dust, fur and, not the least, airborne and insect-borne infections. All tap water is treated with chlorine to sterilize it. By the time it reaches our houses, most of the chlorine will have become gaseous. Nevertheless, residual chlorine has been blamed for a cat's reluctance to drink plain water. On the other hand, the same cat may readily drink the same water if it is dripping into a sink or bath! This may be an ancestral trait, either because a cat knows instinctively that running water is safer than stagnant water, or because a cat's ancestors normally drank from running rivers or waterfalls. However, this does not explain why some cats prefer to drink rainwater, which is acid and, in some industrial areas, can dissolve toxic gases like sulphur dioxide. Most cats love the smell of chlorine given off by such products as household bleach and rub their heads on surfaces treated with it. Some cats will drink more readily from a bowl of water placed in a warm room, beside a fire, or from a puddle in the road!

We can only return, once more, to the wild cat. He will eat nearly all his prey, obtaining natural water from the body and blood of the prey. Unfortunately for cats, much blood is removed from meats intended for human consumption. Natural prey and canned catfoods contain 75–80 per cent water. When meat is cooked, some water is lost as steam, so extra water should be added to casseroles. It should

CATFOODS COMPARED

The following table shows approximate analyses of some commonly used catfoods – natural and artificial. Please also see the notes opposite.

CONTENT PER 100G (OR %)

	FAT (OIL)	PROTEIN	CARBOHYDRATE (NFE)	WATER (BY DIFFERENCE)	ASH	PLANT FIBRE
NATURAL FOODS						
Young rabbit	4g	14g	–	80g	less than 1g	–
Beef mince	22g	17g	–	60g	less than 1g	–
White fish	1g	17g	–	82g	less than 1g	–
Oily fish	18g	17g	–	65g	less than 1g	–
Chicken	18g	18g	–	64g	less than 1g	–
ARTIFICIAL FOODS						
Canned Whiskas	4g (oil)	9g	5g (est.)	79g	2.5g	0.4g
Canned Gourmet (all meat)	6.5g	12.5g	–	78g	3g	0.1g
Canned 9-Lives	4.5g (oil)	15g	5.5g (est.)	73g	1g	1g
Dry catfood	8g	30g	40g	12g	6g	4g
Semi-moist catfood	8g	27g	22g	34g	4g	3g
Puffed wheat	–	13g	69g	2g	–	15g
Puffed rice	1g	5g	85g	6g	–	2g
LIQUID FOODS						
Queen's milk	4.8g	9.5g (casein)	4.9g (lactose)	80g	less than 1g	–
Cow's milk	3.7g	3.4g (casein)	4.7g (lactose)	87g	less than 1g	–

be remembered that meat juices contain not only water, but also any vitamins remaining after cooking, minerals, fat and protein, and these should always be added back to meals. Some cats, presented with a meal plus juice, will expertly hook out the solid food and leave the juice; others will drink all juice first. Water can be soaked up with puffed wheat. Chicken juice, on cooling, will become jelly, which might prove more palatable.

QUANTITY OF FOOD REQUIRED

The amount of food required per day varies from cat to cat and will depend not only on the cat, but also upon the calorific value (or energy value) of the food. There are thin, active, non-hunting cats who can safely be allowed to eat all they want, unless they suffer from diarrhoea. There are frankly obese cats who make a way of life out of 'tum-filling', prowling around the neighbourhood convincing gullible humans that they are starving strays.

The higher the fat content of food, the higher the energy value. Plant fat (called 'oil') cannot be substituted for animal fat. Pure animal fat provides over twice the calories of protein or carbohydrate. About 3½ ounces (100 grams) of fat provides 898 calories; the same quantity of protein or carbohydrate provides 399 calories. But it should be remembered that few cats can utilize all the carbohydrate in a food, even in high-fat foods, and some cats cannot digest any.

Very approximately, it has been calculated that adult neuters and non-pregnant females require about 350 calories a day. Pregnant, lactating queens and kittens require around 500 calories a day.

The calorific value of a large can of catfood (405 grams) is about 335, whereas that of an equal weight of raw beef mince is 1,075!

The higher the calorific value of food, the *less* food will be required. Again, very approximately, an adult will need four heaped table-spoonfuls per day of beef mince, oily fish, chicken or offal, plus any associated animal fat; but eight heaped tablespoonfuls per day of low-fat foods like canned catfood, young rabbit and white fish. In view of the low water content of dried foods, they should only be used as toppings to extra juicy meals. High-carbohydrate foods should not comprise more than one quarter of the total volume of a meal. If chopped, raw animal fat is added to low-fat meats such as young rabbit and white fish, then, again, four heaped tablespoonfuls per day of this mixture should be sufficient. High-fat foods, like beef or lamb mince, old rabbit and chicken, can be 'diluted' with white fish or canned catfood. A good diet must be found by trial and error. As many varieties of food should be served as possible; raw can be mixed with cooked, artificial foods can be mixed with natural foods.

Because artificial catfoods are low-calorie foods, manufacturers sometimes state that cats are self-regulatory and can be allowed to eat all they want at each meal. Faced with that idyllic state of affairs, many cats would eat until they vomited!

Whatever diet is decided upon, it must be *balanced*. Wild cats eat most of their prey, including much of the bone, according to need. Some cats neatly extract the gut of their prey (often leaving it where humans are likely to tread on it!). This may be because the gut of herbivores contains plant-derived raw food which a cat cannot digest and which is a gut irritant. Most cats eat the liver of prey first, followed by other offal; they seem to sense instinctively that those parts are high in vitamins and minerals.

For the domestic cat the rule is that all lean meat, fat, bone, skin, blood vessels, and so on, should be served in the proportions in which they occur in the prey animal. A comparison of, say, the proportions of lean meat on a chicken to the size of its offal in the polythene bag, and an examination of the carcase of lamb in the butcher's shop beside lamb's kidneys, will help you to avoid the very common mistake of feeding cats entirely on heart, liver or kidney. You will also thus be made aware of the mistake of feeding choice (and expensive) lean cuts of beef, which are all protein, to pampered felines. Do not remove fat from kidneys or hearts before feeding, nor skin from fish. It is not suggested, however, that even butch, powerful-jawed tomcats could eat cowhide or want to eat chicken feathers, although these are a source of protein! Remember that individual meals do not always have to be balanced: cats enjoy one meal entirely of, say, kidney perhaps twice a week.

THE APPETITE

A cat's appetite is a barometer of his health. The healthy domestic cat begins to harass for a meal at least an hour before it is due. He will remain well within hearing range of the kitchen and know exactly when meal preparation begins. He will arrive promptly and consume all his food rapidly.

The wild cat hunts at dusk when the desert or jungle is cool. Since cat lovers and non-cat lovers often dislike cats catching birds, this tendency in the domestic feline could be overcome by keeping cats in during the day, when most will sleep, and allowing them out at dusk, when birds are inactive.

For the wild cat a 'kill' may be made every other day, or even less frequently. Cats may eat the entire prey, or they may bury the carcase and return to feed later. Thus cats are naturally occasional feeders. This accounts for the fact that domestic cats can often gorge on a much-favoured food and reject a less-favoured food for three days at no inconvenience to themselves. It is also how a domestic cat manages to convince a human that only lamb's heart will suffice. If a cat refuses one type of food, this should be offered at subsequent meals – it should be kept fresh in a refrigerator between meals (raw food may be stored thus for one day; canned or freshly cooked food for two days). If it is still not eaten, continue to offer food of the same type until the cat does eat it. This will avoid the emergence of the feline food faddist, who will suffer dietary deficiencies from consuming only one or two kinds of food. Genuine dislikes should be respected, of course: canned oily fish and even roast chicken are not universally liked. No healthy cat, however, has ever starved to death because he did not happen to fancy the food on offer!

Slow eating, or picking pieces of food out with the paw, usually mean that the cat is not hungry enough. But these can be the symptoms of the onset of an infection, mouth ulcers, decayed teeth, inflamed gums (gingivitis) or foreign matter (for instance, string or gristle) stuck in the mouth.

Often a disliked food can be 'disguised' by being mixed with a favoured one, thus ensuring that a wide variety of foods are accepted. Any foods can be chopped up and well mixed with others, but if *raw* foods are mixed with cooked, these meals should not be stored for longer than twelve hours as bacteria can grow in ageing, raw food. All raw food must be absolutely fresh or freshly defrosted. Cats will not eat stale, raw meat. A cooked food has a different texture and taste from the same food raw. Thus, although raw food is preferable from the point of view of nutritional value, cooking the same food may make it more palatable to some cats – raw meat can even cause vomiting in some cats. The natural texture of catfood, is, of course, the texture of raw meat.

Cats not only smell food, they can also *taste* the odour by means of a gland (called Jacobson's gland) inside their mouth, and can often be observed 'tasting' the odour of a hostile cat with open mouth! Heat always develops odour and may make a food more palatable to a non-eater. Meals served directly from a refrigerator, unless in very hot weather, are less palatable. Cats with respiratory infections may not eat simply because they cannot smell. To tempt them try mixing small amounts of strong-flavoured food (such as Marmite, Bovril, Oxo or other gravy cube, chopped grilled bacon plus drippings, sardines, fishpastes) with their normal food and then warming the result. Cats with sore throats need very soft, well-mashed, cooked foods, like white fish mashed with chicken liver. It may be necessary to put a little food in the mouth or on the lips before the cat will eat.

Two meals per day are usually served to domestic cats, but some cats eat only at dusk and may consume the whole day's ration at one sitting. Kittens need frequent, small meals. Pregnant and lactating cats, the old and the pampered and the delicate may require many small meals spread over the day, and some, dare I add, like to have a dish of food on view at all times! Some cats normally eat only once every other day, particularly during hot weather, when most have reduced appetites, for then less food is required as a heat source.

It is very important that cats receive the right amount of food for them, but the amount a cat needs, as opposed to the amount he will eat if given the chance, varies enormously. Size is no criterion: there are slim, miniscule cats who can eat mountains of food without gaining weight, vomiting or suffering diarrhoea; there are huge, flabby cats who maintain their weight, however much an owner tries to cut down their food. Wasted food means wasted money and disposal problems. In the case of unknown cats, or as an occasional experiment on familiar domiciled cats, it is a good plan to put an empty dish before each animal and serve spoonfuls of food from a large, pre-prepared quantity, noting the amount each cat consumes with speed and relish, and the point at which he slows down, or starts to pick pieces out, or use his paw. To gain an idea of what foods a boarded cat, newly acquired cat or rescued stray likes, serve tiny portions of a variety of foods on the same plate and note the order of preference in which these are consumed and which, if any, are not eaten. This is very useful when boarded cats refuse to eat the food advised by the owner!

Some cats refuse to eat in the presence of strangers and should be left to eat in complete privacy. On the other hand many domestic cats, when boarded, need stroking, rump patting or neck scratching, or a human presence during eating.

Fur and animal roughage collects in the stomach and is regurgitated periodically as a fur sausage. An impending fur sausage may cause a cat to appear hungry but, after a few mouthfuls, seem satiated. This may last for two days.

For owners of holiday boarding catteries, the cat who will not eat is a major problem. Loss of appetite is a stress symptom, which can lead to vitamin deficiency and a consequent high risk of succumbing to infection. Everything possible should be done to induce a cat to eat.

FOOD IN PRACTICE

The types of food and serving suggestions given below are primarily intended for adult, healthy, non-breeding, domestic cats. Special diets are dealt with on pages 33–8.

Additional calcium: All fresh meats, fish and poultry are deficient in calcium if the bones are removed, so your cat must be given this mineral in another form. Cats who can take milk (as has already been explained, some cannot) will receive enough calcium from four tablespoonfuls of milk daily, served normally in between meals. Cats who like pilchard can obtain some calcium if the bones are mashed in with the fish so that they cannot pick them out and leave them: serve this meal at least twice a week. In other cases cats will require a pinch of calcium carbonate (BP) added to two meals per week. All artificial foods (canned, semi-moist and dry) contain adequate calcium.

Additional fat: Use a heaped teaspoonful of chopped, raw fat to supplement low-fat meats like white fish and young rabbit, and canned catfood. Sources safe to serve raw are: fat trimmed from pork, lamb or beef; bacon fat; fat associated with lamb's heart and kidneys; oxtail; *small* portions of cheese, cream, butter or margarine.

Rabbit: A very digestible, low-fat food, well accepted by most cats. Rabbit sold for human consumption is safe to serve raw (for example, in diced, boneless form). Wild rabbit should be cooked in a low oven until the flesh falls from the bone. A whole rabbit is easier to debone than portions, and this can be done rapidly with fingers, with a little practice. There is no need to chop cooked rabbit for adults; simply shred it with fingers. Raw rabbit may require cutting into strips for some small or old domestics. Local farmers may be able to put cat owners in touch with hunters who shoot rabbits on farmland. These are usually sold cheaply.

Pigeon breasts: Another cheap meat source from human hunters. Cook and serve as for rabbit.

Chicken: Serve roast chicken with skin. Refrigerate chicken juices and, when set, remove solid white fat (which few cats enjoy) and add the remaining high-protein jelly to meals as a moistener.

Lamb and beef: These are ideal foods for cats, and they should always be served with the fat left on. Mince is very quick to serve, supplemented with calcium if necessary. In one- or two-cat house-holds, mince may be divided into individual portions, wrapped in cling film and stored in a freezer; these may then be thawed for use as required. Soyabean minces must be cooked, as cats cannot digest raw vegetable. Offals safe to serve raw are: heart, kidney, liver and tongue. Mixed offals (ground lamb bone, ox cheek, lights, ox heart, and so on) sold 'for pets' must be cooked. Avoid ox cheek (which may carry tapeworm cysts) and ox liver sold 'for pets' (which may contain steroids – artificial fatteners fed to the animal). Always serve the entire offal – not just the lean portions – having first chopped it or cut it into strips.

Fish: Ideal food for cats. Avoid exclusive feeding of oily fish (pilchards, mackerel, sardines, tuna, herrings) because of the danger of yellow fat disease that such a diet carries. If canned oily fish is used, ensure it is preserved in brine. Fresh oily fish, which has small bones, can be chopped whilst still frozen, thus leaving in the bone as a natural source of calcium. If large cuts of white fish (such as coley, whiting or huss) are purchased, the bones are large enough to remove with your fingers once the fish is cooked. Serve all fish skin. Fishing humans may help out by providing freshwater fish like pike, roach or bream. Fish can be served raw, but there are two possible dangers: because it is a natural prey animal of the cat, it may contain cysts or eggs of parasites to which the cat is susceptible; and freshwater fish contains thiaminase, an enzyme that destroys thiamine (vitamin B_1) but which is deactivated by cooking. It is very important, however, not to overcook fish. It can be poached, steamed (retain the juices in this case by placing the fish in a roasting bag) or lightly boiled. Defrosted fish, if chopped, can be cooked by simply placing in just-boiled water until the flesh turns white.

Plant-derived foods: These can comprise up to one-quarter of the bulk of a cat's diet. Sources are human pre-cooked breakfast cereals – puffed rice, puffed or shredded wheat, cornflakes and oat flakes. These contain vitamins which cats need but, of course, not necessarily in the right proportion for cats! Other vegetables and seeds must be cooked: oats, barley, rice, maize, peas, broad beans, soya beans, haricot beans, carrots, turnips. Leaf vegetables are useless to cats, but all *confined* cats need a blade of couch grass daily.

DAIRY PRODUCE

One-twelfth of a pint of milk per day is ample. Milk is a food, not a drink to be given without limit. As has already been explained, it tends to form an indigestible curd in the stomach and causes vomiting and/or diarrhoea in many cats. But even if your eat can take unlimited quantities, obesity could soon be the result, for 1 pint (568 millilitres) of milk provides 350 calories – the approximate daily calorie requirement of the average adult cat. During illness it is useful as a liquid food for short-term use, administered to a non-lapping cat by Brunswick syringe (see page 44) at about 2 millilitres every four hours, or as advised by a vet.

Tiny portions of butter, cream, natural unsweetened yoghurt, cheese and cooked eggs add variety to the diet. Vegetable 'dairy products' cannot replace the animal variety as they contain only plant oil and plant protein.

ARTIFICIAL CATFOODS

Apart from the Gourmet range of canned catfood, all contain similar ingredients, varying only in the flavouring used. A partial analysis appears, by law, on the label. The ingredients are listed, and these include: slaughterhouse waste products unfit for human consumption; knacker's yard meats from animals slaughtered because of disease or old age; broiler fowl; waste products from the fish canning industry; meat from abroad not sold for human consumption – horsemeat, kangaroo, whalemeat; vegetables; wheatflour; cornflower; etc. Colouring, flavouring, preservatives and odours are added, together with vitamin pre-mixes. The whole is well mixed and firmed by the addition of gelling agents (such as gelatine, agar-agar or pig's blood) to make them appear firm. Some foods contain whey powder or skimmed milk powder. Dry and semi-moist catfoods are made to the same formula, but with less water.

Like all convenience foods, canned catfoods are expensive for what they contain, taking into account the cost of processing, addition of vitamins, canning and the fact that food sold for pets is subject to VAT. But they are invaluable for use in an emergency and for those who feed cats in large colonies without kitchen facilities nearby, or without deep-freeze units. They are sometimes described as time savers, but it should be remembered that no food is quicker to serve than raw beef or lamb mince. The use of canned food gives rise to disposal problems – open cans can be both dangerous and offensively odorous. Place lids inside empty cans and flatten if possible.

Once a can is open, its contents should never be stored longer than forty-eight hours and must be transferred to a glass or earthenware container for storage, since air reacts with both the contents and the can. This applies also to semi-moist catfood. When buying cans, reject any with dents or punctures for the same reason; and if you feed canned, dry or semi-moist food which is more than a year old, remember that it will be deficient in vitamins as a result of ageing and that you should serve it with a vitamin supplement (see below). Dry catfood must be kept dry: once it becomes wet, bacteria and the poisons they produce will make the food dangerous!

Benzoic acid, a preservative used in certain canned foods sold for human consumption, is cumulatively toxic to cats, so always check labels before sharing your food with your cat. It is important not to use canned or dry dogfood for cats because the meat protein is far too low.

Finally, remember that cats' teeth are designed to tenderize flesh. An artificial food cannot replace a cat's natural food in flavour, colour, texture or composition. Because they contain plant fibre and sometimes lactose, canned catfoods can cause vomiting and/or diarrhoea in some cats and cannot be used. Canned catfoods are *not* cheaper than most fresh foods: canned foods are needed in greater quantity than fresh foods because of their low calorific value.

SUPPLEMENTS

A healthy adult cat, fed on the diet described on the preceding pages, needs no artificial supplements. The dangers of over-supplementation have already been stressed. Supplements should be used only in cases of dietary deficiency, during periods of stress, during kittenhood, pregnancy and lactation, and in other special circumstances.

A vast array of supplements are available from vets and manufacturers of pet products. Although they are mainly vitamin/mineral supplements, many have a palatable protein or glucose base. The following are a few examples.

Pet-Tabs Feline: Obtainable from vets only, and claimed to be specially formulated for cats. Very comprehensive information is given on the label. Although they are described as vitamin/mineral supplements in a palatable protein base, many cats will not take them whole, nor accept them crushed in food. They are very hard and difficult to powder.

VH B-Sorb: Obtainable from VetHealth, this is a liquid tonic containing B vitamins and iron. It is used in cases of stress, infectious diseases and convalescence.

VH100 Hyper-Nutrient: Also from VetHealth, this is a vitamin/ mineral powder.

ABIDEC: Manufactured by Parke-Davis, obtainable from most chemists, this is a liquid vitamin supplement that is useful in cases where only fresh *cooked* food is served (for example, for kittens). The dose is three drops a day for adults and six drops a day for kittens.

Halibut liver oil: A liquid source of vitamins A and D.

Marmite, Bovril, yeast: Sources of B vitamins and protein. Do not cook.

Calcium carbonate (BP): Pure chalk, obtainable from chemists. It is a source of calcium for those cats fed on fresh food, but *not* given milk or chopped bones.

USE OF SUPPLEMENTS

Stray cats: Rescued strays often have gut infections, respiratory infections or chronic diarrhoea as a result of eating unsuitable food. It is a common mistake to allow ex-strays unlimited food, and this, coupled with the unavoidable (but, naturally, desirable) change in diet, often exacerbates the problem. A liquid vitamin/mineral supplement, without extra solid food, will correct the low absorption levels of vitamins and minerals caused by an inflamed gut.

Healthy adults normally require no supplements, with the following exceptions: (a) if fed entirely on cooked fresh food with chopped bone, they need a vitamin supplement – for example, ABIDEC; (b) if fed entirely on raw or cooked fresh food without bone, they require four tablespoonfuls of milk daily or a pinch of calcium carbonate twice a week.

Teenage cats and particularly those with chronic nephritis (see page 108) may require a high-dosage vitamin/mineral supplement.

Cats on long-term antibiotics: Give these a quarter-teaspoonful of unsweetened natural yoghurt per day.

Cats under stress need a vitamin/mineral supplement.

Sick and convalescent cats: See 'The Isolation Unit', page 160.

Pregnant and lactating queens: These cats will need three to four times more food than non-pregnant queens or spayed females, supplemented where applicable with vitamins/minerals. They should all be given additional calcium. It has been estimated by researchers that pregnant and lactating queens need about 200–400 milligrams of calcium per day. Cow's milk contains about 125 milligrams of calcium per 100 millilitres, but most cats could not tolerate this amount of milk without ill effects. Extra calcium can be provided, if bone is not used, by adding ½ gram calcium carbonate per 100 grams of fresh or canned food. This is equivalent to about half a teaspoon of calcium carbonate per 909 grams (about 2lb) of wet food. For example, 909 grams of raw mince can be spread on a plate and half a teaspoon of calcium carbonate sprinkled on top – and there is the perfect food, ready to serve!

Confined cats: Those which stay indoors in houses, flats and catteries for longer than a fortnight will need vitamin D, in the form of about one drop of halibut liver oil per day, if not exposed to *direct* sunlight regularly. Normally free-roaming cats, confined to the house for long periods during a severe winter, will also need vitamin D.

FEEDING KITTENS

WEANING KITTENS ON TO SOLID CATFOOD

Hand-reared kittens can be weaned from two and a half weeks old; kittens fed by a queen from three weeks old. Wild kittens are not weaned completely until about six months old, which explains why most domestic kittens up to this age can tolerate a high proportion of cow's milk, cereals and vegetables in their diet. However, as in the wild, domestic kittens over the age of six months change to a natural protein/fat diet and may become partially or wholly intolerant to carbohydrate foods as they mature.

Queen's milk contains, per 100 grams, approximately 5 grams of fat, 10 grams of protein and 5 grams of lactose (milk sugar); the same quantity of cow's milk contains approximately 4 grams of fat, 3½ grams of protein and 5 grams of lactose. It will be noted that both the fat and protein figures are higher for queen's milk than for cow's, so whilst weaning it is advisable to enrich cow's milk as described for hand-reared kittens in the following section. Alternatively a commercial kitten milk replacer can be used (for example, Cimicat).

Kittens should grow rapidly. Periods of intense activity are interspersed with deep sleep, a kitten often falling asleep wherever he happens to be playing.

All foods as described for cats earlier in this chapter under 'Food in Practice' are suitable for kittens, but they should be given extra fat, particularly if fed canned catfood, and supplements containing vitamins and minerals will be necessary up to about nine months of age, when kittens officially become cats – although most continue to grow for a further two to three years. All food should be cooked and finely chopped for kittens up to about six months old. Semi-moist or dry foods are not generally advised. Introduce raw beef mince and raw lamb's liver gradually, mixed with normal cooked meals.

If kittens do not learn to lap milk or water, moisten their lips with milk. Once they learn to use their tongues, they will soon learn to lap and hence to eat soft, moist, mashed food.

Feed small meals about six times a day, leaving a meal down for the night. Always provide a bowl of freshly run water. Most kittens will eat the right amount, but some will continue until they vomit – these must be separated from the rest of their family at mealtimes and fed a limited quantity. Weaning should be complete at six to eight weeks and, depending on development, domestic kittens are ready to go to new homes. New owners must be given details of their present diet and informed that any changes must be made gradually: new foods should be introduced alongside familiar ones.

The amount of food required by each individual kitten will vary, but on average, when on six meals a day, two heaped teaspoonfuls per meal should be about right. The amount of food per meal should be increased as the kitten grows, while the number of meals should gradually be decreased. A satiated kitten will usually wash, use the toilet tray and sleep. An unsatiated one will miaow. Kittens over about four months old will generally need about 500 calories per day, equivalent to eight heaped tablespoonsfuls of fresh food or sixteen heaped tablespoonsfuls of canned catfood.

HAND-REARING KITTENS

Kittens may be orphaned at birth; or a queen may be unable to feed her young or may have too many to feed adequately. In such circumstances kittens will have to be fed artificially by humans.

Newborn kittens can be fed liquid food, drop by drop, by means of a kitten's feeding bottle (from pet shops), a dropper bottle or a Brunswick syringe (from vets), a piece of plastic tubing or even pieces of sterilized muslin bandage which can be dipped into the food and squeezed to release drops into the kitten's mouth.

Kitten milk replacers, such as Cimicat, which are formulated to simulate a queen's milk, can be obtained from your vet. Alternatively, enriched cow's milk can be used, as follows. Mix together 1 cup cow's milk, ¼ cup fresh double cream, ¼ *raw* egg yolk, ¼ teaspoonful glucose, Dextrose or honey and 1 drop halibut liver oil. Beat well, warm slightly and introduce the liquid drop by drop into the kitten's mouth. The amount needed will be about ½–1 teaspoonful *per feed* for the first three days, gradually increasing to about 2½ teaspoonfuls *per feed* at two and a half to three weeks old. Kittens should be fed every two hours, day and night; but, as they grow, some feeds can be phased out. If a kitten miaows and does not fall asleep after a feed, give more. Food must be made up freshly each day.

If the queen is available, she will wash the kittens, keep them warm and induce them to pass urine and faeces. If not, this must be done by humans. After feeding wipe the kittens gently with cotton wool moistened with warm water, dry with paper tissue and return to bed (a draughtproof cardboard box lined with newspaper covered with soft sheet). Keep them warm by means of a hot water bottle or safe heated bed, well covered with an old blanket or sheet; or, preferably, keep the room at an even temperature of 75°F (24°C) with some form of safe ambient heating, such as an electric oil-filled radiator or central heating.

To induce elimination, stroke the anal region under the tail with cotton wool between fifteen minutes and one hour after, say, every other meal. Hold the kitten over a tissue. Continue for a few days, until urination and defecation are automatic. A kitten will use a toilet tray at about two to three weeks old; until then, disposable bedding should be used.

If in any doubt, obtain veterinary advice.

All utensils used for feeding must be sterilized with a sterilizing fluid, obtainable from chemists, as used for human babies' feeding bottles – for example, Boots' or Milton. These are solutions of sodium hypochlorite and salt, and must be used exactly according to the manufacturers' instructions.

OBESITY

Obesity kills! Excess weight means that a cat is carrying more weight than his heart, lungs and skeleton were designed to carry. Excess food will mean extra work for the gut, extra work for the liver and kidneys converting and excreting protein as urea. A fat cat is less likely to make old bones than one who remains slim, and therefore active, into old age.

Most domestic cats, particularly de-sexed ones, are overweight simply because they eat too much. This does not necessarily mean that their owners overfeed them. Many cats roam the neighbourhood, convincing gullible humans that they are starving strays! Most free-roamers have alternative food supplies, raiding dustbins, birdtables and even other cats' plates, thus thwarting any attempts by their owners to limit their food intake. Is it better to feed a cat until he is satisfied, rather than have him eat potentially dangerous rubbish? The truth of the matter is that, however well-fed a cat may be, he will still forage for more food. The fact that stray cats can exist at all is a tribute to a cat's ingenuity in searching out food. The idea that cats are self-regulatory and will not overeat is a myth as far as most of them are concerned.

The average adult male weighs about 10lb (4.5 kilograms), the average female about 8½lb (4 kilograms), but the actual weight is not important. It is the appearance which indicates overweight. A cat is overweight if he bulges out at the flanks (or sides) when viewed head on, or if he sports an unsightly 'undercarriage' which wobbles from side to side as he shuffles along. Such a cat is receiving too much food, from whatever source, and all that his owner can do is reduce the amount of food *she* gives him. Unfortunately this may result in a domineering, hectoring, bad-tempered, aggressive animal, who will never let his owner out of his sight!

Cats are at high risk of becoming obese once they reach full size, at around two or three years old. Up to this time, hunting, fighting and climbing keep them slim, and they can eat all they want with impunity. After three years old, however, some cats tend to slow down but continue to eat the same amount, thus gaining weight. Food should not be shared, even in a multicat household. The feline vacuum cleaner who eats his own meal extra fast and then finishes the left-overs is usually overweight.

Once a cat has become obese, there is very little the owner can do. Prevention is far easier than cure. Quite simply, a fat cat is receiving too many calories. Loss of weight occurs naturally in cats of thirteen years and upwards as part of the ageing process.

It may be possible to reduce the *amount* of food your cat consumes by giving frequent small meals. If the problem of obesity is worsened by the fact that your neighbours leave food down for their own cats where it is accessible to yours, try discussing this with them. It may be that they feed their cats outside, in which case find out their mealtimes and keep your own cat in until the food has been eaten.

The number of calories in the diet is best reduced by serving less fat, since fat provides twice the calories of protein or carbohydrate. A cat's diet must consist of a minimum of 12 per cent protein, so low-fat/high-water foods containing a minimum of 12 per cent protein can be served – for example, white fish, rabbit, canned Gourmet or 9-Lives. Lights and tripe, puffed rice and puffed wheat contain plenty of air and it is to be hoped that this will create the illusion of bulk and result in a satiated cat! Such a diet should be imposed only for a short period: say, one month.

It is difficult to be certain where genuine hunger begins and greed ends. Try serving less attractive foods that your cat will not eat, unless really hungry. Limit milk to two tablespoonfuls a day.

Never allow a young fat cat to sleep all day. Prize him out of his day chair and into the garden on fine days.

3 Anchoring Your Cat for Treatment

It is generally acknowledged that cats – big or small – are the most difficult animals to hold and treat. One touch of a comb, one whiff of a flea powder, one hiss of an aerosol spray can transform a normally cosy domestic cat into a completely unmanageable, frenzied animal. Cats are particularly liberal with their claws and teeth when they have had an accident, or a severe fright, or are in an aggressive mood following a cat fight. Most domestic cats and most ex-strays (provided they have not been away from human contact for more than about a year) can be managed easily provided training is carried out methodically and in stages. Ideally training should commence at about six months old. Young kittens are too fragile for you to use the force necessary to handle and treat adult cats, and such treatments are not normally required. A few cats will never submit to handling, and special techniques for them will be dealt with later.

It is unwise to rely on another person being around to hold your cat while you give any necessary treatment. Emergencies never occur at convenient times! The ability to hold your cat, carry out simple treatments and give pills unaided and at once can save a cat's life, to say nothing of the saving in vets' bills! Methods suggested in this chapter should be practised *before* they are needed. Once a cat is ill, injured or poisoned it is often too late for an owner to learn to carry out treatment.

It is important that all cats, preferably from kittenhood as explained above, be accustomed to human handling. As a first step, place both hands underneath the cat and lift him about 1 foot (30 centimetres) from the floor. Gradually increase the height, and once he accepts this without struggling or becoming tense, try lifting him up with one hand underneath. Curl his tail over his hindquarters with the other hand and sit him on this hand, resting his front paws first on your forearm and at a later stage on your shoulder. Beware of raising a kitten more than 1 foot as falls can so easily result in broken bones.

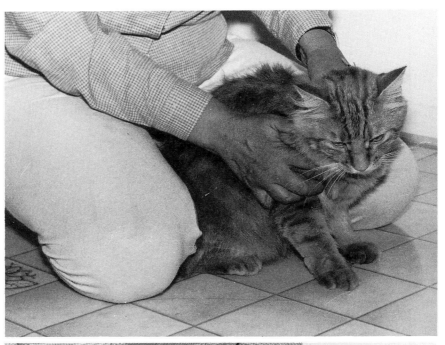

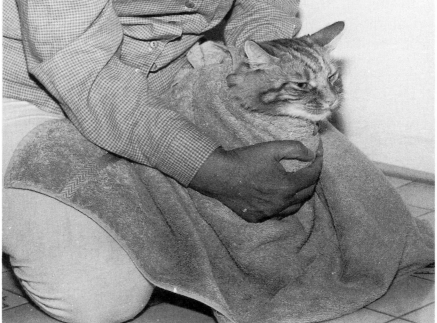

Top FIGURE 3   Anchoring your cat.
Above FIGURE 4   Anchoring your cat with a towel.

Cats escape from human hands by twisting their bodies, using their heads as wedges and flattening their bodies, clawing at clothing for leverage, sliding backwards or sinking teeth or claws into human flesh. When practising holding methods, remember that one hand, at least, must be free for treatment. Cats vary enormously in the amount of restraint necessary.

To anchor your cat for treatment, place him on a non-slip floor with head facing outwards. Kneel down behind the cat, wedging his body between your thighs. This will be sufficient to hold some cats. Otherwise grip the loose fold of thick skin at the back of the neck (called the scruff) and bear downwards towards the floor, thus immobilizing the most dangerous part – the head end! One or both forearms can be used, if required, to further restrain the cat (see Figure 3). Variations can be tried until a method for restraining an individual cat is arrived at.

Some cats, when held in the above way, raise their front legs and tear at human hands. Wrap such cats in a large towel, head exposed (see Figure 4). Parts of the body needing treatment can be exposed.

To examine a cat's hindquarters, or to apply ointment or a laxative suppository into the rectum, reverse a towel-wrapped cat, using forearms to bear down on the rump to avoid kicking back legs.

Finally, remember that treatment may have to be carried out wherever a cat happens to be – even in the garden!

EXAMINATION OF THE MOUTH

The following instructions are for a righthanded person, although many people may find it easier to use the left hand.

The first stage is to accustom the cat to having his mouth opened. Place the left hand over the cat's temples, raise his head slightly and press gently on the jaws with thumb and first finger. Using the first finger of your right hand press gently on the front of the mouth to open the mouth, as shown in Figure 5 (overleaf).

GIVING A PILL

Once a cat allows his mouth to be examined, observe the back of the mouth (base of tongue) where a pill needs to be placed. Never try to place a pill beyond this point, as there is a danger it will enter the windpipe and cause choking. The cat should not be totally surprised

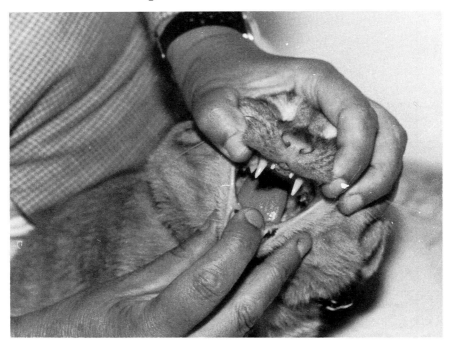

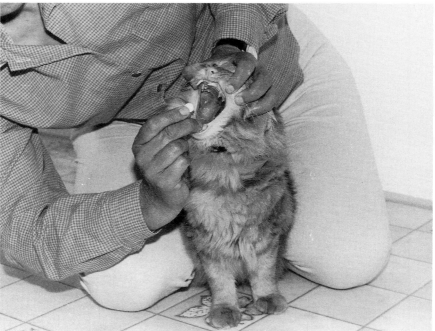

Top FIGURE 5   Examination of the mouth.
Above FIGURE 6   Giving a cat a pill.

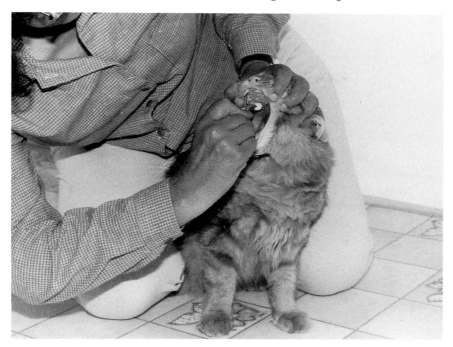

FIGURE 7   Giving a cat a pill using blunt-ended tweezers.

by your action and unaware of what to expect, for in such a case the pill could cause choking. This is the danger in using devices claiming to be specially designed for giving pills to cats.

After a few weeks' training in mouth opening, pill giving can be practised, using small vitamin/mineral supplement pills like Tibs tablets, or portions of larger pills. To avoid the risk of overdosage, use only one tablet or part of a tablet a week, unless the cat is receiving pills under veterinary supervision. Speed, confidence, firmness and plenty of praise for the cat are essential.

Stage 1
Pills are easier to give if broken up into small portions. Hold the cat's head as already described and tilt slightly upwards. Hold the pill between your thumb and first finger and press on the front of the cat's mouth with your middle finger (see Figure 6). Nervous humans can hold the pill with long, blunt-ended tweezers, as shown in Figure 7. Talk to the cat, using the use same phrase each time, for example, 'Sooty, pill'.

Stage 2
Place the pill at the back of the cat's mouth, giving a slight push on

the pill with your first finger. Allow the mouth to close naturally, and the head to lower. If the pill has been placed far enough back, the cat will swallow it involuntarily. If he manages to spit it out, try again another day.

The ability to give a pill to your cat will bring enormous confidence. It is very important only to give pills supplied by, and recommended by, your vet, including routine worming pills and other tablets prescribed by him for recurrent, previously diagnosed illnesses. The advantages of being able to administer a pill are numerous. Although many pills are claimed to be 'palatable', cats may not eat them. Cats are hypersensitive to any additives to their food and if a pill is crushed in it they may either refuse to eat any of the food, or eat insufficient for the treatment to be effective. A sick cat, of course, may not be eating at all. In cases of poisoning, the ability to give a solid antidote or a crystal of washing soda, on veterinary advice given over the telephone, can save a cat's life.

GIVING LIQUIDS

It is impossible to administer pills to some cats, but all is not lost. Pills can be crushed and made into a suspension (they rarely dissolve in water) and introduced into a cat's mouth with a syringe. A Brunswick polythene syringe can be obtained for the purpose, in 2 ml and 5 ml sizes, from your vet – minus the injection needle, of course. The liquid is filled to the correct graduation (if applicable) and the nozzle is inserted between the cat's teeth at the side of the mouth, as shown in Figure 8. Give the liquid a few drops at a time, allowing plenty of time for the cat to swallow. This type of syringe is a boon for giving cats all kinds of liquids, such as water, milk, meat or fish juices, glucose solution and liquid medication in cases of illness.

EXAMINATION OF THE EYES

If damage to the cat's eye is suspected (for example, piercing by a rose thorn), examine the eye by gently holding it open, using the thumbs of both hands (see Figure 9). Medication prescribed by a vet will usually take the form of eye drops or eye ointment. Eye drops are easier to apply, but it is essential that the eye is held open and upwards, otherwise the drops will simply fall out if the cat is allowed to blink. In the case of eye ointment, the nozzle of the tube must never point inwards *at* the eye. The tube must be held horizontally,

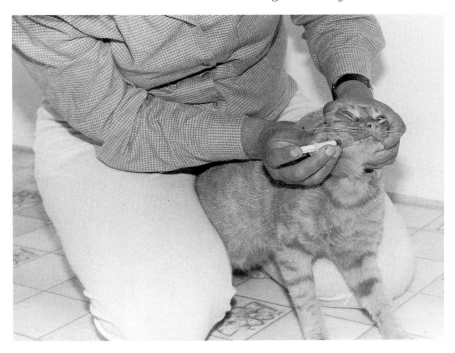

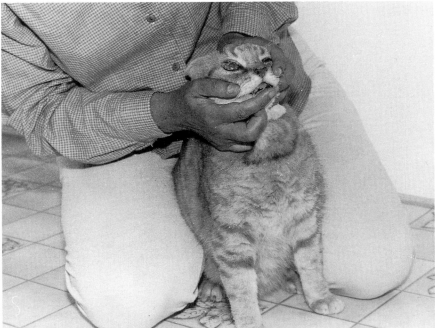

Top FIGURE 8   Use of a Brunswick syringe.
Above FIGURE 9   Examining an eye for possible injury.

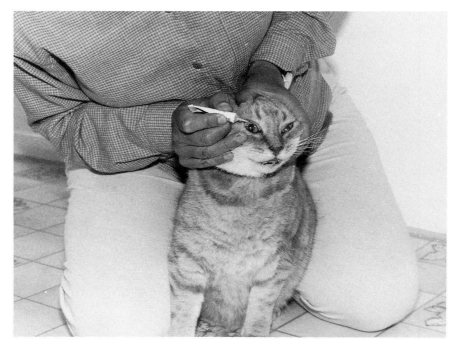

FIGURE 10   Applying eye ointment.

parallel with the face (see Figure 10). The eye is held open a few
seconds to allow the ointment to liquify and drain into the eye socket.

EXAMINATION OF THE EARS

The first stage of training a cat to allow examination of his ears is
to get him used to your holding his ear flap between your thumb and
first finger (see Figure 11). This can be followed by gentle cleaning
with a cotton bud moistened with water, as shown in Figure 12.

Cotton buds are useful for cleaning ears, but it is very important
never to probe further than you can see.

If your vet prescribes ear drops, remember that those which are
in a dropper bottle are far easier to insert into the ear than those
which require the plastic bottle to be squeezed whilst the nozzle is
inserted into the outer ear. Figure 13 shows how to give ear drops to
a cat using a dropper. After the drops have been inserted, the cat
usually shakes his head, so the ear flap is held down over the ear
opening to prevent them from running out while the base of the ear
is massaged to assist penetration of the medication and loosen wax.

Further information is given on page 84.

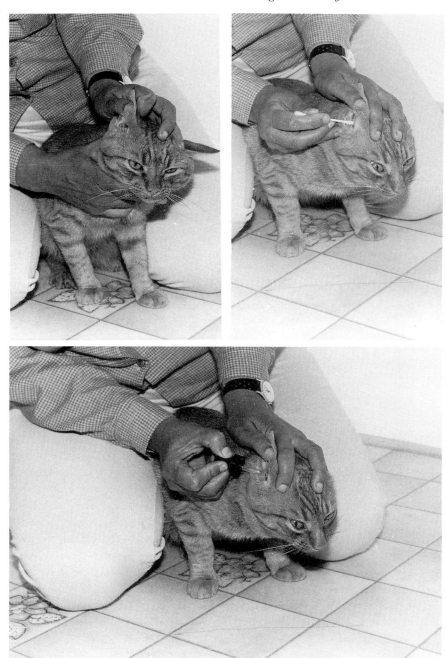

Top left FIGURE 11   Holding the ear flap.
Top right FIGURE 12   Cleaning the ear with a cotton bud.
Above FIGURE 13   Inserting ear drops.

4 Accidents and Emergencies: First Aid

CAUSES OF ACCIDENTS AND INJURIES

Owners should be aware of the type of accidents to which free-roamers and housebound (or cattery-confined) cats are exposed. Some injuries are consistent with specific accidents, and an informed guess as to the possible cause of an accident may help your vet's diagnosis.

FIGHTS

Cat fights are by no means confined to full toms and queens in kitten or queens nursing (and therefore protecting) kittens. De-sexed cats (neutered males and spayed females) engage in territorial fights. Often there is a powerful neighbourhood bully who wreaks havoc among local cats and engenders monstrous vets' bills. But courting disputes among full toms are more serious, as a rule, than territorial disputes. It is, therefore, wise to de-sex domestic cats, and keep them in from human bedtime until dawn, for entire cats (that is, those which have not been de-sexed) are most active at night-time. During the day there is often a caring human around who will stop a serious can fight by aiming a jug of water at the combatants, or making a loud noise, or throwing a coat over them. It is unwise for a human to intervene directly in a cat fight as wounds from cats' claws and teeth can be equally dangerous to humans as to cats because of the potentially harmful (pathogenic) bacteria on them. Bites on a cat's legs, body and face can penetrate deep into the skin, allowing bacteria to enter the bloodstream. Claw wounds can cause abscesses (painful, pus-filled swellings) on any part of the body, though they occur most frequently on the head. Young cats are particularly susceptible to abscesses; older cats have acquired some immunity.

ROAD ACCIDENTS

Traffic accidents are the commonest cause of serious injury and death in urban free-roaming cats. Injured cats will attempt to distance themselves from an accident, and be vicious with fear. Roads, and gardens bordering roads, should be searched immediately a cat is missed because prompt veterinary attention can save an injured cat's life. Some die of shock, if untreated, even if their injuries are slight. Road accident victims often show no external signs of injury, or they may have a little blood on the nose or mouth, indicating internal bleeding. When a cat is hit by a car, he immediately tries to cling to the road by his claws which will, therefore, often appear shredded.

A cat owner is very likely to have to cope with a road accident victim – her own animal, a neighbour's cat, or an unknown feline. Although an injured cat should not be moved, there may be no choice. A stunned or unconscious cat must be removed from the road, and a split-second decision will have to be made whether to scoop the cat into your arms or stop the traffic first. An unconscious cat should be gently slid on to a coat and carried to the vet. In the

FIGURE 14 A cat will maintain his claws in peak condition by drawing them down a convenient tree or along a piece of wood. Shredded claws on a shocked and/or injured cat indicate that he has been in a road accident.

case of a slightly injured cat all that is possible is to throw a coat over him, gather up the edges beneath him and call for help. Enclose the cat with your body to 'anchor' him as described in Chapter 3. An injured cat is very dangerous and unpredictable, and a would-be rescuer may have only one chance to catch him before he disappears into a hedgerow, possibly to die alone.

Internal injuries, a fractured skull and broken bones are the most likely results of a road accident, and the injured cat should be immobilized as soon as possible in an escape-proof cat carry basket. Before setting out for your vet's surgery, always telephone first to ensure that he or someone else will be there to help.

Road accidents, in most cases, are non-preventable. Some neutered cats insist on crossing main roads, and travelling long distances, even if there are 20 acres of woodland in another, safer, direction. It may be possible to fence off the front of the house, so that your cat cannot dart out into the road. Some cats acquire traffic sense, but others have no fear of anything, and for the latter a harness and lead or enclosing a portion of the garden may be the only options. It should be borne in mind that old cats, over ten years, may be unable to jump or move as fast as they could in their younger days, and hearing, sight and smell will begin to deteriorate. These animals will need supervision when outdoors.

INJURIES FROM REFUSE

However well fed cats are, they are natural predators, scavengers and carrion-eaters. The practice of using polythene refuse sacks makes their contents easily accessible to cats, who can claw the bags open, thus exposing such potentially dangerous items as milk bottle tops, plastic bags, meat string, empty cans, old bones and decaying food. Tongues can be slit on empty cans, swallowed meat string can cause death, decaying food can cause vomiting and diarrhoea – though it is amazing how much rotting food cats can consume with impunity. All that can be done is to keep your cats indoors until the refuse has been collected.

POISONING

Cats are normally very careful not to eat poisons, but there is a danger they will walk over or brush against a poison, lick their pads or coats and thus ingest it. Most products used in the home and garden are potentially dangerous to cats, unless manufacturers' instructions are slavishly followed. In general it may be said that liquids, once dry, are safer than powders which can contaminate a cat's fur. The *safe* drug, weedkiller, slug bait or insecticide does not exist: everything in this line which is breathed in by a cat, walked upon by a cat, brushed against, sprayed upon or eaten by a cat is potentially dangerous in excess. It is only the *dosage* of a therapeutic drug, or the concentration of a disinfectant or flea spray, which makes it safe to use. Slug pellets must be placed at the rate of one pellet every foot (30 centimetres) so that, if a cat walks over treated soil, he will only pick up one on his pads, not a dozen. Better still, cover the pellets with wire mesh.

RURAL HAZARDS

Country cats are at risk from farm machinery, poisonous plants, poachers' guns, air rifles, crop sprays, traps and snares, wandering dogs and foxes, bites from prey like rats, moles and squirrels, falling into ponds or rivers, insect stings, thorns, barbed wire and bonfires.

MOVING HOUSE

Moving house is always traumatic for a cat because he is wrenched from his well-known territory and placed in a strange environment, inhabited by potentially hostile cats and other animals. It should be remembered that a cat tends to travel in one direction, and a safe direction at one house may be a dangerous direction (for example, towards a main road) at another. Cats tend to become completely disorientated and lose their way when familiar scents and landmarks are missing. They may seek to return to their old homes, often becoming victims of road accidents, or becoming strays, in the process. The homing instinct of cats is vastly overrated!

Curiosity or, dare I say, stupidity causes cats to enter garages, sheds and other houses, where they can so easily be locked in. On the other hand cats are born escapologists, able to squeeze their way through 2-inch (5-centimetre) gaps in high windows, or flatten themselves and escape through damaged wire mesh in boarding catteries.

RISKS IN THE HOME

Of all the obvious dangers, however, accidents in the home are probably the most common: falls, perhaps because some cats can open windows; burns from cooking fat or boiling water; walking over grills, gas burners or hotplates; biting through electric cables; high-placed heavy ornaments knocked down by one cat on to another; pins and needles; unguarded fires; houseplants; contamination from household or garage products. No cat should ever be allowed in a kitchen whilst cooking is in progress.

EMERGENCY PROCEDURES

When a cat is seriously injured a vet is the only person who can diagnose, treat, prescribe effective drugs, anaesthetize, treat for shock and, if the condition is terminal, painlessly end your cat's life. Vets are understandably reluctant to visit small animals since all their life-saving equipment is at the surgery, and most owners can transport their cats. It is essential that cats can be transported speedily, safely and without the aid of another person. Transport is dealt with in Chapter 10.

Choose a vet and make contact with him well before you need to call on his services. If possible, select a vet with a special interest in cats – perhaps one who is also a cat owner. Local cat owners' opinions and vet preferences should be sought. Keep the following information near your telephone: names, addresses and telephone numbers of local vets, including particulars of all surgeries in a practice; day-time numbers and emergency numbers should be included, together with surgery hours. All vets can refer a client to a specialist if necessary.

Always telephone your first-choice vet prior to arriving with an accident victim. He may be able to suggest an antidote for a suspected poison, or appropriate first aid, over the telephone. In an emergency it is important to keep calm, coherent and observant, and write down any symptoms or theories to aid diagnosis.

If you go out to work or are likely to be away from home for a whole day, it is important to leave a note on your door giving a telephone number where you can be contacted, or leave a neighbour's address, and perhaps leave a key with a neighbour. These precautions will ensure prompt attention to your cat if he is brought home injured.

A cat's natural reaction to illness or accident is to hide, as he feels vulnerable to his jungle enemies! He should be shut in a room, isolated from other cats, and left alone whilst you prepare for transport to the vet.

TREATMENT FOR SHOCK

The shock syndrome, as its name suggests, is a collection of symptoms with various causes. Cats are highly susceptible to shock and have been known to die of shock even if unharmed. All cats involved in any kind of accident or frightening incident should receive the following standard treatment for shock:

(a) Confine the cat in a carry basket in a warm, dark, quiet, well-ventilated room. Use disposable bedding, like newspaper, which can be buried in the garden, since shock relaxes bladder and bowel muscles and may result in vomiting. Keep all visitors at bay.

(b) If the cat is unconscious (that is, in a coma) and is not breathing, give artificial respiration (see page 55).

(c) A lack of oxygen results in rapid, shallow or even irregular breathing. This can result from damage to the lungs, being shut in a hot, unventilated building or car, or major loss of blood. (See 'Heat Stress', page 57, and 'Wounds', page 62.) Ensure that the cat receives as much fresh air as possible, high in oxygen.

(d) Shock may result in an initial rise in temperature indicated by panting or a hot, dry nose. This may be followed by a contraction of surface blood vessels, in order to divert blood to vital organs like the heart and muscles used for breathing. A cat in shock may therefore have a pale skin, eye sockets, tongue and gums. The limbs will feel cold. Place the cat in a position where the head is lower than the body, if feasible, to encourage blood flow to the brain and prevent irreversible brain damage. Massage the limbs, provided there are no signs of broken bones – limb held in unusual position, outline of bone visible below skin in unusual position (compare, if possible, with uninjured cat to confirm), limb dragged along uselessly. Provide a well-wrapped hot-water bottle.

(e) Shock results in salt retention. This, together with loss of blood, causes thirst. Only if the cat is conscious and will lap voluntarily should water or glucose be given.

(f) Lactic acid may concentrate in the blood and muscles, so a pinch of bicarbonate of soda can be added to water or glucose.

(g) Since blood, and thus white cells, may be diverted away from the gut to essential organs of life support – heart and lungs – gut infections are possible. Food absorption may be lowered and hence a vitamin deficiency may occur. All these factors contribute to a lowered immunity to infection. Give a vitamin/mineral supplement for a few days after shock.

FELINE FIRST AID

All medications, whether given internally or applied externally, should be prescribed by a vet. Those purchased from chemists or pet shops will in general not be so effective: drugs such as antibiotics, for example, may only be supplied by a vet. Use only drugs, ointments and so on that are *specifically for cats*: no medications prescribed for humans, or other animals, should ever be used for cats.

Some cats are allergic (hypersensitive) to drugs, and all should be watched carefully for such intolerance (shown, for example, by frothing at the mouth or vomiting). Antibiotics are usually administered in tablet or liquid form every twelve hours – say, at 8am and 8pm. If there is no improvement in a sick cat's condition overnight the prescribed drug may not be the right one and the cat should be taken back to the vet. Check and double-check that the correct dose is being given. Ensure also that the expiry date of a medication has not passed, especially if you are treating a recurrent condition with a 'left-over' prescription.

Unless advised to the contrary, no external medications should be used near the eyes, mouth, or the delicate orifices below the tail: these areas must always be protected with hands or a towel. Finally, never try to give food or liquid to a sick or injured cat without veterinary advice, unless the cat will take it voluntarily.

FIRST AID KIT
The following items will probably be collected over a period of years. They should be kept in a strong, waterproof tin.

Obtainable from veterinary surgeons:
An antiseptic ointment for use on small wounds.
A stomach/intestine corrective for use in minor conditions, for example, neosulphentrin (neomycin and other antibiotics).
Ear drops effective against ear mites and bacteria.
Eye ointment or drops for minor infections, scratches and irritation, for example, Neobiotic eye ointment
Veterinary recommended laxative for occasional use.
A supply of relevant drugs for any *previously diagnosed* condition, so that treatment can be instituted at once, for example, Clamoxyl for bacterial infections.
Brunswick syringes – a supply of 2 ml and 5 ml sizes.
A supply of dropper bottles.

Obtainable from chemists:
TCP – an antiseptic and analgesic (pain and inflammation reducer); this must be diluted to half-strength with water before use on cats.
White petroleum jelly.
Cotton buds.
Roll of medicinal plaster.
Crystals of washing soda (sodium carbonate) in air-tight bottle.
Hydrogen peroxide.
Bicarbonate of soda.

Glucose.
Blunt-ended and sharp-ended scissors.
Long, blunt-ended and sharp-ended tweezers.
Medicinal cotton wool.
Absorbent lint.
Box of paper tissues.

ABSCESSES

These are a constant problem among young, fighting cats and are caused by the entry into a wound of bacteria normally resident on cats' teeth and claws. Thus cat fights should be stopped quickly, if possible! An abscess will sometimes reveal itself as a soft, swollen, red area. The cat will growl when the abscess is touched, and probably take to his bed. Often, however, the first sign is odorous, yellow or white pus on the coat, indicating that the abscess has burst. As soon as signs of an abscess are noticed the cat must receive a systemic antibiotic (that is, introduced into the body by mouth or injection). Topical application (that is, putting ointment on the abscess) is insufficient, for you must avoid the danger of a general blood infection by bacteria (septicaemia). If constant cat fights are a problem, a vet may be prepared to prescribe an antibiotic which will prevent abscess formation for use *immediately* after a fight.

ACCIDENTALLY SHUT-IN CAT

Cats have been known to survive for as long as six weeks without food or water when accidentally shut in a strange house, shed, or some other building.

Conscious cat: Give small amounts of water at a time. Feed on liquids only for the first three days, for example, glucose or honey dissolved in water, milk, milk beaten with raw egg yolk, oatmeal drinks, Brands Essence or (from your vet) Cimicat, Protogest or any kitten milk replacer. After three days, give small meals of poached white fish. If advised by your vet, give a vitamin/mineral supplement.

Unconscious cat: Must be rushed to the vet for intravenous drip feeding.

ARTIFICIAL RESPIRATION

If a cat has stopped breathing as a result, for example, of partial drowning, electric shock or suffocation in a burning building, try to restart breathing as follows:

(1) Place the cat near a window for the maximum amount of fresh air.

(2) Make sure that the cat's airways are clear. Open his mouth, extend the tongue and remove any debris such as vomit, silt or waterweeds.

(3) If the cat has suffered partial drowning, water must be removed from the lungs: leaving the mouth open and tongue extended, hold the cat firmly by the hocks (or ankles) of the back legs, well clear of the ground, and swing him downwards about five times. This action is similar to shaking a small mat and must be done positively.

(4) Now give artificial respiration using one of the following methods:

Method 1 (mouth to mouth): Open the cat's mouth and extend the tongue. Cup your hands to form an airtight tube over the cat's mouth and nose. Blow air through the 'tube' until breathing commences.

Method 2: Lay the cat on his right side with the head lower than the body. Extend the head and neck, open the mouth and extend the tongue. Place one hand over the ribs and push down firmly, but gently, to expel air from the lungs. Release immediately to allow the chest wall to expand naturally and the lungs to fill with air. Count to five slowly, then repeat as necessary.

(5) In the case of a cat which has been immersed in water, dry his fur by blotting off as much water as possible with paper tissues; then, using fresh tissues, gently raise the fur in sections and massage it.

BROKEN BONES

Broken bones often result from road accidents and falls from high buildings. The bone may be visible in an unusual position under the skin, a limb may be dragged along uselessly, or be held in an awkward or unusual position. Immobilize the cat in a strong carry basket containing soft bedding and take him to the vet as soon as possible.

BURNS

Burns are the result of *dry* heat, scalds of *wet* heat. The commonest cause of burns is hot cooking fat; corrosive poisons will also burn the mouth, lips and tongue.

If a cat's fur is fire, smother the flames by excluding air with a thick rug, coat or blanket. Signs of minor burns, which are often caused by the cat getting too close to a hot stove, are: singed whiskers and fur; a smell of burning hanging around the cat; limping (look for blisters on the pads); bald, blistered, raw, red patches, constantly licked.

Treat burns as follows:

Major burns: Splash as much cold water as possible over the cat, wrap him in a clean sheet and rush him to the vet.

Minor burns: Dab the burn with cold water. If the burn is on a paw, hold the paw under a running tap if possible. Dry gently and apply white petroleum jelly frequently. Keep the cat in until the burn heals to avoid the entry of dirt and associated bacteria.

Corrosive chemical burns: Concentrated chemicals such as battery acid, caustic soda or ammonia may be brushed against or walked over by a cat, thus contaminating the coat or pads, which are then licked and the chemical taken on to the lips and tongue or into the mouth and throat. To treat, flood the affected areas – coat, paws, lips and/or mouth – with as much cold water as possible. If it is certain that an acid has been ingested, follow by flooding with a solution of sodium bicarbonate (2 parts made up to 100 parts with water). If the offending chemical is an alkali, such as caustic soda or ammonia, follow by flooding with vinegar (5 parts made up to 100 parts with water). Never force liquid down a cat's throat. Seek veterinary help.

EAR PROBLEMS
See page 84.

EYE INJURIES
If the eye appears damaged, perhaps by a rose thorn, or a white area is apparent, or blood is seen, or a flattened area appears on the cornea, urgent veterinary treatment should be sought. A flat area on the eye may be the first symptom of a developing corneal ulcer which, unless treated in time, may prove incurable.

If the eye is partially closed and watery, the cat may have blundered into a twig, or grit may have entered the eye as a result of a high wind or during the course of a dust bath. Even slight damage to the surface of the eye can allow an invasion of bacteria. The eye should be treated as described on page 44. If there is no improvement visible on the following day, the cat should be taken to the vet. In some cases, ointment may be needed up to three times a day for life!

HEAT STRESS
Cats shut in a chalet or run, in a small, unventilated room, in a parked car or even in a carry basket in full sun may suffer from heat stress. Cats have sweat glands only on their paws and cannot cool themselves by the evaporation of sweat as we do. Cats suffering from heat stress may be panting (breathing rapidly through an open mouth) in an attempt to take in cooler air, or licking their fur to try

to cool themselves by evaporation of saliva. Heat stress is particularly dangerous for short-nosed, long-haired pedigree cats, the asthmatic and the overweight. Affected cats should be taken to a cool, airy place and sponged with cold water or wrapped in wet sheets. In hot weather cats must be kept in well-ventilated, shady conditions and be provided with lots of iced drinking water.

MOUTH DAMAGE

Cats occasionally catch a bee or wasp in the mouth. This is very dangerous as the swelling resulting from a sting can cause difficulty in breathing. In such a case urgent veterinary treatment is required.

If you notice your cat pawing his mouth, carry out an examination of the inside using the technique described on page 41. Foreign matter, such as gristle, decayed meat, string, grass, a needle or prey bone, may have become stuck. This can sometimes be removed with tweezers; if not, a visit to the vet will be necessary. A prey bone may have punctured the mouth, causing an ulcer, which may clear up without treatment.

PAD PROBLEMS

To inspect a cat's front pads, hold him as shown in Figure 15 facing outwards, and bend each front leg in turn backwards towards his tail, thus turning each pad upwards. To inspect the back pads, reverse the cat and bend each back leg in turn away from you towards his tail, again turning the pads upwards (see Figure 16.)

Pad injuries may be indicated by limping, licking the pads, holding the paw up, or blood spots where the cat has walked. Road accident victims may have shredded claws. Inspect the pads for splinters of wood, metal or glass; thorns, cuts and blisters. Sometimes a claw is wrenched in a cat fight. Foreign bodies may be removable with tweezers. Bathe minor cuts with dilute TCP, apply antiseptic ointment frequently and keep the cat indoors until the wound has healed.

POISONING AND CONVULSIONS

A convulsion (also called a fit or seizure) may last only a few minutes, never recur and the cause may never be found. The most common causes are poisoning, brain tumours or infections of the central nervous system (brain and spinal cord).

The symptoms of a convulsion are very frightening for the cat's owner. The cat may cry out, bite, become restless, begin to travel in circles; the legs and body may twitch; the neck may be extended, curved and rigid; breathing may become rapid and shallow; the

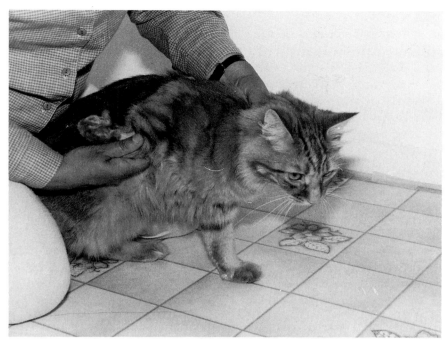

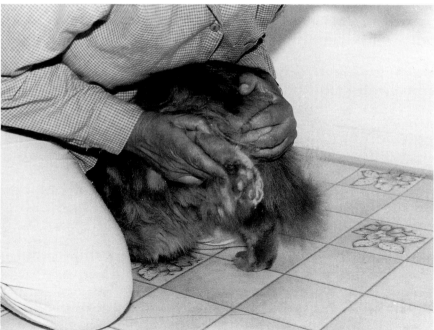

Top FIGURE 15   Inspection of a front pad.
Above FIGURE 16   Inspection of a back pad.

pupils (the black part of the eyes) may enlarge; the cat may jump at the slightest noise and shun light; he may fall on his side, be unable to co-ordinate his leg movements, may become temporarily paralysed, may paddle his legs in the air, grind his teeth or foam at the mouth; he may vomit, and urination and defecation may be involuntary; unconsciousness (coma) and death may follow quickly.

In such a case do not handle the cat, block all means of exit, turn off any heaters, remove any furniture which could cause injury if bumped into, darken the room, and leave the cat alone to recover. Contact your vet for advice. The cause may be trivial and no treatment may be needed.

If poisoning is suspected, and the cat has recovered from the convulsion and is conscious, it may be possible to induce vomiting, although this usually occurs spontaneously upon ingestion of poisonous material. Vomiting can be induced by *one* of the following:

Giving equal parts of hydrogen peroxide and water, about 20 ml in total, from a Brunswick syringe, until vomiting occurs, *or*

Placing a crystal of washing soda into the mouth, so that the cat swallows it, *or*

Giving a mixture of salt and water from a Brunswick syringe, *or*

Giving a mixture of mustard and water from a Brunswick syringe.

It will probably be very difficult to discover exactly what has caused the poisoning. Take to the vet samples in glass jars of any recent meal the cat has eaten, his vomit, and anything you think might be the cause of his sickness, to assist in identification of the poison and thus the choice of an antidote.

SOILED COAT

Never bath a cat for pneumonia can easily result, and never use cleaning fluids or detergents on the coat. If the fur is contaminated with poisonous and/or solid matter, the best course is to cut away the affected portion as rapidly as possible. If the contaminant is not poisonous, remove as much as possible with paper tissues. Then, if it is water-soluble, wash in plain warm water and dry thoroughly. If the contaminant is not water-soluble (for example, tar, grease, oil, petrol), use melted butter applied with cotton wool. To remove mud, allow to dry, rub between the fingers and brush off the coat. Sometimes a stray cat has such matted fur that there is no alternative but to have it cut away under anaesthetic. If grooming has been neglected by the cat, stiff tufts of matted fur may form, which have to be cut out. The tuft to be removed in this way should be held carefully between the fingers to avoid nicking the cat's skin.

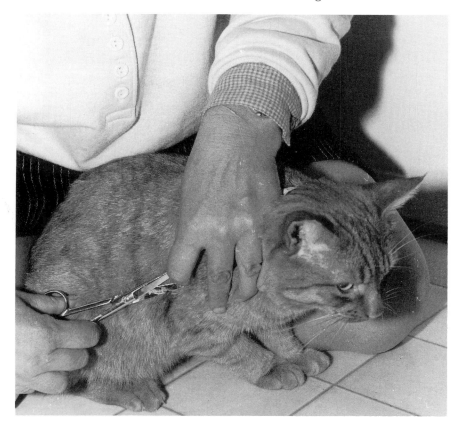

FIGURE 17   Soiled or matted fur should be cut out with blunt-ended scissors. Always hold the portion to be cut between finger and thumb to avoid nicking the skin.

STINGS

If possible locate a sting on the body and carefully cut away the surrounding fur. Bee stings are quite visible because they are black in colour: these should be removed with tweezers. Apply dilute TCP or antiseptic ointment frequently.

For advice about stings in the mouth see under 'Mouth Damage' on page 58.

STRAINS AND SPRAINS

A *strain* results from damage to a muscle; a *sprain* from damage to ligaments which hold joints together.

Kittens and active young cats are especially prone to these injuries because they are most often caused by falls, fights and rough play. Indications are limping, walking with an arched back and inactivity. If no improvement is noticed after a few days' rest, a pain-killing, anti-inflammatory injection may be required, and possibly an X-ray. An X-ray usually necessitates an anaesthetic, so do not feed the cat after 6pm on the day preceding a veterinary examination.

WOUNDS

The treatment of minor surface cuts, scratches and war wounds in areas which the cat can reach with his tongue may safely be left to him, for his saliva contains a natural antiseptic. Scratches on the face, ears and back of the neck should be bathed in dilute TCP, and antiseptic ointment frequently applied.

Serious wounds with extensive bleeding need urgent veterinary care. As an immediate measure, make a pressure pad of lint about ¾ inch (2 centimetres) thick, apply it to the wound and secure in place with medicinal plaster as firmly as possible. Plaster will not stick to fur, so it must be passed round the body or limb so that the overlapped ends can be stuck. (This will only be possible with amenable cats!) Torn ears may need stitches to avoid disfigurement.

5 Feline Infections and How They Are Treated

Infections are the silent, often unseen enemies of all cat owners. It is important to know what is meant by 'infection', to know how to 'disinfect' or kill infections in cat accommodation and give simple treatments to infected cats. A cat owner's aims should be to reduce the number of infections in the cat's environment and avoid their transfer from one cat to another. Infectious diseases should not be confused with the non-infectious type which cannot be transferred from cat to cat (for example, some skin disorders, and tumours).

All infections, although variously classified by biologists, are basically parasites living on or in the cat. They obtain food and protection from the cat, which is called the 'host'. The 'food' may be blood, digested food in the gut, living cells which comprise every organ in the cat's body, or simply dead, outer skin cells. Throughout this book the term 'infection' will mean the same as 'parasite'.

VIRUS INFECTIONS

Cats are particularly susceptible to virus infections. These are by far the most life-threatening infections, since there are no antiviral drugs available at present which will destroy a virus once it is inside a cat.

Viruses are minute protein particles, sometimes with a small 'tail'; they can only be seen with an electron microscope. Viruses are generally regarded as non-living particles since the majority cannot live for very long, grow or multiply unless they can actually enter a living cell (the basic unit which, in great numbers, makes up the cat's body). Every organ of the body consists of several different kinds of cells. The blood is a liquid organ, containing white and red blood cells. Viruses infecting these particular cells are very dangerous, since they will be carried to all parts of the body via the blood.

Once a virus particle (or virion, as it is sometimes called) gains entry to a cat's body, perhaps via a flea bite, through a gut pierced by a prey bone, or from saliva from an already infected cat on some shared prey, the virus attaches itself to the cell by its tail. The inside (or core) of the virus enters the cell. Hundreds of viruses are produced, using the protein of the living cat's cell. After about twenty or thirty minutes (depending on the kind of virus) the cell bursts, liberating the new viruses and the toxins (poisons) they have produced.

The virus particles may now infect neighbouring organs, or they may be confined to one organ (such as the nose) because of the cat's own method of defence called the immune system (see page 90). If the virus enters the blood, an overall virus infection may result, called viraemia.

It follows from the above that an infective virus may be present in any of the cat's secretions or excretions, namely queen's milk, mucus coughed up from infected lungs, nasal discharge, vomit, blood, urine, faeces (particularly when the cat has diarrhoea), eye discharge and saliva. It is easy to imagine how these infective discharges are carried by flying insects, fleas, human hands, shared food, toilet trays, high winds, and so on, to healthy cats. This transfer process is called 'transmission', or 'cross infection', and is discussed later (see page 91).

Once shed from a cat, a virus can remain infective (that is, able to infect, or grow in, another cat) for varying periods of time depending on the type of virus and the environment. Viruses remain infective longer in hot, damp conditions than cold, dry conditions, and longer in poorly ventilated areas, although they cannot *multiply* outside a cat's body. The feline panleucopaenia virus (the cause of a disease of the same name, which is also known as feline infectious enteritis) can remain infective for a year at room temperature. Fortunately, a vaccine is available for this invariably fatal kitten disease. Adults who survive feline panleucopaenia will never show symptoms of it again. The respiratory tract (also known as cat flu) viruses can remain infective for about twenty hours at room temperature. These can be fatal to kittens by causing viraemia; fortunately a vaccine is available. The invariably fatal feline leukaemia virus can survive up to four hours in average conditions outside a host. Once outside a host, however, a virus is easy to kill with the right disinfectant.

The dozens of viruses which can infect cats are usually grouped according to which organs they commonly infect. The many upper respiratory viruses are grouped under two main headings – the feline rhinotracheitis viruses and the feline caliciviruses. Rabies is an example of a virus which infects the brain and spinal cord (that is, the central nervous system, or CNS). General viruses, affecting the whole body, are: feline leukaemia, feline sarcoma, feline peritonitis and feline panleucopaenia. The feline sarcoma virus can infect any cells of the body, causing them to divide out of control. These cells of the cat's body are now cancerous, and malignant tumours will result. Pieces of the tumour may break away and be carried to other focal points in the body.

Viruses cause inflammation of an organ. This means the organ is swollen, painful and sometimes bleeds. For example, a gut virus will cause inflammation of the gut, resulting in vomiting and/or diarrhoea and sometimes bleeding showing in the faeces or vomit. A general gut infection and inflammation is called gastritis. Inflammation of the small intestine is called enteritis, of the bladder cystitis, of the kidneys nephritis. Toxins produced by viruses, or accidentally ingested, are removed by the kidneys; if these are excessive, permanent kidney damage results. The very thought of the feline leukaemia virus strikes fear in the heart of everyone who has rescued the local tatty stray, who rescues and rehomes cats in need, who owns a boarding or breeding cattery or breeds pedigree cats. Its tragic effects will inevitably be encountered sooner or later. Here the virus infects the bone marrow, and hence the red and white blood cells which are made in the marrow. The white cells, vital agents in the fight against viral diseases, are rendered unable to fight *any* infection.

A knowledge of the transmission, detection and treatment of virus diseases and how to reduce their numbers in the cat's environment is vital to everyone owning cats.

A cat who has contracted a virus may in fact show no symptoms, or may be only slightly lethargic or off his food. The incubation period may pass unnoticed. But once a cat has programmed the correct antibody to a particular virus, it cannot be assumed that he is completely free of that virus, nor can it be assumed that such a cat is incapable of 'shedding' the virus in saliva, faeces or urine, and thus infecting other cats. Every admission to a multicat establishment must be assumed to be a source of potential infection to the other felines. This is why all cats are kept permanently separated in holiday boarding catteries, and why newly introduced cats are isolated from domiciled ones for at least a fortnight. In the case of boarding catteries, all equipment and vacated premises are disinfected before the admission of a new boarder.

The symptoms of a virus infection are, of course, dependent on whether the virus is general (that is, affecting the body generally) or localized (specific).

If your cat does show symptoms, the first will probably take the form of one or more of the following: dull coat, clumpy fur, loss of appetite and a tendency to sleep in a quiet, unobtrusive place. These are easy to spot if a cat's behaviour is known, but if a cat is in an unaccustomed environment a loss of appetite may be due to a change of diet, or a sudden decrease in activity as a result of confinement or the arrival of hot weather. Later the haw (or third eyelid) may be seen, like a white curtain partially covering the eye. A rise in body temperature may be indicated by trembling, rapid breathing, and lying flat or hunched on a cold floor. There may be sneezing, dribbling, panting, raised heartbeat, vomiting and diarrhoea. Any cat who constantly catches infections, with seemingly no hope of a permanent cure, must be suspected of being infected with the deadly feline leukaemia virus. A blood test may indicate the presence of live bacteria and an increased white blood cell count because the white cells are not maturing and dying normally – they are non-functional.

Viruses are easy to kill on surfaces (by disinfectants) and in the air of indoor accommodation (by virucidal sprays or vaporizers), but there are no anti-viral drugs currently available to destroy them once they have entered a cat's body. Antiseptics containing phenol can penetrate the skin, but are of doubtful value against viruses, which usually enter via the nose and mouth.

Some treatment of virus infections is possible, however. Your vet can give an injection containing hormones (or chemical messengers) called corticosteroids which stimulate the appetite, raise the blood glucose level and help, in some cases, to reduce eye and nose discharges. The injection may also contain vitamins, for a lowered or non-existent appetite results in a decrease in the body's vitamins. A reduction in vitamins, particularly vitamin A, favours the growth and multiplication of all viral, bacterial and larger parasitic infections. To combat secondary bacterial infections, an antibiotic is also injected, followed by a five-day course of oral antibiotic tablets (that is, given by mouth), which may be crushed on the food. If the cat is not eating and inflammation of the gut is present, any tablets given orally may be vomited. In this case, a daily injection may be necessary. Antibiotic injections act much faster than oral antibiotics. The injection lasts for twenty-four hours, by which time the normally healthy cat with a competent immune system is well on the way to recovery. An injection can be intramuscular (for example, into the muscle of the back leg), or sub-cutaneous (just under the skin), usually into the thick skin at the back of the neck called the 'scruff'.

Antibiotics, and other injected or orally administered drugs, reach all parts of the body via the blood – except the eyes, which have to be treated separately (see pages 44 and 57). They are not selective, and when long-term oral antibiotics are necessary the gut flora (bacteria) may be killed as well. To offset this, ¼ teaspoonful of *natural*, unsweetened yoghurt should be given daily on food – yoghurt contains bacteria similar to the gut flora.

Remaining treatment consists of keeping the cat isolated in a quiet, warm room and feeding high-protein, easily digested food like casseroled rabbit and lightly steamed white fish.

FELINE LEUKAEMIA VIRUS

As usual it is the stressed, strays, ferals and cats in sub-health living in city colonies that are at risk. When any cat is challenged by active virus, either the cat develops immunity or the virus persists, perhaps to activate only under stress. In cats where the virus persists, 90 per cent die within four years.

The virus is thought to infect the salivary glands first, but the main infection site is the bone marrow where all types of blood cells are made. The effect of the virus is to prevent maturation of white blood cells. Like all cells, white blood cells are constantly being destroyed and replaced, but when infected with the virus they do not mature and are not destroyed. This results in blood containing a vast number of immature non-functional white cells – in fact, the word 'leukaemia' means 'white blood'. Red blood cells are destroyed by the virus and thus the oxygen-carrying capacity of the blood is reduced.

The white blood cells called lymphocytes, occurring in the lymph nodes and in the blood, may become infected simultaneously by a similar virus called feline sarcoma. This virus, which has not been proved to be transmittable, causes lymphocytes to divide continuously, resulting in tumours in the lymph nodes. Infected lymphocytes may be carried via the blood to any organ – for example, the stomach, liver, kidneys or lungs – where tumours may form. Tumours of the lymph nodes are often an end stage symptom of the leukaemia syndrome.

Diagnosis

Symptoms occur so gradually that they are often not recognized in the early stages by vets or cat owners, but in any event there is no cure at present.

(1) A blood test can only demonstrate the presence of feline leukaemia antibody. It cannot tell whether a cat has overcome the virus, or whether the cat will infect under stress or whether the cat is actively infected. Spontaneous recoveries have occurred. Owners should, of course, prevent breeding. Infected entire cats are unlikely

to exhibit sexual behaviour, and it is inadvisable to have likely
leukaemic cats de-sexed because of the 'trigger' effect of the anaesthetic. Because of the danger to other cats, and the danger that other
cats will transmit infections to leukaemic cats, to which they have no
immunity, all leukaemic cats should be confined to the house.

(2) A gradual change in behaviour not accounted for by age will be
noticed, as will the cat's inclination to sleep more and eat less. The
incubation period is uncertain but three to twelve months has been
suggested. Episodes of infections of the upper respiratory tract, lungs,
kidneys, liver and gut may respond to antibiotic treatment, or the
cat may appear to make a spontaneous recovery, but response lessens
because of the waning immune system. Wound healing may be slow
– for example, there may be permanent scratch marks on the temples.
Bacterial gingivitis, particularly at the angle of the jaw (sometimes
called 'rodent ulcer'), may cause mouth discomfort and loss of appetite but may respond to antibiotics at first. Corticosteroids may be
prescribed, but although these reduce inflammation, they can further
damage kidneys already damaged by poisons or infections. No antibiotic can destroy all bacteria: the immune system must finish the
job. Live bacteria may be identifiable in the blood.

(3) Vaccines against other infections will not work. A leukaemic cat
may die of cat flu or feline panleucopaenia. A general viral infection
called feline infectious peritonitis is, itself, immunosuppressive, and
often proves fatal to leukaemic cats.

(4) A leukaemic queen does not automatically infect her kittens, but
is unlikely to carry kittens to full term.

(5) As the disease advances, the cat will become weaker, with a
permanently high temperature.

Treatment

If medication, easily digestible food, complete rest, disinfection and
isolation can maintain a good quality of life, the leukaemic cat may
survive for up to five years.

A vaccine has been developed in America by the Cornell Feline
Health Center, which in trials has proved effective in the case of
feline leukaemia negative cats – that is, those who are believed not
to have active feline leukaemia virus. It is not known when this will
be available in the UK.

For those cats with persistent virus, hope lies in the work of
Professor Jarrett at the University of Glasgow Veterinary School. He
is working on monoclonal antibody, which is produced initially in
the blood of rats and mice artificially infected with feline leukaemia
virus. Monoclonal antibody can be produced in a laboratory outside

the body of a rodent, so these creatures are not used in great numbers. When large quantities of the antibody have been produced, clinical trials on infected cats can begin.

The feline leukaemia virus is fragile outside the host, and may remain infective for only three to four hours on a dry surface at room temperature. Nevertheless, a thirty-day waiting period is recommended before reoccupation of units vacated by leukaemic cats.

The human virus which causes AIDS (acquired immune deficiency syndrome) shows very similar symptoms in humans. But it is stressed that cats cannot catch AIDS from humans, and humans cannot catch feline leukaemia from cats.

FELINE PANLEUCOPAENIA VIRUS (FELINE INFECTIOUS ENTERITIS)

Vaccination has practically eradicated this virus, but pockets remain in feral and stray cat colonies. All rescued cats should be vaccinated before introduction into a healthy cat community. Even a vaccinated cat may carry active virus and thus pose a risk to others, particularly kittens, old cats and leukaemic cats. Booster vaccinations are necessary, at least until a cat is eight years old. The feline panleuco-paenia virus is a 'strong' antigen (substance which causes an immune response) because it causes the cat to make large quantities of anti-body quickly. Protection is, therefore, rapid, taking about three days to become effective, and boosters are normally only necessary every two or three years to ensure that a cat challenged by live field virus can respond rapidly.

Diagnosis

Death occurs within twelve to twenty-four hours from the onset of symptoms. The disease is invariably fatal in kittens; about 50 per cent of adults recover and are then immune for life. The infected cat is too weak to move, often hanging over the water bowl, too weak to drink. He may lie on a cool surface, legs outstretched, indicating a high temperature. There is vomiting, dehydration, rapid weight loss, and an inability to eat or drink. Diarrhoea usually occurs only at the end of the course of the disease, at which stage recovery is a possi-bility. Large quantities of liquid faeces are passed, dark with digested blood from the inflamed gut. There is a severe loss of white cells at the infection sites all along the gut. The word 'leucopaenia' means 'low white blood count'.

Treatment

Veterinary care, hospitalization and convalescence in an isolation unit are necessary. Transmission of the disease is by all usual methods. The virus (a parvovirus) can remain infective for up to a year at ordinary room temperatures. Vacated premises, disinfected with sodium hypochlorite, should be left vacant for at least six months. No unvaccinated cats or kittens should be housed in a previously infected cattery or multicat accommodation for at least two years.

UPPER RESPIRATORY TRACT (CAT FLU) VIRUSES

Many variations on feline rhinotracheitis (feline herpes) virus and feline calicivirus exist, and are constantly undergoing slight changes, but all are antigenically similar, and the same vaccine can be used for all. Some strains of virus cause more severe symptoms than others and vaccination may have the effect only of reducing those symptoms, giving limited immunity. Vaccines for the cat flu viruses cannot protect against viral lung infections.

The cat flu viruses are 'weak' antigens, antibody being produced slowly in small quantities. Protection takes six weeks from vaccination, although the nasal drop vaccine works more quickly since antibody is produced at the most vulnerable site – that is, in the nose and throat. Protection by nasal drop takes about one week and is used mostly for those cats who have to be unexpectedly boarded. Symptoms of sneezing and eye watering may follow such vaccination. Frequent boostering is necessary, every six to twelve months, because the cells lining the nose, throat and mouth (called mucosal cells) cannot maintain protective immunity for longer periods. This is beyond the financial resources of those with many cats, and the best solution may be to have kittens vaccinated every six months for, say, one and a half years.

In fact, cat flu viruses are so common in the environment that natural boostering must occur. Dormancy and activation under stress are common. Cats who have recovered from feline calicivirus often shed virus continuously, but feline rhinotracheitis-recovered cats are more likely to shed virus intermittently under stress. Cat flu viruses can remain infective for up to twenty hours in average moist room temperatures.

Diagnosis

The wide variation in symptoms is dependent on several factors: the degree of stress the cat is suffering; the quality of his food; the concentration of the challenge virus (that is, the quantity of a particular virus to which the cat is exposed); the duration of contact between donor cat and susceptible cat; the type of virus (feline calicivirus usually gives rise to more severe symptoms); and the method of transmission (see page 91). Infection may be through the skin, if it is punctured by a cat bite, prey bite, broken glass or, say, a blow from a moving car; or it may enter via the lungs if they become damaged by smoke or air polluted by chemicals.

Symptoms include: clumpy, dull fur; loss of appetite; sneezing; sore throat, indicated by red stripes in the throat, frequent swallowing, gulping and extension of the tongue; white or yellow spots on the tongue (ulcers) called glossitis, usually associated with feline calicivirus; ulcers and redness in the mouth (stomatitis); pawing at the mouth; loss of smell and taste contributing to a depressed appetite, rapid loss of weight; inactivity; tendency in the cat to make himself unavailable and conceal himself; unusual thirst; protruding haw, giving the eyes a 'tired' appearance; croaky miaow or purr, or absence of both; hot, dry, sore nose, with discharge, clear at first but becoming yellow (an indication of secondary bacterial infection); ocular (eye) discharge, watery or thick yellow; dribbling; noisy breathing (snuffling); breathing through an open mouth; coughing; mouth odour; nosebleeds; raised temperature (see page 102).

Treatment

A normally healthy, non-stressed, adult cat, having spent a night out stalking a vole, may simply sneeze, sleep and carry on eating, and need no treatment other than confinement, warmth and rest. For cats more seriously affected, however, veterinary treatment will probably be necessary.

RABIES VIRUS

Cats have more resistance to the rabies virus than man and dogs but, once they are infected, the disease is terminal. The virus infects the brain and spinal cord (central nervous system, or CNS). Transmission of rabies to cats is normally via the saliva of an infected dog biting the cat.

The virus is easily destroyed by heat, chlorine, formalin and phenol. A 1 per cent Domestos solution (see page 128) is recommended for treating infected surfaces, which should be allowed to dry without rinsing, thus ensuring rapid destruction of the virus and a residual, persistent disinfection. The virus loses its infectivity in a few hours on surfaces contaminated by saliva from an infected animal.

The UK is free from rabies, but all that is necessary to introduce it is for someone to take pity on a stray cat or dog during a continental holiday and try to smuggle it into this country. If rabies should reach our shores, all cats and dogs will have to be confined. It is against the law to smuggle any animal into the UK. To import any animal, an import licence must be obtained from:

In England and Wales
Ministry of Agriculture,
    Fisheries and Food,
Hook Rise South,
Tolworth,
Surbition,
Surrey.

In Scotland
Department of Agriculture and
    Fisheries for Scotland,
Chesser House,
500 Gorgie Road,
Edinburgh,
EH11 3AW.

On arrival in the UK, all animals must be quarantined for six months. Full information concerning the import of animals and a list of licensed quarantine accommodation can be obtained from the relevant ministry.

A rabies vaccine is available, and all cats taken out of the UK should, for their own protection, be vaccinated.

BACTERIAL INFECTIONS

Bacteria are one-celled plants, not all of which are pathogenic (harmful). Those that *do* infect cats do not enter cells, like viruses, but they are able to use the liquid foods (fats, proteins and sugars) present in the gut, blood and in the fluid between the cells. But, like viruses, they produce waste products which are toxic to living cells.

Bacteria can be seen with an ordinary microscope. In favourable conditions they can divide and so reproduce themselves every 30 minutes. Some beneficial bacteria are free-living; some, which live in the small intestine of the cat, are called the gut bacteria or gut flora. These manufacture some of the B vitamins required by the cat, aid digestion and produce antibiotics which kill some of the harmful bacteria present on decayed prey, dustbin refuse or birdtable scraps. It is always an amazing revelation to the cat owner when she realizes how much revolting rubbish her cat can consume with impunity!

Available to vets are a large number of antibiotics which kill many of the bacteria causing disease in cats. Some of these drugs, which kill a large number of bacteria, are called wide-spectrum antibiotics. Some are specific or narrow-range antibiotics, which kill only one or two types of bacteria. Any skin surface initially damaged by a virus is liable to attack by bacteria. Such an attack is called a 'secondary' bacterial infection. Not all bacterial infections are treatable with antibiotic, or the appropriate antibiotic may not be found in time to save the cat.

An alarming trend is the increasing use of antibiotics by farmers. These are given routinely to poultry and farm animals and are thus present in fresh and canned catfood. Continual use, or continual consumption of antibiotics in food, may result in resistant strains of bacteria against which usual antibiotics will be ineffective. For this reason penicillin, once so effective, has had to be largely replaced by new antibiotics.

Harmful, or potentially harmful, bacteria abound in the environment, and some are actually resident on a cat's teeth and claws. Normally they are harmless, but should they enter the skin as a result of a cat fight or a deep cut or gash, a general bacterial infection of the blood may result – called septicaemia. If a wound is not too deep, the infection is only a local affair. Immediately bacteria enter the skin, below the dead outer layer, the skin cells produce chemicals called histamines which cause the surface blood vessels in that area to enlarge, thus bringing extra blood and hence white cells to the infection site. Special white blood cells, called macrophages, engulf and break up the bacteria and any other foreign particles. Young, fighting cats in particular may develop red, hot, swollen, painful areas which eventually burst, liberating an odorous white pus which consists of dead white cells, dead bacteria and toxins. These swellings, which are very common, are called abscesses. In multicat families or rescue centres habitually aggressive cats may have to be housed separately to protect their fellows from damage which might result in these painful abcesses.

All bacterial (and viral) infections may result in a rise in body temperature, production of toxins (poisonous waste products), death of cells, and other symptoms, depending on the organ infected.

Bacterial eye infections are common. The eye can be damaged by another cat's claws, bonfire smoke, dust, grit, high winds, fly sprays and flea sprays or powders. The initial damage allows entry of bacteria. Fortunately, eye bacteria cannot reach the rest of the body.

Bacteria grow on rotting food, rancid fat and dried catfood which has been stored in a damp place. Cats, being scavengers and carrion eaters, as well as carnivores, often eat revolting waste food, which may have been contaminated by the saliva and urine not only of other cats, but also rats, mice, voles and other animals. Cats usually get away with it, because the stomach generally repels such food by vomiting. Prolonged diarrhoea can occur if bacteria and their toxins reach the intestine. Most cats recover in a few days, but, again, neighbours' cats should be protected by keeping your own cat in. Antibiotic treatment, possibly by injection, may be necessary. The importance of cooking all food other than meat and offal sold for human consumption has already been stressed.

In view of the wide variety of bacteria which may be present on a fighting cat's teeth and claws, even an old fighter may not have immunity to a particular bacteria not previously encountered. Prompt antibiotic treatment and bathing wounds (if they can be found!) with dilute TCP may prevent abscess formation or general infection of the blood by bacteria.

It is important to remember that no antibiotic can kill *all* bacteria. The immune system must be competent enough to destroy residual bacteria. The leukaemic cat, whose immune system is waning, will therefore suffer continually from bacterial infections.

PROTOZOA

These are microscopic, one-celled animals. Parasitic protozoa can infect any organ of the cat's body, but are mainly located in the gut, where they cause inflammation, bleeding, vomiting and diarrhoea. The best known is *Toxoplasma gondii*. Specific curative drugs are available once a vet has diagnosed the infection – not always an easy matter. Drugs may have to be administered without a definite diagnosis.

FUNGI (OR DERMATOPHYTES)

These are microscopic, many-celled plants, parasitic on dead cells – fur, skin and claws. The most common is ringworm. Transfer is by spores.

RINGWORM
Strays and ferals are likely to be infected, and all rescued strays must be checked for the presence of ringworm. Ringworm, a type of fungus, infects dead skin, fur, whiskers and claws with minute filaments which produce spores in great numbers – it cannot grow on living skin. Spores are equivalent to the seeds of a flowering plant, and spread by being borne away in the air. Healthy cats develop immunity to ringworm spores and, although in close contact with an infected cat, may not develop symptoms.

An early symptom is the appearance of a round or irregular patch of thinning fur, lighter in colour than the surrounding fur. The fur becomes brittle and later a bald patch may appear. This patch may enlarge, then appear to heal, only to be followed by the development of a similar patch elsewhere. Secondary bacterial infections may result in pus-filled pustules. Infected claws may appear mottled.

A definite diagnosis is difficult. The only certain way is to brush the suspected sufferer's fur with a toothbrush first washed in dilute Domestos, rinsed and dried. Take the fur sample thus obtained to your vet, and he will arrange for a laboratory culture. The vet can check whether the culture is ringworm by examining it under a microscope.

Treatment should always be under veterinary supervision. Disinfection by sodium hypochlorite (see page 124) will be sufficient for routine disinfection of multicat accommodation, but, once ringworm has been diagnosed, a more specific iodine-based disinfectant may be prescribed by your vet.

Griseofulvin is given internally to the cat. This is fungistatic (that is, it prevents the growth of fungus). Iodine-based disinfectant is applied to the fur (kept well away from the eyes, nose and the area beneath the tail). Treatment may take six weeks or more, and is expensive and time-consuming. Any contacts should be traced and treated, just in case they have contracted ringworm.

METAZOA

These are many-celled animals which, in their adult forms, can be seen with a magnifying glass or even the naked eye. They are transferred from cat to cat, or from cat to intermediate host and then to another cat. They begin life as eggs, passing through several other stages before they reach maturity and are themselves capable of egg-laying.

Parasitic metazoa are divided into two groups: ectoparasites, which live on the outside of a cat, on dead (outer) skin, or by biting the skin and sucking blood; and endoparasites, which live inside the cat, commonly in the gut.

The commonest ectoparasites in the UK are fleas, biting lice, ticks, body mites, ear mites. The commonest endoparasites in the UK are roundworms and tapeworms.

Metazoa have at least one vulnerable stage in their lives when they can be easily killed, but treatment must be prompt because, like all parasites, they breed rapidly.

FLEAS

My cat isolation room had been vacant for a week, pending a thorough disinfection. Only a sheet of polythene covered the floorboards. Late one night I heard a curious clickety-click coming from beneath the polythene. To my horror, hundred of fleas were trying to hop out! That's where they all were, inaccessible and waiting . . .

Some cat owners refuse to acknowledge that their cats are ever infested with fleas. At the other end of the scale, some owners become almost paranoid at the mere thought of these parasites. It is hoped that this section will help owners to realize that all cats are liable to flea infestation, but that, once detected, their presence need be no cause for alarm. Modern anti-flea preparations are quick-acting and effective, but over-frequent treatment must be avoided as it is all too easy to give a cat an overdose of insecticide.

FIGURE 18   An adult flea (actual size about the size of a pinhead).

Fleas cannot fly; they can only jump. Nevertheless, they are insects, with a life cycle similar to that of a butterfly. Adult fleas vary in size according to the species, but all are about pinhead size, reddish-brown, always around yet seldom seen. The life cycle begins when adult fleas lay their glistening, white eggs on carpets, between floorboards, under carpet edges, in damp places in the garden and, occasionally, on the cats themselves. The eggs, barely visible to the naked eye unless in a group, are highly resistant to adverse weather conditions and can survive for up to eight years! Under favourable conditions – a hot, humid atmosphere – the eggs hatch into minute, white larvae (the equivalent of butterfly caterpillars). The larvae feed only on animal-derived material: faeces, wool, fur, adult flea excreta ('flea dirts') consisting of dried blood, and, of course, any carrion in the garden. After a period of feeding and maturation, the larvae change to pupae, another highly resistant form, equivalent to butterfly chrysalids. The pupae hatch (sometimes in response to vibration, perhaps caused by a moving animal) to become immature fleas. At this stage, cat fleas will bite the skin surface of cats (their preferred hosts if they are cat fleas, but, in the absence of cats, dogs or humans will do!), inject their saliva which prevents the cat's blood clotting, and suck a minute quantity of the host's blood. After several skin changes (or moults), immature fleas become mature and capable of laying eggs.

Like all parasites fleas breed with breathtaking speed, and once their presence has been recognized prompt treatment is vital. It is far, far easier to kill a few young fleas than a few hundred mature ones!

Under hot, humid conditions, the whole life cycle will be completed in about thirty days. Outdoors only eggs and pupae can survive very cold, wet winters, and the life cycle is therefore slowed down. But breeding will continue unabated in centrally heated houses. Thus, all stages in a flea's life history will usually be present in the house or in the garden in summer. Even if a house is kept flea-free the chief reservoir of infection will be outdoors, and all free-roamers will contract fleas.

Adult fleas can survive without food for up to 124 days in warm, humid environments, and under laboratory conditions have been shown to survive without food for 250 days. An unoccupied house may therefore contain large numbers of very hungry fleas and prompt treatment of the environment before reoccupation is essential.

How can we recognize the presence of fleas? Adult fleas may occasionally be seen hopping off cats or emerging from well-furred areas on to paws or temples. Infected cats may wake suddenly from sleep, scratch, run a few paces and give frantic grooming nibbles. But the most reliable guide is examination, under a bright light and with a magnifying glass, of those areas most frequented by fleas and inaccessible to a cat's tongue – under the chin, on the back of the neck and along the spine. Minute, crescent-shaped flea dirts may be seen which, when placed on a damp, white tissue, will stain the tissue pink. Groomings can also be shaken over a damp, white tissue, and any specks collected examined in the same way. In addition to flea excreta, eggs, larvae and pupae can be observed in cat's bedding, on windowsills and, in cases of heavy infestation, even on the cats themselves.

As cats mature their skin becomes more resistant to fleas by producing chemicals which repel them. In some cats this anti-flea reaction leads to excessive irritation, scratching, inflamed skin, fur loss, self-inflicted skin damage and small pustules over large areas, usually the spine. This non-infectious skin condition, sometimes called miliary eczema, is usually attributed to the presence of fleas, yet this has not been conclusively proved to be the cause and some affected cats have been kept indoors and worn flea collars but with no improvement. Treatment is usually by sex hormones, although it is unclear why these work. The condition often disappears after a few years.

Fleas are transmission agents for the commonest kind of tapeworm infecting dogs and cats called *Dipylidium caninum*. The tapeworm eggs, shed from the anus of an infected cat, are swallowed inadvertently by flea larvae whilst feeding. These eggs become encysted in adult fleas, and if a flea is accidentally swallowed by a cat the cysts become tapeworms.

Whilst the odd flea or two cause little inconvenience to healthy, adult cats, heavy infestations in kittens can result in anaemia because of the loss of blood suffered.

However, there are far more sinister reasons why we should try to eliminate, or at least reduce, the number of fleas around cats. Fleas are travelling insects, moving from one feline to another. As fleas inject their saliva, they also inject blood of previously bitten cats. Thus the flea is transferring blood infections, such as viruses and bacteria, from cat to cat. Feline leukaemia virus can be transmitted in this way. Some bacteria thus passed on may prove resistant to all antibiotics and the cat may die of septicaemia. A minute organism called *Haemobartonella felis*, parasitic on red blood cells and responsible for the occasionally fatal disease called feline infectious anaemia, is also carried by fleas. It is generally believed that infection transfer requires close, prolonged contact between cats, but, since they are not gregarious animals, the flea must be implicated in transmission in multicat households and feral colonies. This also applies to any other travelling, blood-sucking parasite – including ticks and biting lice.

The task of eliminating or at least reducing flea numbers in the environment can be approached in two ways: we can treat the cats or the environment. It is unsafe to treat both, since some insecticides are incompatible and can cause dangerous side-reactions if mixed.

As already pointed out, there is no such thing as a 'safe' insecticide or a 'safe' drug. Everything that is used on, in or around cats is potentially dangerous. It is only the correct concentration which renders a chemical 'safe' and therapeutic. Many cats are poisoned because owners do not read manufacturers' instructions carefully enough, or do not listen to and write down veterinary instructions. Manufacturers are often blamed unfairly for selling poisonous chemicals when, in actual fact, the user is to blame for poisoning incidents. Even preparations made up strictly according to instructions and applied correctly may cause adverse effects in some cats, so *any* cat under treatment for *any* disease must be watched closely for signs of distress: panting, excessive salivation, frothing at the mouth, enlarged pupils, skin irritation, lethargy, loss of appetite, trembling, vomiting, diarrhoea, lack of limb co-ordination and so on.

Most insecticides in current use against insects like fleas and arachnids (mites and ticks) are based on Dichlorvos, a type of chemical compound called an organo-phosphorus compound. All such compounds are potentially harmful if inhaled, ingested or absorbed into the skin, to both animals and humans. Although they are harmless in the quantity needed to de-parasitize a cat, humans treating large numbers of cats are advised to avoid inhalation and skin contact where feasible.

Cats detest any defilement of their fur and lick it constantly. In view of this, environment treatment is preferable to applying sprays or powders to cats' fur. The environment method is, of course, the only method available for powerful or unmanageable cats, provided they can be enticed into enclosed accommodation! The most effective treatment is by an electric volatilizer (see page 136). The room or cattery is vacated and the appliance switched on to do its work. All parts of the accommodation can be reached by the now vaporized Dichlorvos-based insecticide given out, and a film of it is left on surfaces. It remains toxic to fleas for about a fortnight, after which the product biodegrades (decomposes). After the Vortex is switched off, the room is aired thoroughly before reoccupation. Use of the appliance for two hours per week in the summer is sufficient: evidence suggest that all stages in a flea's life cycle are killed by Dichlorvos.

Disposable bedding which can be burnt, or easily washable bedding, such as the 80 per cent acrylic/20 per cent polyester fabric with fluffy pile, are the most practical for cats. Theoretically, since flea larvae can feed only on organic material (that is, material derived from animals), if woollen carpets, curtains, upholstery and so on are replaced by cotton, nylon, vinyl or plastics, there is little, in a *clean* indoor environment, for the larvae to feed upon.

Vacuuming is of limited use as fleas, larvae, eggs and pupae may be residing well out of reach, but it will reduce parasite numbers. The vacuum bag should be sprayed or powdered inside, or burnt after use.

Staykil, obtainable from vets, is an environment treatment based on Dichlorvos. Instructions and safety precautions on the aerosol container must be followed to the letter.

New products based on insect growth hormones are reaching the market – for example, Acclaim, available from vets. This is an aerosol spray used on pet bedding, carpets, curtains and upholstery, and in cracks and crevices in a closed, vacated room or house. After one hour, the room is aired. The product is consumed by feeding larvae, and it is claimed that fleas do not emerge from the pupae.

If it is essential to keep cats flea-free (as, for example in the case of those suffering from miliary eczema) they must, if they are free-roaming, be treated with a preparation obtained from a vet. Nuvan Top and Zeprox are aerosol sprays. Nuvan Top and Wellcare are available as powders. Wellcare is based on permethrin and much safer to use, even on kittens, but it kills only fleas – no other parasites. Remember to use only a *minimum* of any preparation.

Thin-furred cats and kittens can be groomed with a light-coloured comb which will show up any reddish-brown fleas on the teeth. The grooming comb, with fine and coarse teeth long enough to reach the skin (where fleas reside), can be plunged into water and any fleas caught will drown easily.

Most cats are terrified of aerosols – hissing, to a cat, means 'Keep away from me!' Since fleas travel, it is only necessary to give a one-second burst along the spine. Alternatively the infested animal can be groomed with a comb that has been sprayed. The cat is restrained as described on page 41. Shake the aerosol and check that the nozzle is working, and the direction in which to point it. Run the fingers through the cat's fur *against* the lie of the coat to raise it (see Figure 19). Cover the cat's face with one hand and give a one-second burst of the aerosol as shown in Figure 20.

Powders are easier to use. The fur is raised as described above and the powder sprinkled as near the skin as possible, then the fur is ruffled to spread the powder. Kittens should never be treated unless absolutely necessary.

Whilst it is unlikely that a cat will eat one of its own fast-moving fleas, or even another cat's fleas during mutual grooming, it is possible that a cat will ingest *dying* fleas, with the risk of tapeworm infection. It is, therefore, important to groom the cat, if he is available (!), fifteen minutes after any treatment. Excess powder will be removed, but a minute amount of insecticide will stop fleas biting for up to a fortnight. Treatment should never be given more than once a fortnight, and then only if the presence of fleas is confirmed.

Some owners find flea collars very effective for their cats, but these have limitations. First, the cat is continuously exposed to the insecticide near the mouth, nose and eyes; this may cause symptoms of poisoning in some cats, lethargy, or discoloration and/or loss of fur. Second, in case of incompatibility no other insecticide should be

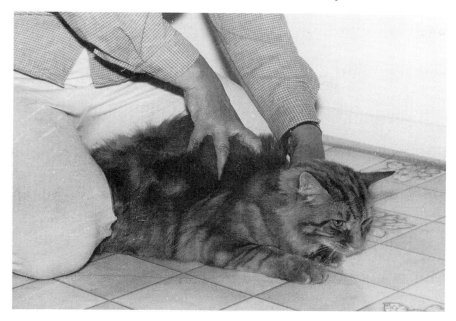

FIGURE 19   Raising fur before applying powder or spray against external parasites.

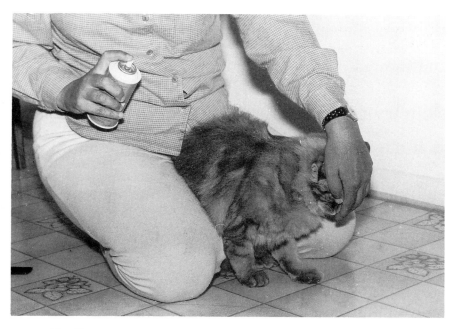

FIGURE 20   Use of flea spray: note that the cat's eyes are covered.

FIGURE 21   Using a flea comb. This has very close teeth and sometimes fleas can be trapped in it during grooming and drowned in a conveniently placed container of water. Cats who are resistant to grooming can often be groomed when sleepy. Chin scratching will help to disguise your true intentions.

used on the cat or in the house, including fly sprays, fly papers and so on. Third, a flea collar can only kill fleas living in, or traversing, the neck region; the insecticide cannot be spread by the cat's tongue (as is popularly believed) because a cat cannot reach the back of his neck, or underneath his chin. Fourth, ordinary cat collars, particularly those without an elastic insert, are dangerous if they catch in tree branches, cats' mouths or claws and are particularly dangerous for active, young, climbing and hunting cats. Cats have been strangled by such collars. If a quick-release safety collar (available from the Cats Protection League) is used, it can be powdered or sprayed on the *inside* only.

Herbal flea remedies are not strong enough actually to kill fleas. At best they repel fleas, which will go elsewhere. The best-known herb (or green plant) with insecticidal repellent properties is pyrethrum. The flowers are dried, crushed and used to fill fabric bags to place in cats' bedding.

Some vets prescribe Cyflee tablets, administered orally over a period of a few weeks. In view of the fact that they are organophosphorus-based and enter the blood, I would not recommend them.

PARASITES MORE LIKELY TO BE FOUND ON STRAY, FERAL AND FARM CATS

The powder or spray used to treat the following parasites (infections) must be an insecticide *and* acaricide, supplied by a vet. The Vortex unit containing Dichlorvos, described in the section on fleas, can be used in enclosed accommodation, but it is unlikely that this will result in complete eradication of the parasites discussed below. This is because, for safety reasons, the concentration of insecticide is not high enough.

BITING LICE (INSECTS)

The light grey eggs of lice may be seen in groups attached to the base of a cat's fur. These hatch directly into lice, with no intermediate forms. Lice are non-jumping, non-flying, light grey or brownish, fast-moving, blood-sucking insects, capable of travelling from cat to cat in search of pastures new, and are thus transmitters of blood-borne infections. The adults are treated in the same way as fleas. Eggs grouped at the base of fur can be cut out along with the fur itself and burnt.

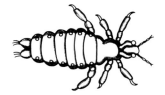

FIGURE 22   An adult louse (actual size slightly larger than a pinhead).

TICKS (ARACHNIDS)

When newly attached, ticks resemble minute pinkish outgrowths of skin, usually on the cat's head. They are contracted as cats stalk through pastures grazed by farm animals. They attach themselves by means of sucker-like mouthparts to the skin, puncture the skin and, as they engorge themselves on the cat's blood, enlarge to pea-size, changing in colour to purplish grey. Catching sight of ticks in this state, a cat owner may be forgiven for thinking her cat has lead shot embedded in his temples! After a few days' intensive feeding, the ticks drop off and live freely until all the blood has been used. Having shrivelled to their former size (after about a year), they reattach themselves to another animal, not necessarily a cat. After about three years, ticks produce eggs and die.

During routine grooming, it is advisable to feel all over the cat's body with fingertips and check any protuberances, for ticks may crawl up a cat's legs and attach themselves under the legpits. Take care over their removal, however: if ticks are jerked off with tweezers, there is a danger that the mouthparts will remain, causing a damaged area which may be invaded by bacteria or viruses. The best way to remove a tick is to raise its body with tweezers in order to locate the mouthparts, and dab these with Nuvan Top (or an equivalent) using a cotton bud. About an hour later, hold the tick at its mouthparts and gently pull: a dead tick is easily removed. If it is resistant, repeat the treatment. Some vets simply hold the tick at the mouthparts and give a sharp tug – the element of surprise is important; others cut a tick's body in half, when the attached half will die and drop off. Whatever the method, the area should be dabbed with antiseptic ointment. Heavy infestations are usually treated with Nuvan Top spray, as described for fleas; but, unlike fleas, ticks can infest any part of the body, and most areas will require treatment.

BODY MITES (ARACHNIDS)

The commonest are harvest mites and dandruff mites (cheyletiella). Resembling minute spiders, they live on dead skin, where they cause thickening of the skin and intense irritation. Harvest mites are bright orange, and may be found in the small pouch at the base of the outer ear. Dandruff mites are brownish and may live between the pads, or on the surface of the skin, where they cause excessive sloughing off of dead skin (dandruff). Transfer is by close contact between cats, for example, bed sharing in the garden or house, or mutual grooming. Treatment is by insecticidal/acaricidal powder or spray.

EAR MITES (ARACHNIDS)

These very common, minute, glistening, white creatures reside out of sight deep in the inner ear. Kittens are often infected by the queen. Although they live on dead skin, ear mites set up intense irritation which causes the ear to produce an excessive amount of brown wax. This dries on the outer ear, looking like brown scale, and is shed during scratching. An infected cat is obviously in great discomfort, shaking his head, scratching his ears and holding his head on one side, if parasite numbers are high. Stray cats are liable to suffer self-inflicted skin damage, baldness and a haematoma (blood blister) which, if untreated, can leave a cat with a permanently deformed ear. In cases of light infection no discomfort will be evident, the only signs being brown wax in the ear.

Ear mites are easy to treat. All that is necessary is a few drops of a veterinary-supplied acaricidal oil (also containing antibiotic against possible secondary bacterial invasion of the damaged ear) squirted into the ear twice a day for about a week. Application with a dropper bottle is the easiest method. The brown wax will slough off, but if you want your cat to look smart quickly *visible* brown scale may be removed with a cotton bud moistened with oil. Heavy infestations will probably require initial veterinary treatment.

ROUNDWORMS

The commonest species of roundworm affecting cats and dogs is *Toxascaris leonina*. The adult worm is white, 2 millimetres in diameter and 2½–4 inches (6–10 centimetres) long. The species affecting cats only is *Toxocara cati*, which is a little larger. Both species inhabit the stomach and intestines of cats, living on the liquid food around them.

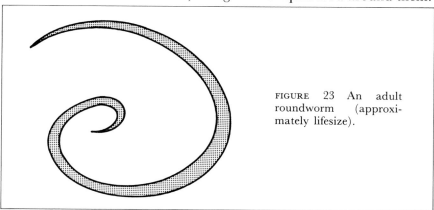

FIGURE 23 An adult roundworm (approximately lifesize).

Infection of the cat is by eggs passed in faeces and it is therefore present in soiled toilet-tray filler and garden toilet areas. In multicat establishments hygienic disposal of waste material is very important to avoid infection risk to free-roaming residents or neighbours' free-roamers. The surface of roundworm eggs is uneven, thus enabling them to stick to a cat's paws whence, on washing, they are transferred to the mouth. In both types of roundworm, eggs swallowed by prey animals of the cat remain as larvae in the liver of the prey, only maturing when swallowed by the cat.

Heavy infestations are uncommon among domestic cats, who are often able to vomit roundworms with the aid of couch grass. Kittens can be infected by roundworm eggs in toilet areas or by sharing infested prey. Normally queens are roundwormed just before being sent to stud, and it may be considered necessary to confine them thereafter, since they cannot be roundwormed once pregnant. It is possible, but not proven, that kitten infection via a queen's milk may occur, or immature worms may be transferred across the placenta to the unborn foetus.

As cats mature they develop the ability to produce chemicals in the gut wall which interfere with the maturation of roundworms, which may therefore be inactivated and remain as larvae in the gut wall or muscles. Although by the time the cat reaches the age of five or six years, roundworms may be parasites of the past, larvae can remain and reactivate under stress. This may account for a cat becoming infected with adult roundworms on entry to a boarding cattery, or after a period of homelessness, or the reappearance of roundworms in very old cats, when immunity is on the wane. Pregnancy is stressful, and reactivated larvae may infect kittens as described above.

Stressed cats are far more likely to show symptoms of infection and carry heavy burdens. Healthy cats may have one or two in the gut and show no symptoms whatever. Symptoms observed in cats and kittens may include: vomiting live or dead worms, or passing them in faeces; protruding haw; watery eyes; bloated stomach; loss of weight; lethargy; insatiable hunger; persistent diarrhoea; sparse, dull coat; heavy moulting. Positive identification can be made by a vet, by examination of a faecal sample for eggs (the vet will provide a suitable container).

Treatment of roundworm infection is very easy. A vet may prescribe tablets such as Citrazine or Endorid. Some cats will take these crushed in food, others have to be given entire pills as described on page 41. The normal dosage is 1 tablet per 10 lb (4.5 kilograms) of cat. Kittens from four months old need ¼ tablet, adolescents up to nine months old need ½ tablet and outsizes 1¼ tablets. The treatment is repeated after ten days, and again after a further ten days if symptoms reappear. Treatment can result in temporary diarrhoea. Unfortunately, hunting cats may become reinfected almost immediately, but suffer no ill effects. Overdosage is more harmful than the worms, so, as a routine measure in the case of hunting cats, roundworming should be carried out twice a year only.

TAPEWORMS

The commonest species of tapeworm shared by cats and dogs is *Dipylidium caninum*. Transfer is via the cat and dog flea and biting lice. A species preferring cats as hosts is *Taenia taeniaeformis*. The intermediate hosts are prey. No direct transfer of tapeworms can take place by a cat eating tapeworm eggs shed by another cat.

Eggs eaten by the intermediate hosts (flea larvae, biting lice or prey animals) become cysts which cannot develop unless eaten by a cat or dog. Once inside the cat's gut the tapeworms attach themselves

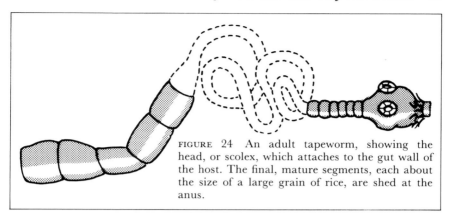

FIGURE 24 An adult tapeworm, showing the head, or scolex, which attaches to the gut wall of the host. The final, mature segments, each about the size of a large grain of rice, are shed at the anus.

by hooks to the wall of the intestine. From this 'head', segments grow which, when mature, contain eggs. These may be expelled with the faeces, or they may crawl from the anus when they can be seen easily as tiny, glistening, pure-white segments, capable of limited twisting movement. They may also appear in vomit. They dry rapidly, become immobile and cream-coloured, and resemble tiny grains of rice or grass seed. In infected cats, these grains will be abundant in cats' beds or favourite sleeping places.

In the case of *Dipylidium caninum*, the intermediate hosts are the cat and dog flea and biting lice. While feeding flea larvae and adult lice accidentally consume tapeworm eggs which become cysts in the adult. If a flea or louse is accidentally eaten by a cat, perhaps whilst grooming another cat, since fleas usually reside well out of reach of a cat's tongue, the tapeworm attaches itself to the cat's intestine wall and may reach 30 inches to several yards in length. The adult tapeworm is never seen, only the segments. Once the tapeworm is killed, it is digested along with all the other protein in the gut, and nothing will appear in the cat's faeces. Dead and dying fleas are most likely to be swallowed by a cat, and for this reason the cat should be groomed after flea treatment if possible.

In the case of *Taenia taeniaeformis*, eggs scattered in gardens are eaten by prey animals, chiefly voles and mice. The eggs hatch in the stomach of the prey, the larvae migrate to the liver and the liver reacts by forming a cyst around each larva. Nothing else happens until a cat swallows the prey's liver, then the tapeworm matures. Domestic kittens rarely contract tapeworm, unless the queen or another cat share prey with them.

Nowadays treatment of tapeworm infection is very simple as fasting is unnecessary. Droncit tablets can be crushed in food, or put into the mouth. Dosage is ½ Droncit per average 10 lb (4.5 kilogram) adult. Kittens must not be treated under six months old without veterinary advice. Since reinfection with both types of tapeworm can occur at any time, routine treatment should be given *twice a year only*. Droncit can also be given by a vet as an injection in the case of a heavy infestation, indicated by loss of weight and unusual hunger. Tapeworms are harmless to healthy, non-breeding, adult cats who, as usual, develop immunity.

All parasites can be very frightening to new cat owners, but they are easily eradicated and are in most cases harmless.

HOW CATS DEFEND THEMSELVES AGAINST INFECTIONS

Since cats are obviously surrounded all the time by infections of many kinds ('field' infections), it might be expected that they would constantly suffer from their effects. This, clearly, is not so. The normal, healthy, unstressed, well-fed, adult cat, roaming free in a domestic, routined environment is often challenged by infections shed from other cats, directly or indirectly (carried by wind or insects), but he usually resists the infections without exhibiting any symptoms. Cats can inactivate viruses, bacteria and some forms of the larger parasites, but this does not mean that they are not present, liable to activate in cats under stress. Some authorities state that dormant infections in a healthy cat can be passed on to susceptible cats, with whom they come into contact – the sick, the very young and the very old – though this is not proven. However, it is true that, as in the case of humans, those most at risk are the stressed, unfit, young and old.

How, then, do cats defend themselves? The first line of defence is the thick, elastic, difficult-to-puncture, dead outer skin. The skin is further protected by fur. Where the fur is sparse or non-existent, the skin is correspondingly thicker, for example, on the temples and pads. All organs in contact with the outside have a strong protective lining – the nose, windpipe, lungs, gut and urinary bladder.

It is important that all cats (and their accommodation and equipment) receive some *direct* sunlight, as ultra-violet light is a natural disinfectant which does not pass effectively through glass. Saliva and eye lubricant (tears) contain the antiseptic lysozyme. A cat fed a natural diet of protein from a meat source, together with ground bone and fat, will have an acid urine which is antiseptic. It is important for cats to drink enough liquid to ensure a dilute urine, for bacteria grow less in dilute, acid urine. The stomach contains hydrochloric acid which, besides being an antiseptic, also enables a cat to digest bone and gristle. Any infection invading the nose and lungs is 'fixed' in the natural lubricant called mucus. This travels, or is coughed up, into the throat, is swallowed and removed via the gut. The gut flora, as already stated, produce an antibiotic effective against the bacteria of putrefaction present in decomposed food.

Couch grass (*Triticum repens*) is essential to cats, because it is an emetic (causing vomiting) and a laxative. It is thus an aid in expelling unsuitable food and other indigestible materials (for instance, ingested fur, prey bones). All plant material contains fibre which acts as a gut irritant. Excessive eating of grass is an indication of a gut infection. Cats occasionally chew herbs (such as sage), catmint and catnip and various other plants which may assist in reducing bacteria and other gut parasites, but the role played by green plants is not clear. Certainly cats roll around in catmint and catnip and these plants contain an insecticide called nepetalactone, which may repel fleas and lice.

Despite all the above 'barriers' and precautions, there are many ways in which infections can gain entry to a cat's body. If they do, however, all is by no means lost: two other defence systems swing into action.

DEFENCE SYSTEM 1: THE WHITE BLOOD CELLS AND OTHERS

White blood cells of many types are made in the bone marrow. One type, called a lymphocyte, is located in a network of tubes and swellings all over the body. This network is called the lymphatic system. Blood plasma (blood minus red cells) leaving every organ enters the lymphatic system before returning to the heart and lungs via the veins. The lymphatic system acts as a filter where bacteria, viruses and any other foreign material are filtered out and destroyed by the lymphocytes. Lymphocytes are also present in the blood. Other white cells, called phagocytes and macrophages, engulf and destroy infections. White cells can pass through thin-walled blood vessels called capillaries.

Other body cells produce substances which render toxins harmless; some produce flea repellants; gut cells produce substances which interfere with the bodily functions of gut parasites, or prevent maturation of roundworm larvae. Cells in damaged skin produce histamines which increase the blood supply to that part.

This response to the challenge of infections by white blood cells and other types of cells is called the 'cell mediated response'.

However, if the cell mediated response is unable to cope with the invading infections, there is another line of defence, known as the 'antibody response' or 'immune system'.

DEFENCE SYSTEM 2: THE IMMUNE SYSTEM

One type of white blood cell manufactures a blood protein called globulin. When a virus or bacterium enters the blood, lymphocytes 'programme' a supply of globulin which is specific to a certain virus or bacterium. This globulin is shaped so that it locks on to the infective particles and thus identifies them as foreign (or 'not-self') material. Once it has been identified, lymphocytes home in on the infection and destroy it. Thus a cat's blood will gradually build up a stock of differing globulins, specific to those infections to which the particular cat has been exposed. Stocks of globulin remain to deal with any reinfection. As time passes, however, these stocks slowly diminish, unless the cat receives a further challenge from a field infection. Then the stock of globulin which matches the specific infection is topped up. Thus further attacks of an infection (or 'boosters') are necessary to maintain maximum immunity. Even if a particular globulin almost disappears, due to lack of boostering, 'memory' cells will have stored information about the infection which it matches, ready for reprogramming further specific globulin. In this case, the immune response may be too slow, and mild symptoms of the infection may be apparent.

It follows that, as a cat grows up and roams free in his natural environment, he receives challenges from many kinds of field infections present locally. Infections vary according to the locality. Each time he is challenged, white cells programme the correct antibody, as the specific globulin is called. Thus, by the time a cat is about three years old, his blood contains supplies of relevant antibody against, say, feline leukaemia, cat flu, and the varied bacteria on cats' teeth and claws prevalent in his particular environment.

A healthy, well-fed, free-roaming, adult mongrel cat has little to fear from the normally low concentrations of infections present around him. He can be protected artificially by injection (given by a vet) with a quantity of inactivated cat flu virus or feline panleuco-paenia virus. Lymphocytes programme the right antibody, responding to an inactivated virus in the same way as to an active one. An injection of harmless, inactivated virus in order to promote the formation of antibody is called a vaccine.

At present, vaccination is 100-per-cent effective against feline panleucopaenia. Vaccination against cat flu viruses is available, but the immune system does not remain effective on the lining of the nose, throat and mouth for more than a few months, and so vaccinated cats are liable to become reinfected. Although complete protection is impossible at present, vaccinated cats which do become reinfected show milder symptoms or even none at all. However, it is believed that cat flu-vaccinated and feline panleucopaenia-vaccinated cats can still be carriers of active virus, although immune themselves, and can thus be.a source of infection to susceptible cats. This is called the 'carrier state'. All boarding catteries will insist on vaccination against cat flu and feline panleucopaenia. A vaccine against feline leukaemia virus is available at the time of writing in the USA, but it is very expensive and not completely effective. There are, of course, dozens of other viruses and bacteria for which no vaccines are available, many of which are invariably fatal if they are able to overcome a cat's immunity.

While a cat is producing antibody, he may not exhibit any symptoms of the infection which is attacking him, or he may show mild symptoms which pass unnoticed. When the usual symptoms of a virus infection appear – for example, lack of appetite, attacks of sneezing, nasal discharge, vomiting, diarrhoea, lethargy, a tendency to hide in a cupboard – all is not lost, for there is much a vet can do to help the cat produce antibody.

Sadly, even a healthy cat is sometimes unable to produce antibody in time, and he will die. Many kittens and adult cats are at particularly high risk: these will be considered on page 96.

TRANSMISSION OF INFECTIONS FROM CAT TO CAT

It is impossible for anyone to know whether a particular cat is carrying an infection if he shows no symptoms, which is why bringing cats together in large numbers in catteries or exhibition halls is potentially hazardous.

Most free-roaming cats are challenged by a range of infections. If they happen to be housed in (by their standards) overcrowded accommodation or in unfamiliar surroundings, if they have become strays, or if they are under stress of any kind, we know that they are *less* likely to develop immunity. In such cases their immune systems are said to be 'compromised' or 'less competent'. We also know that, once contracted, an infection may not be shed completely, and if the immune system should become less competent because of stress, the infection may reactivate. This is seen in practice, for example, when a cat becomes overtired or spends a cold, wet day huddled over a mole hill, waiting. . . The next day he may begin to sneeze, or dig numerous toilet holes, suggesting that he is suffering an attack of cystitis (inflammation of the bladder). It is clear, therefore, that a cat does not have to be in contact with an infected cat to become infected. The obvious conclusion is that some viruses or bacteria are present all the time, harmless so long as the cat is in his normal, routined, unstressed environment. Moreover, it is not only viruses and bacteria which can activate in this way: roundworm larvae present in a cat's body may suddenly develop into adult roundworms during stress, or during symptoms of another – perhaps viral – infection.

As might be expected, the concentration of a particular infection is highest in the immediate vicinity of a cat showing symptoms of that infection. The concentration lowers in the general environment, but the infection is still airborne, or present in excreta, vomit, saliva on food dishes, and so on. It is therefore the duty of everyone who suspects that their cat may be infected to confine him immediately, to protect neighbours' cats and other cats in the same house, boarding or breeding cattery or rescue sanctuary.

We can only guess at the mechanism of transfer of infections from cat to cat, because no one knows all the answers. What is known is that infections *are* transferred from cat to cat. This is called 'horizontal transmission'. Queens can infect their kittens, because of the very close, prolonged contact between them. This is called 'vertical transmission'. In some cases the transmission of infections from cat to cat requires an intermediate host. This is called 'indirect transmission'.

All cat owners will need a knowledge of disinfectancy, the means whereby the concentration of infections in the environment is reduced. Food bowls and toilet trays are high-risk infection items. In these cases complete removal of *all* infections will be necessary and feasible. This process is called sterilization.

THE INCUBATION PERIOD

Consider the following examples of transmission: a cat is bitten by a flea which has just bitten a cat infected with the feline leukaemia virus; a cat has just raided a local dustbin and eaten some rotting food containing bacteria which may cause vomiting or diarrhoea; a cat has just eaten a vole, the liver of which is infected with the larvae of roundworm; a cat has just rolled in a catmint bed previously rolled in by a cat infected with a cat flu virus. What happens next depends on the cat:

(a) The cat may have already been challenged by the latest infection circulating in his neighbourhood and already have the appropriate antibody or natural repellant to reject the infection. Food may be vomited immediately, thus ridding the stomach of potentially harmful bacteria. The cat's owner will be unaware of the infection.

(b) The cat may suppress the infection, but it may remain dormant. This is particularly true of those viruses, of which feline leukaemia is one, which infect white blood cells. This type of virus suppresses the immune system and is called, therefore, an immunosuppressive virus. Dormancy may last up to five years; then, suddenly, if the cat is stressed, symptoms appear.

(c) The cat may not have the correct antibody because he has not been previously challenged by this particular infection. Or he may not have received a booster vaccination or a natural booster from a local virus for some years. In this case the cat may show slight symptoms of infection, while the immune system is getting mobilized. At this stage it is very difficult to know whether to take the cat to a vet or not. The cat may merely be off his food, or slightly less active than usual. The rule here is isolate, watch and wait for two or three days. If the condition of the cat deteriorates, see the vet at once. The cat may completely recover without any treatment beyond keeping warm and quiet indoors.

(d) The cat may develop all the symptoms of the infection, for example, sneezing, loss of appetite, lethargy, high temperature, vomiting, diarrhoea, and so on. Without veterinary treatment, and sadly sometimes even with treatment, the cat may be unable to make antibody in time, and may die.

The period of time between the initial contact with an infection and the appearance of symptoms is called the incubation period.

The length of the incubation period for some infections is known and this can be helpful in tracing a possible source of infection – perhaps an infected cat which shows no symptoms because of an efficient, uncompromised immune system. The incubation period for respiratory viruses is about two to four days; for feline panleucopaenia (likely to be encountered in a rescued, and very probably unvaccinated, stray) about five to seven days. For feline leukaemia the incubation period is very uncertain, but believed to be on average three to twelve months; however, cats which have contracted the virus five years earlier may have gradually developed symptoms of immunosuppression. Roundworm larvae from prey may develop into adult roundworms in two months.

The incubation period of any infection will vary according to the concentration of the infection received, the method by which it gains entry to the cat and the length of time the cat is exposed to the source.

HORIZONTAL TRANSMISSION

The following are methods by which horizontal transmission of infections can occur:

(1) Active infections can be in: faeces, urine, vomit, saliva, nasal and eye discharge, mucus from lungs; on teeth, claws, whiskers, coats; and shed in the blood of battle. They are everywhere. It is easy to visualize that anything an infected cat has brushed against, slept upon, sneezed upon, licked or occupied, and any human who has nursed or handled him, is a possible source of active infection to other cats. Inanimate sources of infection can thus include carry baskets, beds, toys, grooming equipment, accommodation, food dishes and left-overs, and, in the case of free-roamers, all their territory.

(2) It is believed that close, prolonged contact between infected and non-infected cats is necessary for the transfer of some viruses (for example, feline leukaemia). This particular virus is believed to enter the salivary glands of the mouth, so saliva is believed to be the instrument of transfer. Mutual grooming, playing, fighting and food sharing are thus possible means of transfer.

(3) Exposed food, and the dustbin rubbish that free-roamers or strays love so much, is a constant source of infection. *All* flying insects can carry infections by flying from food dish to food dish, or between toilet trays, contaminated soil, and so on, and food. Hygienic food storage, preparation and cooking and food-dish sterilization are vital in all homes containing one cat, or many. Food sharing is not recommended, particularly if some members of the family are ex-strays.

(4) When a cat with an upper respiratory infection sneezes, the heavier droplets fall to the ground, but the smaller droplets become airborne. Thus the concentration of infective mucus will be highest near an infected cat, and decrease with distance. For this reason, an infected cat should be isolated in a room of his own in the home, or as far away as possible from healthy cats in catteries.

(5) Cats are normally unsocial animals, and it is difficult to under-

stand how a virus can be spread by direct, prolonged contact in feral colonies and among strays. But in these communities, such fatal viruses as feline leukaemia, feline panleucopaenia and infectious peritonitis are very common, and limit the population. All stray cats, when taken into care, should be de-parasitized and kept in isolation for at least two weeks. They should not be de-sexed until they have had a period of rest and good food. Travelling parasites and food contaminated by flies and rats must account for cross-infection in some cases.

(6) A cat's outer skin (and that comprising the lining of the gut) is tough and elastic, but once it has been punctured, infections can enter. A puncture may not be easy to find, but a clue may be given by the cat licking the injury; if you do notice one, bathe it immediately in dilute TCP and (because cats lick off ointment rapidly) apply antiseptic ointment frequently, gently massaging it into the skin. Fur should be cut away, to assist finding the damage again.

TRANSMISSION FROM QUEEN TO KITTEN (VERTICAL TRANSMISSION)

It has been stated that those viruses which infect the bone marrow and hence the white blood cells can be transmitted from either parent to their offspring because the genetic cells in their ovaries or testes are infected, but this is as yet unproven. It is true that kittens can be infected at birth, and quickly die, from a virus similar to that of feline leukaemia. It is true that feline leukaemic kittens are born and may survive for a year. On the other hand, queens have died from feline leukaemia shortly after giving birth to healthy, long-lived kittens. A queen with very advanced feline leukaemia, however, would be unlikely to conceive in the first place.

It is possible for a kitten to become infected via the placenta before birth, and via the queen's milk after birth, but a more probable explanation of why a kitten is at such great risk from infections is that its immune system does not begin to function until it is about ten or twelve weeks of age. It is possible that a queen may contract any virus during pregnancy and produce antibody against it, but she can still infect her kittens because of the close, prolonged contact between her and them. If there is any possibility of a queen having been exposed to a virus, a breeder may decide to remove the kittens immediately after birth and hand-rear them (see Chapter 2). The stress of pregnancy and birth depresses antibody formation and hence immunity.

The first milk kittens receive is called colostrum. As well as possible infections, this contains antibody against many of the infections to which the queen has been exposed in the past. For about one hour after birth the antibody (which consists of protein particles) can pass through the wall of the kitten's small intestine and enter his bloodstream. The kitten does not make this antibody; the queen does. This type of immunity is called 'passive immunity', as opposed to 'active immunity' when the kitten begins to make his own antibody on receiving (hopefully!) low concentrations of field virus from his environment. As they pass the age of six to ten weeks kittens' passive immunity wanes, but until it does vaccination will not work. So kittens may need to be vaccinated at ten weeks and twelve weeks, on veterinary advice. It will be obvious that kittens are at very high risk from transfer of infections from adult cats, human hands and so on, and well-separated, escape-proof maternity units are essential, coupled with a high standard of disinfection/sterilization. Kittens should be introduced gradually to other domiciled cats, and into the garden after vaccination, so that they are challenged by infections at a moderate rate and have a chance to programme antibody. Thus by the time a cat is about five years old most infections, even intestinal worms, will be crises of the past.

INDIRECT TRANSMISSION

Transmission by flying, jumping or travelling insects (called 'vectors') has already been mentioned. Prey animals of the cat accidentally eat parasite eggs. Nothing happens until the prey animal is eaten by a cat, or a queen shares her prey with her kittens. Roundworm eggs will also develop if swallowed directly by a cat (having stuck to paws walking over infected faeces). In the case of tapeworms, however, transmission must be indirect. In one kind of tapeworm, the eggs infect the liver of prey, and develop when consumed; in another kind, the cat must eat infected fleas.

HIGH-RISK CATS

Every cat owner will, at some time, be faced with the problem of a cat which is a high risk where infection is concerned. Boarding cattery owners and rescue sanctuaries must recognize high-risk cats and keep them in isolation. These animals may even be considered too high a risk to accept for boarding. People looking after such cats while their owners go on holiday should also be aware of the dangers.

The risks may be summarized as follows: the cats may be carriers of dormant viral or bacterial infections contracted up to five years previously which could infect boarders under stress; they may be able to resist a few virus particles (that is, a low viral concentration) but have immune systems unable to cope with a high viral concentration such as may occur in multicat situations.

Accepting responsibility for their welfare will involve special disinfectant procedures, special diets and isolation from other cats. Cats recognized as being high-risk fall into the following categories:

Pedigree cats: It is often stated that inbreeding (that is, allowing close relatives to breed) results in less infection-resistant offspring. This is true to some extent, for when inbreeding is practised, progeny may inherit the same defects from both parents and have no chance of avoiding them. Inbreeding occurs in farm, feral or stray cat colonies. Such cats may lose all their teeth early, or have very thin coats. All reputable breeders are careful to avoid inbreeding, and other reasons must be sought for the shorter-than-average life, susceptibility to infections, higher kitten mortality and incidence of feline leukaemia in pedigree cats.

It is unlikely that a pedigree queen with active feline leukaemia would conceive, let alone carry kittens to full term, but feline leukaemia can be inactive in a queen and the virus can be passed to kittens through the placenta before birth or via the mother's milk after it. The so-called fading kitten syndrome (FKS) or kitten mortality complex (KMC) is often found in pedigree kittens, and is believed to be associated with the feline leukaemia virus.

Studs, because of their many contacts, must be considered high risk, as must queens returning from studs. These cats will have to be kept in isolation for at least two weeks following an outside contact, and in normal but separate accommodation thereafter.

The main reason why pedigree cats are high risk is probably associated with the law of nature which decrees the survival of the fittest. This precludes *any* artificial selection.

Kittens: These receive some maternal antibody via the colostrum, or first milk, but only against infections to which the queen has been exposed. All kittens are at very high risk of contracting infections from adult cats in their household, and from neighbours' cats frequenting their garden. Hand-reared kittens (whose mothers have died or had mammary infections) will be extra high-risk. Until the maternal antibody wanes, vaccination against cat flu and feline panleucopaenia will be ineffective. Thus all kittens should be kept in isolation, indoors, until vaccination at ten to twelve weeks.

Young cats: At four months old, cats begin to explore the environment and contact (hopefully) low concentrations of local virus. But young cats up to about three years old, if plunged into a high-density cat population, may meet unnaturally high concentrations before the immune system is fully operational.

Indoor cats: Cats which spend all their lives indoors have no opportunity to contract field virus, and will thus have little immunity.

The rescued tomcat: The rescued tom and, to a lesser extent, the stray queen will have travelled over a wide area. Although potentially healthy (only the fittest can survive without veterinary treatment and the right food), they may have viraemia or septicaemia as well as heavy burdens of larger parasites. Any additional stress, like a neutering operation before a period of rest and recuperation, can activate latent viral and bacterial infections, which may set up infection sites in any organ of the body, such as the gut, lungs or kidneys.

Suspected leukaemic cats: Stray cats who do not respond to rest, good food and veterinary care with wide-spectrum antibiotics must be leukaemia suspects. Since the sex urge may be diminished, such cats, if possible, should remain entire. Leukaemic cats may live up to five years if kept in strict isolation in aseptic conditions. It is infections other than the feline leukaemia virus that kill, because such a cat has no immunity. Leukaemic cats must be kept isolated indoors, to protect free-roamers.

Pregnant and nursing queens.

Tomcats neutered too early (under one year).

Teenagers: Particularly those suffering from chronic or recurrent infections (for example, sinusitis, cystitis), or those requiring routine treatment. As well as needing frequent, easily digested, high-protein meals, cats of this age group need to be kept under supervision or confined, as they may have failing sight and/or hearing. Chronic kidney disease is likely. They are at high risk from infections as their immune system is waning.

All unvaccinated cats.

First-time boarded cats who don't know what to expect.

All exhibited cats: It is impossible to tell whether cats admitted to cat shows are carrying dormant infections. They are exposed, in a high-density cat population, to infections possibly not present in their home environment. Under stress, cross-infection is more likely. After showing, cats should be quarantined for a fortnight. It should be remembered that lack of symptoms is not evidence of freedom from infection or from risk to other cats.

THE ROLE OF HUMANS IN TRANSMISSION

We have see that close, prolonged contact is necessary for cat-to-cat (horizontal) transmission, but in the case of susceptible cats (very young, very old, sick or stressed) contact with infected human hands carrying a low concentration of, say, a virus from an infected cat, could result in transfer. Fighting and mating cannot be described as close, prolonged contact, but mutual washing and contact between a queen and her kittens can be. Close, prolonged contact occurs mainly between kittens, who play with, bite and wash each other. Once adulthood is reached there is often little rapport.

Since viruses and bacteria can usually remain infective for periods varying from four hours to one year, it is obvious that positive methods are necessary to disinfect human hands, clothing, shoes and equipment in contact with infected cats, to avoid passing on infections to healthy cats. This applies to those owners with one sick cat in isolation, who may inadvertently transfer an infection by stroking a neighbour's cat, and it applies equally to those with several cats, one of which may be infected and in isolation, and to all people in charge of cats confined in breeding, boarding and rescue sanctuaries. Visitors to boarding catteries are not allowed to touch cats other than their own. Visitors to cat shows receive constant pleas over the loudhailer systems not to fondle exhibited cats. In the case of free-roaming cats, all animals, particularly rats and mice, can contaminate exposed food with their own, possibly infected, saliva, urine and faeces, and transfer feline infections around the environment.

All this may sound frightening, and control seem impossible. In multicat households and catteries time is at a premium, but cats need fondling. The best plan may be to serve food to each isolated cat without touching the cat, then set aside a separate time to clean each unit, remove faeces and soiled urine patches from toilet trays, fondle the cat and then thoroughly scrub the hands with detergent and rinse well, before passing on to the next cat. Cattery owners may prefer to wear rubber gloves, keeping a separate pair for each unit, thus avoiding the need to scrub hands after cleaning each one. Most cattery owners use footbaths containing disinfectant, in order to destroy infections on rubber shoes. A separate overall may be kept for each unit.

An appreciation of the danger of cross-infection and how quite simple precautions can be taken will prevent a virus, such as cat flu, sweeping through a multicat household or cattery, or a high-density cat population in, say, a road in a built-up area.

Where a cat's ability to resist parasites is concerned, correct nutrition is probably the most important factor, and here the human role is a vital one. Young cats contract most protozoan and metazoan parasites from eating raw meat; most older cats develop immunity.

Here is a dilemma. If we *do not* feed cats raw meat, raw fat, animal roughage and finely chopped bone (the nearest equivalent of their food in the wild), we are depriving them of a natural source of vitamins A, B, D and E (the only vitamins cats need), for vitamins are mainly destroyed by cooking. Vitamins are vital for developing resistance, or, in some cases, complete immunity to infections. If we *do* feed raw meat, our cats may become infected with a protozoan called *Toxoplasma gondii*, or metazoa (roundworms or tapeworms).

The best course in this case is a compromise. Do not allow cats to eat raw fish, raw rabbit or, indeed, raw vole or bird (if they can be prevented), because these are close to their natural prey (there is a fishing cat, whose diet consists partly of raw fish). A cat's *natural* prey is far more likely to contain cysts (parasites surrounded by a protective sac) and eggs of those parasities which infect cats. Serve instead raw beef, lamb and associated offals sold for *human* consumption, as not only are these free from cat parasites but they are also veterinary inspected at approved slaughterhouses to ensure that they are free from all cysts. The exceptions to this rule are ox cheek (which may contain parasite cysts) and ox liver (which may contain cysts or be contaminated with steroids often fed to cattle): exclude these from your cat's diet.

Meats which are sold 'for pets only' should never be served raw. They may contain metazoan cysts and eggs parasitic on man which, should they infect the cat, cause more severe symptoms as the cat is not the favoured host. Always cook these meats.

ARE HUMANS VULNERABLE TO CAT INFECTIONS?

Anyone caring for cats obviously loves them and tends to believe that no cat infection, microscopic or visible with the naked eye, could harm him or her. Transfer of *Toxoplasma gondii* oocysts from cat to human is very rare, and nearly always the result of lack of hygiene. Equally rare is human contraction of feline ringworm or fleas. But there are cat infections which can be caught by many animals, including man. These infections (or zoonoses) may be regarded as 'shared' by cats, dogs, cattle, man and so on.

Toxoplasma gondii infects cats, humans and nearly all other warm-blooded animals in the world. The chief source of infection is raw meat sold 'for pets only' which is derived from old and diseased cattle and horses slaughtered in knackers' yards.

Most humans who have handled raw meat (and that is the majority of people) will have already been exposed to *Toxoplasma gondii* cysts. Most of us are able to produce antibody to this protozoan and are therefore immune to it. However, once again, those humans who *are* at risk are the pregnant women who have not been exposed to the cysts before pregnancy, and who therefore have no immunity. The unborn foetus and young babies of such women are also at risk. So, too, are stressed and exhausted humans and those with the immunosuppressive disease called AIDS.

Research into *Toxoplasma gondii* infection suggests that only cat faeces contain a special kind of cyst (or oocyst). Therefore a very strict régime for the handling and disposal of cat faeces is necessary for susceptible humans.

The fungus ringworm, which can infect humans, can only become established in the scalp, and those cat owners having to deal with ringworm in cats would be advised to keep their hair covered. Infection with roundworm larvae is possible only via dog faeces, causing the very rare disease in man called visceral larva migrans.

PRECAUTIONS TO BE TAKEN BY ALL PEOPLE WHO HANDLE CATS

(1) Handle raw meat as little as possible – use a spoon to serve mince, chopped liver, and so on, to cats. After handling raw meat, scrub hands thoroughly with a soft brush and bactericidal/virucidal soap (obtainable from chemists). Rinse in warm, running water.

(2) Cook meats at a minimum temperature of 151°F (66°C). Steam fish. *Never* serve meat sold 'for pets only' in its raw state.

(3) If pregnant, wear rubber or disposable polythene gloves when handling raw meat, or removing waste from toilet trays. Faeces can be flushed down the lavatory. Remove faeces promptly, for parasite eggs do not become infective immediately they are shed.

(4) Keep raw meat at the bottom of the refrigerator, well wrapped and well away from other foods. If possible, keep raw meat, fresh or frozen, in a separate refrigerator/freezer.

HOW TO DECIDE WHEN TO TAKE A CAT TO THE VET

It is easy to note a sudden change in the behaviour of a cat you know. He may refuse to eat, lie under the bed or disappear into the shrubbery to sleep all day. If nightly lock-up and toilet tray are the rules, diarrhoea or vomiting will give an owner early warning of any health problems. Catteries and people adopting strays are dealing with cats whose normal appetite and behaviour are unknown. Anyone looking after unfamiliar felines should obtain all the available information about a cat from his owner, or the person who has been feeding him, and write it down. An advantage of owning several cats, especially if more than one are of the same breed or colouring, is that suspected infected cats can be compared in appearance with the healthy ones.

The following are indications of health problems that may require veterinary treatment:

Loss of appetite: Usually the first symptom of ill health, followed quickly by loss of weight. A cat may not eat because of a nasal infection, or an uncomfortable mouth (due perhaps to bad teeth or bacterial gingivitis). But loss of appetite can be due to the sudden onset of hot weather, a sudden reduction in exercise, dislike of food or the formation of a fur sausage prior to regurgitation. Watch for excessive drinking of plain water and excessive grass eating. Note if vomiting and/or diarrhoea occurs and the colour of the urine, and whether there is constipation.

A subtle change of behaviour: Old cats sleep most of the time, and there are also young cats who normally sleep twenty-two hours a day. But if a cat begins to slow down and sleep indoors over a period of months, it may be a symptom of an immunosuppressive virus, or bacterial infection (possibly septicaemia).

A change in appearance: The fur may become 'clumpy', the coat dull. A heavy moult may begin, there may be a protruding haw, and excessive licking, nibbling or scratching. Watch also for discharges from the eyes, ears and mouth.

A rise in temperature (pyrexia): An indication of viral or bacterial infection. A cat's normal temperature hovers around 101°F (38.3°C). This is measured by a special rectal thermometer and should never be taken by an untrained person as the thermometer could shatter in the rectum. Signs which can indicate a raised temperature are: lack of appetite; lethargy; self-concealment; rapid breathing; trembling; lying flat, legs outstretched, on a cool surface. The cat may feel hotter than a healthy cat; his nose is unusually hot and dry; his skin, ears, nose and pads (if pink) appear deeper pink than those of a healthy cat.

Increased pulse rate: The heart beats faster after an accident, a cat fight, after running or jumping. The heartbeat is slower when the cat is asleep. The normal heartbeat is about 110–130 beats per minute.

The pulse should be measured when the cat is at rest, awake but not purring. Place your fingertips on the cat's chest, near the 'elbow', and move your fingers until the heartbeat can be felt. It is difficult to keep a cat still enough to count the number of heartbeats, even in thirty seconds. The beats are less easy to feel in the average plump domestic, but far easier in thin cats. It helps to accustom your cat to having his heartbeat measured, and to know his normal pulse rate. A feeble heartbeat, a very slow or a very fast beat are causes for concern.

Breathing (or respiration) rate: The expansion and contraction of the chest wall is far easier to see and measure than heartbeats. As in the case of the pulse, it must be measured when the cat is not purring or sniffing the air for the scent of prey! The normal breathing rate is 20–30 'ins' (or 'outs') per minute. As a guide, that of an unknown cat can be compared with that of a known healthy cat. Rapid breathing indicates a lung infection, a raised temperature, shock, a chest tumour, or some obstruction that makes breathing laboured, such as fluid collecting in the chest cavity or abdomen. Any condition which results in a reduction in red blood cells (which convey oxygen round the body) will result in a faster heartbeat and rapid breathing. A reduction in red blood cells, for whatever reason, is called anaemia.

Occasional vomiting and/or diarrhoea are no cause for alarm. They are a cat's way of expelling indigestible food or fur, or remains of prey, often with the aid of grass.

Continual squatting or digging toilet holes, with or without apparent straining, could indicate cystitis, feline urolithiasis or acute constipation and *emergency treatment is imperative.*

If a cat of any age, from kittenhood onwards, exhibits one of the above symptoms and shows no improvement on treatment, or your vet is unable to give a reasonable diagnosis or prognosis, or if you are simply not satisfied with treatment, you should go to another vet for a second opinion. If you are then still not satisfied, ask to see a specialist or request referral to the Feline Advisory Bureau at Bristol University.

6 Other Common Ailments

DIARRHOEA

Diarrhoea is a very common feline problem. Sufferers have odorous, matted, soiled 'trousers' which have to be sponged down and dried. The anus may be bright pink and sore, necessitating the application of white Vaseline. Cats may miss toilet trays, or have uncontrollable diarrhoea, so that bedding will be soiled. Floors may have to be protected with polythene sheeting. All litter will have to be changed after each use of the toilet tray, and the waste material flushed down the lavatory or incinerated in case the diarrhoea is infective. If it is, transfer to other cats in the house or neighbourhood is very likely. An affected cat must be isolated to prevent cross-infection and toilet trays and food bowls must be disinfected after each use, as must hands after ministering to the patient. Diarrhoea should be prevented at all costs: it involves endless work and expense, causes unpleasant odour and, once contracted, can last for up to a year!

Diarrhoea is most often the result of gastroenteritis, a condition in which the skin lining the stomach and intestines is inflamed, swollen, painful and bleeding. The causes of this gastroenteritis are numerous: the cat may eat bacterially contaminated rotten meat, together with the toxins produced by bacteria; the gut may be pierced by a prey bone, thus allowing in virus and bacteria; the cat may be heavily burdened with gut parasites; he may have eaten unsuitable food, like raw vegetable waste from a compost heap; he may have consumed food to which he is allergic, such as milk, cream or cereal-containing foods; long-term administration of antibiotics for another condition may have destroyed the gut flora and allowed any pathogenic bacteria present to multiply; he may have accidentally consumed poison; he may have experienced a sudden change of diet or have contracted a general viral disease like feline panleucopaenia.

A healthy cat's faeces should be dark brown, firm, sectioned (though not separated into too small segments), and passed without straining, usually daily or every other day. When the gut is inflamed, water absorption from the food in the intestine is reduced, resulting in the passing of large volumes of liquid or very soft faeces, sometimes containing fresh blood, or brown granules of clotted blood. Thus, lack of water (or dehydration) is a symptom of diarrhoea. A cat who drinks large volumes of plain water is a diarrhoea suspect (or may have chronic kidney failure – see page 108). A protruding haw and excessive grass eating are also signs of gut discomfort, though not necessarily diarrhoea. In long-term diarrhoea, low gut absorption levels of food, vitamins and minerals will result in malnutrition, weight loss and low immunity.

Rescued strays, probably not vaccinated against feline panleuco-paenia, may have diarrhoea when over the crisis point and when recovery is probable. The faeces are passed in large quantities, and are dark brown due to partially digested blood. A more common cause of diarrhoea in strays is a sudden change of diet, or too much food. It is a temptation to give strays all they can eat. The resulting diarrhoea may be accompanied by a clear, thick mucus. A limited amount of white fish, with plenty of juice, and a vitamin/mineral supplement is the best treatment, but a bacterial infection may need an antibiotic prescribed by a vet, and may tend to recur.

Very watery, blood-containing faeces passed eight to twelve hours after a meal may indicate an allergy to a particular food, usually milk, cream or foods high in carbohydrate (see page 18). In this case it is usual to give water and white fish only until the diarrhoea clears up, and then introduce variety gradually into this diet until the allergen is identified. Some unsuitable foods are easily identifiable, since they may pass through a cat in record time, practically unchanged!

A bacterial infection may be suspected when several cats in a family lose their appetites and pass fluid faeces, often bright yellow. They usually recover without treatment but, if antibiotics are necessary, problems occur because the normal gut flora are killed and other bacteria may therefore flourish. The antibiotic may be changed and, as explained earlier, ¼ teaspoonful natural unsweetened yoghurt added to the diet daily, but sometimes a vicious circle is set up and it is best to stop all treatment and resort to plain water and white fish, with a vitamin/mineral supplement. (It should also be remembered that some cats are intolerant to yoghurt because of its high lactose content.)

Other causes of diarrhoea are: shock, due to an accident or serious cat fight; eating raw meat (try cooked instead); eating too much liver, fat, meat juice or chicken juice, oily fish (sardines, pilchards); or simply eating too much food in general. Often the reason for an attack can never be discovered and, although the diarrhoea may persist for months, the faeces eventually return to normal.

CONSTIPATION

It is very important for owners to know what their cats' faeces look like when the cats are in good health so that abnormalities, when they occur, can be quickly noticed. The faeces of most cats are dark brown, firm and sectioned but not completely divided. Constipation, even among confined cats, is uncommon. Some cats normally defecate every other day, some every day.

Constipation may be due to one of a number of causes. Old cats may be constipated because the muscles of the large intestine, which move food on towards the rectum, have become lax due to age. Chronic nephritis results in extra reclamation of water from faeces, which become hard, black and difficult to expel. Cats suddenly confined in catteries, or in the house because of illness, may appear to be constipated, but this may be due simply to lowered food intake, and defecation will occur at longer intervals (say, every four days). Loss of appetite, perhaps during hot weather, may cause *apparent* constipation, but in fact the cat will simply be defecating less because he is eating less. Fur in the digestive tract during heavy moulting may delay defecation. Inactivity caused by old age or obesity may bring on constipation, as may too much dry or hard food; swallowed objects like rubber, string or polythene bags; a blow to the pelvic region; or a tumour.

If a young, otherwise healthy cat appears to be constipated, a simple change of diet to laxative foods may be all that is required: raw liver, chopped raw animal fat, milk, cream, oily fish canned in brine (pilchards, sardines, mackerel, herrings).

For temporary constipation during boarding or illness, a few drops of liquid paraffin can be added to meals. Increase the number of drops until defecation is normal. Never use liquid paraffin for long-term constipation, as fat and fat-soluble vitamins will be leached from the food in the intestine and paraffin coats the intestine wall, interfering with food absorption.

Old cats with chronic constipation need a regular laxative such as Vi-Siblin Granules (available from chemists). Give ¼ teaspoonful daily, or as required.

The symptoms of constipation are: continual straining over the toilet hole; passing small portions of shrivelled, hard, black faeces, or just mucus; dragging the hindquarters along the ground; continual licking of the anus. If cats are confined at night, it is easy to check that all is well by looking at the toilet tray in the morning. If in doubt, shut the cat in the house during the day until he defecates.

Once symptoms of serious, long-term constipation appear, which cannot be treated with, say, a saucer of cream, seek the help of a vet *urgently*. The symptoms of serious constipation, as distinct from undue intervals in defecation, are the same as for feline urolithiasis (see page 114), when no urine may be passed. If this condition does not receive urgent treatment, it is fatal.

VOMITING

Continual vomiting of food, and later liquid, and inability to keep even water down will result in rapid dehydration. Continual vomiting is a symptom of nearly every serious illness, ranging from kidney failure to feline leukaemia, and is always cause for *urgent* veterinary treatment.

As already explained, daily eating of couch grass (or other varieties) and vomiting within ten minutes is normal for many cats. Only froth, with fur, should be evident. All cats vomit fur, which collects in the stomach however much they are groomed. This is vomited in the shape of a fur sausage. An impending fur sausage may be noticed by the fact that a cat is satiated after eating a few mouthfuls of food, or a cat appears hungry but cannot eat. Once the vomitus is examined, the cause will be apparent. This applies to any vomiting, and the cause of the vomiting is therefore far easier to diagnose than diarrhoea. Occasionally grass cuts the mouth or throat, and a little fresh blood may show in the froth.

Vomiting is a safety valve, ridding the stomach of unsuitable, irritant or infected food, bones, polythene bags, chewed elastic, shoe laces, currant cake, bacon rind, and any other samples of the wealth of rubbish cats like to eat! The offending item is vomited quickly, usually under half an hour after ingestion.

If food is vomited, it will be evident whether it is food supplied by the owner, filched from dustbins, or stolen from next door's dog. If vomiting occurs several times in a day, this may be due to eating a bacterially contaminated food and indicate that bacteria are multiplying and damaging the gut wall. In some cats the vomitus is bright yellow. This will require an injection of antibiotic, since oral antibiotics cannot be kept down. For one-off vomiting, neosulphentrin tablets, containing antibiotics, are excellent stomach correctives. One should be given every day for five days.

Other possible causes of vomiting are:

(a) Overeating or bolting food, perhaps in order to finish an adjacent cat's food as well! A large quantity of food, mixed with stomach juices, will be vomited, and the cat will appear ravenous and eat again soon after.

(b) Drinking too much milk, meat or fish juice, particularly if served with, or directly following, a meal.

(c) Parasitic worms. Dead or living roundworms may be vomited; or minute, moving, white, glistening, tapeworm segments. The cat should be wormed.

(d) Eating prey. Parts of this, particularly the indigestible remains such as feathers, skulls, claws, bones, may be vomited. Some cats cannot keep raw prey down, or indeed *any* raw meat.

(e) Eating raw vegetables from compost heaps; or sometimes cooked vegetables (mainly potatoes).

(f) Accidental eating of poisons, or poisoned prey (for treatment see 'Poisoning and Convulsions' on page 58).

Treatment, as indicated, should be based on an examination of the vomitus. Most cases of vomiting of food clear up in a day without treatment.

CHRONIC NEPHRITIS (CHRONIC KIDNEY FAILURE)

Approximately one-quarter of all old cats over the age of twelve are likely to die from a non-infectious disease of the kidneys called chronic nephritis. Once diagnosed, it is important to accept that there is no cure, but a nephritic cat can, with correct veterinary care, enjoy two or more years of high-quality life. The kidneys appear to be the 'weak' organ in cats, comparable to the 'weak' human organs – heart and lungs. All cats are susceptible: entire, de-sexed, domestic, feral, pedigree and the big wild cats.

Chronic nephritis is a degenerative disease in which healthy kidney cells are gradually replaced by non-functional fibrous cells. The cause is unknown. It is important to distinguish chronic nephritis from acute nephritis, which can occur at any age. In the latter case, the cause is often traceable to an injury to the kidneys in a road accident, or by a blow, fall or kick; an infection of the kidney; a tumour; or accidental poisoning. The cat will obviously be ill and require urgent veterinary treatment.

Chronic nephritis is very common, so many cat owners will be faced with coping with a nephritic cat. This section will, it is hoped, help owners to understand healthy kidney function, recognize the early stages of chronic nephritis, understand the theory of treatment, cope with feeding and accept that the disease is always terminal.

Always bear in mind, however, that a hormone deficiency disease may give identical symptoms. Correction is easy, and the cat will have a new lease of life. Your vet will advise you.

THE KIDNEYS

The easiest way to appreciate the position of a cat's kidneys is to purchase a whole, de-gutted rabbit from the butcher. The kidneys of the cat are in the same position as the rabbit's, about midway along the back, one on each side of the spine, just after the last rib, well protected by the thick back muscles and encased in protective fat.

The function of the kidneys is to remove waste products from the blood. Like all organs of the cat's body, the kidneys are composed of many different kinds of body units, called cells. Some of the kidney cells form the outer skin. Just below these, in the cortex, are the nephrons – cells arranged in groups to form a means by which some of the blood entering the kidneys can be 'washed' of poisonous waste.

Nephrons work rather like the well-remembered filter funnels of our schooldays. Filter paper, or blotting paper, was placed in the funnel, and if water containing a solid substance, like chalk, was poured on to the filter paper, the water ran through and the chalk stayed on the paper. The now clear, or filtered, water passed down the stem of the funnel and could be collected in a beaker. If we can imagine a funnel with a very long, coiled stem, and, instead of filter paper, a knot of very thin-walled minute blood vessels which allow water and any substances dissolved in it to pass through their walls, but not larger undissolved particles; and if we can imagine all this structure to be generously supplied with minute blood vessels, then we are picturing the nephron, the basic unit of filtration in the kidney. Each kidney contains thousands of such units – about 250,000 in fact – many more than are needed by a healthy cat. Figure 25 (overleaf) illustrates how a nephron works.

Dissolved toxins (poisons) which are filtered out of the blood by the kidneys are: urea and creatinine, which are the waste products of protein digestion, including any protein consumed in excess of the body's needs; accidentally eaten toxins absorbed into the blood

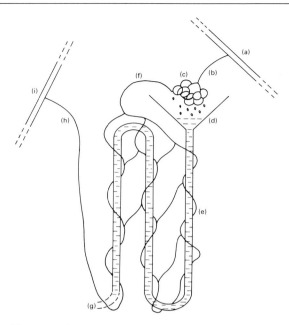

Figure 25   How a nephron works.

This diagrammatic representation of a nephron shows how it removes poisonous substances from the blood.

(a)   Blood is carried to the kidneys in a thick-walled artery.

(b)   The artery divides many times. Some blood carries digested food, oxygen, vitamins, hormones and so on to *all* parts of the kidney; some blood enters the nephrons.

(c)   This is a knot (or glomerulus) of very thin-walled blood vessels, called capillaries. The walls of the capillaries comprising the glomerulus are so thin that water, and any substance dissolved in it (including oxygen now transferred from the red corpuscles), can filter through the walls; but in the *healthy* nephron, red blood cells, amino acids, blood proteins and fat globules cannot.

(d)   About one quarter of the blood water (or plasma – the liquid in which the red and white corpuscles are suspended) is filtered from the blood and collects in the funnel, called a Bowman's capsule.

(e)   The filtered blood water passes down the long stem of the funnel and, as it does so, any substances needed by the body, mostly salts, and most of the water, is drawn from the stem of the funnel back into the filtered blood, which has left the Bowman's capsule via the blood vessel (f).

(g)   The blood water which remains is a concentrated solution of toxic waste products, mostly urea, which the body must get rid of. This part of the stem of the funnel joins up with others and the fluid leaves the kidney via the ureter and reaches the bladder. This fluid is now called urine.

(h)   The 'washed' blood, which still contains a low amount of toxins, is returned to the main vein (i) leaving the kidneys. Here the blood is joined by other blood which has supplied food and oxygen to all other cells of the kidney, and collected toxic waste and carbon dioxide.

through the gut wall (for example, poison from poisoned prey, poisonous leaves and berries); and toxins produced by viral, bacterial or worm infections.

As Figure 25 shows, the blood is constantly 'washed' of impurities and most of the valuable water and salts are reclaimed. The kidneys thus ensure that the composition of the blood remains constant.

Cats, being desert-type animals, need this remarkable ability to concentrate their urine. That is why they can survive for up to six weeks without water – far longer than other animals. Thus a healthy cat is very continent, usually urinating only once or twice a day.

WHAT HAPPENS WHEN THINGS BEGIN TO GO WRONG

The kidneys of a healthy cat contain far more nephrons than are actually used. As nephrons gradually become fibrous and useless, more spare nephrons are called into service. This process is called compensation. When about 70 per cent of them have become fibrous and useless, symptoms will become evident – there will be no early-warning signs.

After this symptoms will gradually develop over a period of months and often pass unnoticed, particularly if the cat has complete freedom twenty-four hours a day and does not have an indoor toilet tray. Several symptoms (called a syndrome) appear as a result of gradual inability to filter out enough toxic waste and reclaim water and salts.

As the number of functional nephrons decreases, the rate of filtration of water, toxins and dissolved salts is diminished. Similarly, there is less reclamation of water and salts. Because of this the cat appears thirsty and will drink plain water, which is unusual except in very hot weather or after eating salty foods such as canned pilchards. Excessive drinking is called polydipsia. Since the water cannot be reclaimed, there is an increase in the volume and frequency of urination (polyuria). Thus a cat who previously has not used a toilet tray when shut in for the night may come to need more than one tray. Loss of toilet training may occur, particularly if trays, or the garden, are not immediately accessible.

As less and less blood is filtered or 'washed', the concentration of toxic products builds up. This condition, called uraemia, causes other symptoms: vomiting, diarrhoea, loss of appetite and therefore weight, inactivity, poor coat condition, gingivitis (inflammation of the gums) and mouth ulcers (white or yellow spots); the breath may smell of ammonia (a breakdown product of urea) or just smell generally bad. Usually there is no pain.

The kidneys, normally about 1½ inches (4 centimetres) long, begin to shrivel. As the disease advances (sometimes there are remissions of months) the cat becomes dehydrated due to lack of water reclamation. The skin, if pinched, does not return quickly to normal. Extra water is extracted from the faeces, causing hard faecal material and constipation.

Since the composition of a healthy cat's urine is constant, a urine sample can sometimes be helpful in diagnosing kidney problems. It is not reliable for diagnosis of chronic nephritis, but can indicate other kidney diseases. Urine samples are easy to obtain from a cat by putting a large spoon underneath the cat a few seconds after urination has started. This is called a 'mid-stream' sample. If shredded kitchen paper is used as litter in the tray, a sample can be obtained by expression (squeezing the urine out of the paper).

A blood sample can indicate whether the amount of urea in the blood is high. Since urea contains nitrogen, an unusually high amount of nitrogen in the blood will be indicative of kidney failure. This test, performed in special laboratories, is called the BUN (blood urea nitrogen) test. The condition in which the BUN level in the blood is high is called azotemia. Owners should be wary of subjecting an elderly, ailing cat to such a test; testing a young cat is, of course, an entirely different matter.

As the disease advances, loss of salts, glucose, B vitamins and even amino acids occurs and corrective treatment is necessary.

The bone marrow may be affected, resulting in a reduction in the number of red blood cells and hence the blood's oxygen-carrying ability. This is called non-regenerative anaemia. Symptoms will be rapid breathing, weakness and pale, whitish gums (in the case of a cat whose gums are normally pink).

TREATMENT

The cause of chronic nephritis is unknown and treatment can only be symptomatic (that is, the symptoms, not the cause, are treated). Exacerbation of symptoms can result from external factors: insufficient water intake; holiday boarding; veterinary visits and tests, and the use of anaesthetics on the cat; introduction of new cats or dogs into the household; exposure to cold, wet weather and so on.

When early symptoms are noticed (polydipsia and polyuria) all that is necessary is to provide ample fresh water, rabbit juice or fish juice, and ensure that a toilet tray is always near at paw. When there is a uraemic crisis (loss of appetite, gingivitis, vomiting) veterinary treatment may consist of an injection of glucose, water, vitamins, salts, and so on, to bring the composition of the blood back to normal. Gingivitis is a sign of bacterial activity consequent upon high blood urea content, and antibiotics may work wonders. Salts and vitamins (for example, Vi-Sorbin) are now given as regular dietary supplements in high doses. Synthetic anabolic steroids may be injected to assist the use of amino acids to increase body weight and stimulate the formation of red blood cells in the bone marrow.

DIET

The cat owner should always bear in mind the possibility that her cat might fall victim to chronic kidney failure in his later years and should try to accustom him when he is young to accepting *some* carbohydrate food in his diet. It is very difficult to change a cat's diet, and may not be feasible. Canned nephritis diets, glucose with breakfast cereals, and so on, are useless if the cat will not eat them. If a cat will eat only raw red meat and liver, then, since he is on borrowed time, it is best to respect his wishes!

The proteins of white meats (rabbit, chicken, white and oily fish) are composed of shorter chains of amino acids than red meats. These proteins are easier to digest, and the toxic waste products from their digestion are less toxic to the body than the toxic waste products from red meats and offals, and less likely to cause vomiting. Rabbit and white fish also have a high water content. But the essential point about protein is that, once digested (that is, broken down into amino acids), it cannot be stored, and it is converted into toxic waste. This is obviously harmful to nephritic cats, who must not be overfed.

For those cats who can utilize carbohydrate foods, these can be increased slightly and mixed with acceptable meats (see pages 29–30). Milk should not be increased. A vitamin/mineral supplement for nephritic cats should be given under veterinary guidance. A regular laxative may be needed (*not* liquid paraffin for long-term use).

The canned nephritis diets often prescribed for nephritic cats may prove unacceptable and indigestible. In any event the protein content may not be low enough (it is usually about 6½ per cent). A more acceptable diet may be made by mixing 50 grams of high-quality protein such as lean white meat, fish or cooked eggs, with 46 grams of glucose crystals. This food will contain 4 per cent protein.

PREVENTATIVE MEASURES

Since the cause(s) of chronic fibrosis of the kidneys is unknown, it is possible only to theorize on preventative measures:

(a) The importance of adequate dietary water has already been stressed (see page 23).

(b) It would be easy to assume that red meats are more damaging to healthy kidneys than white meats, but those cats fed exclusively on high-carbohydrate canned catfoods are just as susceptible to chronic nephritis.

(c) Obviously, too much food should be avoided, because excess protein cannot be stored and is converted into toxic waste.

(d) A cat's kidneys are high in fat and vitamin A. The quality of animal protein in the diet has been found to influence kidney size. Correct nutrition may hold the key.

BLADDER DISEASES

Cystitis (inflammation of the bladder) can be brought on by exposure to cold, wet, windy or snowy weather which may cause resident bacteria and viruses in the bladder to activate. In other cases, viruses and bacteria are believed to enter the bladder by ascending the urethra (or passage from the outside).

The disease known as feline urolithiasis, or the feline urologic syndrome (FUS) is common in young male cats, but can occur at any age and in both sexes. Sharp crystals or protein material appear in the urine, damaging the bladder wall and paving the way for viral or bacterial growth. In extreme cases in the male cat this deposit forms a plug in the urethra, preventing urination.

The symptoms of cystitis and feline urolithiasis are similar, and can be confused with constipation. Either way, if *any* of the following symptoms are noticed, *emergency veterinary treatment is vital*: a change of toilet habits – a normally clean, non-spraying cat begins to spray urine (possibly blood-stained) on walls or in the bath or sink; the cat constantly digs toilet holes in the tray or garden and squats over the hole for long periods but may be unable to pass urine, or may pass small amounts; straining may be evident, and the cat may lick his hindparts.

If ordinary cystitis is diagnosed it is treated with antibiotics and/or anti-inflammatory drugs. It can become chronic, tending to recur periodically, particularly after exposure to cold, wet weather and low night temperatures. Susceptible cats should be confined in cold weather, and kept in at night. Fluid intake should be increased, if possible, to dilute the urine and thus make it less irritant to the inflamed bladder wall.

To aid diagnosis and treatment, a urine sample will be necessary (see page 112 for how to obtain one). Crystals, which can be seen with the naked eye, are usually struvite (magnesium ammonium phosphate). As these are more soluble in dilute, acid urine, extra juice and urine acidifiers will be prescribed together with antibiotics against secondary bacterial invasion of the bladder wall, damaged by sharp crystals. The less common, protein-type material is more soluble in alkaline urine, so if this is found, treatment will aim to make the urine alkaline.

The cause of feline urolithiasis is unknown. Several theories have been put forward, and the following preventative measures will be of interest to all cat owners, not only those whose cats have suffered from cystitis and/or FUS.

(a) Cats fed raw red meats with plenty of meat and fish juices will have dilute, acid urines in which bacteria are less likely to grow, and in which crystals are less likely to form.

(b) In wild cat colonies fed by humans, and in domestic cats, one method to encourage cats to drink more water is to add 1 per cent of salt (sodium chloride) to their food – that is, 1 gram of salt per 100 grams of food. But remember that cats will not eat oversalted food.

(c) Dried catfood contains only about 8 per cent water, and cats are unlikely to drink sufficient plain water to make up the deficit. If you serve dried catfood, use it as a 'topping' to extra-moist meat or fish meals, or soak it in juice or water for about half an hour.

(d) Mineral supplements and high-ash foods (carbohydrate-containing foods) have been implicated in FUS, so use these with caution.

(e) The old theory that neutering tomcats before maturity (two years of age) results in a smaller urethra, and therefore more likelihood of blockage by insoluble material in the urine, has been largely disproved. What is certain is that the male neutered under one year old is unable to extrude the penis from its protective sheath for cleaning purposes, and debris – providing a potential breeding area for bacteria – is more likely to accumulate. As FUS is prevalent among neutered males, a prudent precaution is to neuter as late as possible (see page 183), and thereafter give half a Sesoral tablet (containing sex hormones) twice a week.

(f) Some researchers have suggested that the cause of FUS is a virus or bacterium, which would explain why they are usually found in the urine of cats affected with FUS, but it is more probable that these infections are in the bladder all the time and multiply in a damaged bladder wall. Try to minimize the conditions under which such viruses and bacteria can grow: remember that cats are desert animals, not adapted to cold, wet weather.

(g) Urine retention will favour the deposition of crystals. Obese, lethargic cats are reluctant to take exercise and this results in the retention of urine. Cats should be slimmed, and regularly prized out of their day chairs to be shut outdoors for a time. Tomcats who keep up a good flow of urine by spraying every few metres are less likely to retain urine!

STRESS

It is not strictly accurate to describe cats as domesticated animals. Not all of them can adapt to living in high-density domestic communities. Any situation in which cats are expected to eat, sleep and share territory is potentially stressful to them. This does not mean that cats cannot exist in harmony – once acquainted. However, in a cattery or sanctuary, animals unknown and potentially hostile towards one another are brought together in what are, to them, overcrowded conditions.

The fact that stress greatly increases the possibility of active infection following activation from dormancy or cross-infection has already been discussed. The multicat owner or carer, in particular, is faced with the daunting task of preventing transmission in conditions which are most in its favour.

Entry to a boarding cattery is not the only cause of stress. Any sudden disruption of routine or change of environment can be stressful – for instance, exposure to cold, wet weather; being lost from home with inadequate or unsuitable food if unable to hunt; rehoming, in the case of strays or cats whose owners have died or entered hospital, or can no longer care for them for some other reason; veterinary visits; introduction to the household of a new baby, dog, cat or adult human; the shock of an accident or cat fight; showing; moving house; the cat's owner being away from home; being sent to stud; long journeys; holidays in caravans or unfamiliar surroundings; unfamiliar or prolonged noise; pregnancy, birth and lactation; chronic illness, such as chronic nephritis.

SYMPTOMS OF STRESS
The first indication of stress in most cats is loss of appetite. Stress lowers a cat's ability to absorb digested food from the gut, and this

in turn leads to vitamin deficiency which favours parasitization by viruses, bacteria, protozoa and metazoa.

Under stress, extra corticosteroids are secreted by the adrenal glands just above each kidney. Corticosteroids cause a drop in the number of white blood cells and hence a lowering of immunity. It may seem paradoxical that corticosteroids are used so often by vets, but in small amounts they are useful for treating infections because they stimulate the appetite, increase blood glucose levels and reduce inflammation.

All cats likely to be stressed must be watched closely, persuaded to eat by every possible means (see 'The Appetite' on page 27) and given a vitamin supplement such as ABIDEC (obtainable from chemists).

DENTAL PROBLEMS

A cat's biting teeth at the front of the mouth are minute and useless. His canine teeth are sharp and curved and designed for tearing flesh from bone into strips. His pointed molars are designed for spiking (tenderizing) meat. The prong-like projections on the upper surface of the tongue remove flesh from bone. The best protection we can give a cat against dental disease, then, is to provide food similar in texture to his natural food – raw meat, liver, kidney, lights, tripe, fat – cut into strips to provide exercise for teeth and jaw.

Yellow plaque and inflammation of the gums are common complaints. Some vets believe these are the result of feeding cats soft-textured, artificial foods, or dried cat food. Inbreeding among farm and pedigree cats has been suggested as a reason for loss of teeth. But the possession of a healthy set of teeth and gums into old age probably depends largely on heredity.

The cat's mouth is easy to open and examine (see page 41). Gingivitis in young cats may be an indication of an underlying secondary bacterial infection consequent upon the presence of the feline leukaemia virus. Cats do need teeth cleaned or extracted under an anaesthetic on occasions, but in the case of an old cat this is not usually advisable, and oral antibiotics may be used to check bacterial infection.

Symptoms of mouth discomfort are: mouth odour (sometimes associated with chronic nephritis in old cats), pawing at the gums, salivating, extending the tongue, vomiting, loss of appetite, slow eating. As a test for mouth problems in an old cat, give him his favourite food, and if he still eats slowly, discomfort is indicated!

OLD AGE

The average lifespan for a cat is twelve to fifteen years. During their teenage years cats should be watched carefully by their owners, using the information on pages 101–103. However, old cats should be treated like antiquated machines – if they are working well, leave them alone and do not service unless absolutely necessary! It should be remembered that veterinary visits, tests for terminal diseases which are in any case untreatable and certainly anaesthetics are particularly stressful to an old cat, whose immune system is on the wane. Any break in routine will cause stress and liability to infection.

The following are a few points to note concerning old cats:

(1) There may be a gradual stiffening of the hindlegs and inability to jump. This does not necessarily mean arthritis or any pain, but, coupled with a deterioration in vision and hearing, indicates that safety precautions should be doubled and old cats should not be allowed out into an unenclosed garden without supervision.

(2) Muscle wastage and loss of weight may be caused by less efficient digestion, chronic nephritis (see page 108) or a hormonal imbalance, and should be investigated by your vet. Ample fresh water should be provided, and perhaps, if tolerated, a change of diet to easily digestible white meats, served frequently in small amounts. An old cat may require more food than in his younger days.

(3) An old cat needs a comfortable bed in a peaceful, warm place, and should be allowed to sleep away his declining years. Many old cats remain active and playful, but there will be a gradual slowing down.

(4) Some old cats become less particular about their personal appearance, so extra grooming may be necessary.

(5) Claws are normally kept short and blunt through exercise and, in the case of front claws, by drawing over wood, but old cats' claws may become very long and sharp and tend to catch in fabrics. This may be accentuated because the ability to keep claws sheathed may also be lost. Claw trimmers, specifically for cats, can be purchased from pet shops. These resemble tiny secateurs. Only the tips of the claws should be clipped.

EUTHANASIA

Cats who have received tip-top care sometimes die young, through no fault of their owners. Longevity depends on luck! But cats are

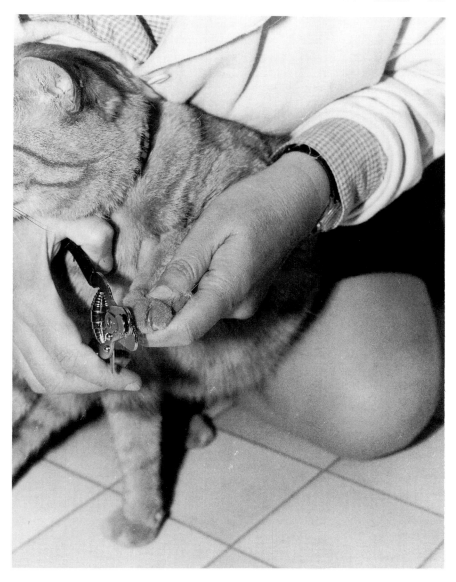

FIGURE 26 Use of claw trimmers. The paw is squeezed gently between thumb and first finger to unsheath the claws.

known to have nine lives. This may be an exaggeration, but it is true that they possess vast powers of recuperation – they rally when all seems lost. Cats, unlike humans, may be afforded a dignified end, made possible by euthanasia. Not for them is the indignity of the life-support machine, or the long-drawn-out terminal illness. It will be obvious when a prolonged treatment has failed and, to save further suffering, the last service an owner can give is to stay with a cat while the vet gives a final injection. The end takes thirty seconds, is painless and the owner has nothing to fear. Making the final decision, will, however, nearly always fall upon the owner, and cats should not be kept alive through selfish love. Vets are, understandably, very reluctant to be more than advisors, when euthanasia appears to be the only option.

Vets will dispose of bodies through specialist firms who arrange mass cremations, or they will put you in touch with private burial or cremation firms for animals. Many people prefer to bury their cats under a favourite tree or bush in the garden. The cat will be placed, by your vet, in a polythene bag and should be buried in this, at least 4 feet (120 centimetres) deep.

CONCLUSION

Cat owners can learn a great deal from their vets by seeking up-to-date information, by seeking explanations of their cat's condition and by watching their vet's handling techniques. Cat care is constantly changing as research probes deeper and deeper into the mysteries of disease and preventative medicine.

We can provide top-quality food, a stable, routined environment, warmth and prompt veterinary care so that, when it is time to say goodbye, as all cat owners have to when their cat reaches his end, we can state with honesty and some consolation: 'I have given him all I have to give; he has had a wonderful life. I've made mistakes through lack of knowledge or experience and I've taken risks unknowingly, but I've always done my best.'

7 Disinfection and Sterilization

It is now clear that a cat owner cannot rely on vaccines to control disease, since only two virus diseases can be controlled in this way. The risk of all types of infection can be minimized, however, by scrupulous hygiene.

Disinfection means killing or inactivating *some* of the less resistant life forms, thus lowering the concentration of infections in the environment, in accommodation and on equipment. These include: bacteria, viruses and protozoa freshly shed by cats.

Sterilization means totally killing or inactivating *all* life forms. This is not always practicable or safe for the cat. All infections, except viruses, have highly resistant forms, designed to survive adverse conditions outside the cat. These include: bacterial spores (the most resistant life form known to science); fungal spores of, for example, ringworm; eggs of intestinal worms shed in faeces; oocysts of protozoa shed in faeces (for example, *Toxoplasma gondii*) and cysts and larvae associated with raw meat.

Both disinfection and sterilization can be carried out by chemical means, details of which are given on the following pages. In warm solution, only a chemical disinfectant/sterilizer can penetrate the outer envelope of protein and destroy living cells of highly resistant life forms. Some chemicals can serve as disinfectants in dilute solution and sterilizers in concentrated solution. The correct concentration for the task in hand is essential as some disinfectants/sterilizers are less effective in concentrated solution. Disinfectants are sometimes called biocides, germicides, bactericides or sanitizers. Many are effective only against bacteria, but it is viruses particularly which must be inactivated in cat environments since these are dangerous to cats. Any product which is not virucidal, or which will render harmless only the less resistant, so-called 'enveloped' viruses and not the 'non-enveloped' or 'naked' viruses, is useless for catteries.

However much we would like to sterilize all cat accommodation and items in contact with cats, this is impractical. We can disinfect

FIGURE 27   Hygiene is of the greatest importance. All bedding should be either protected or washable. Here the bed and mattress are completely covered with a heavy-duty polythene sheet on top of which is a washable valance. Individual washable pillows of polyester foam allow sectional washing in cases of soiling.

accommodation and some equipment, and sterilize items such as food bowls (after every use), toilet trays, grooming kits, waste buckets, scoops and so on. Sterilization, where practicable, should be carried out on high-risk items: that is, those directly in contact with cats' excretions and secretions (urine, faeces, saliva, mucus), including floors and walls up to a height of about 4 feet (120 centimetres). Obviously certain methods of sterilization cannot be used if equipment is to remain undamaged.

Damp dusting is a very useful method of disinfection. The surfaces requiring treatment are wiped over with a cloth dampened in the appropriate disinfectant. This may be done safely during a cat's occupation of a cattery unit or confinement in an isolation room.

Many items can be sterilized only if they can be immersed in the sterilizer for at least two hours; or, in the case of a surface, if it can be kept wet for ten minutes. In the latter instance a more concentrated solution of the sterilizer would be needed.

Food is sterilized by prolonged, dry heat in an oven. Dishes can be sterilized in this way, if necessary. Faeces and soiled toilet-tray fillers can be sterilized in a brick-built incinerator, where they must be exposed to *dry* heat of over 176°F (80°C) for at least one hour.

Most cat viruses and bacteria are inactivated by boiling in water for half an hour. Eggs, larvae, pupae and adult forms of ectoparasites in bedding are killed by washing in hot water, but eggs and cysts of endoparasites are not reliably destroyed by boiling water or even superheated steam.

Freezing does not kill bacteria, nor does it reduce the infectability of viruses; it only suspends bacterial growth and temporarily inactivates viruses.

A component of sunlight, called ultraviolet light, is an important disinfectant outdoors. Its effectiveness is limited indoors, however, if it is received through ordinary glass. Thus it is important that all cats, their accommodation and equipment should receive direct sunlight at some time during the day. Remember also that soiling (that is, a film of dirt, on, say, a cattery unit floor) reduces the disinfecting action of ultraviolet light.

In fact, all disinfectants are inactivated to some extent by soiling which covers and protects infections, even on apparently smooth surfaces. Typical soiling consists of: humus (decomposed animal or plant material); vaporized cooking fat condensed on walls; fluff from wool, cotton or other fabric; cat fur; dust particles.

Disinfectants, then, work best on very clean surfaces and equipment. To help them do their work, they may contain an added detergent which increases the wetting power of water and helps it to penetrate surfaces, lifting dirt away and allowing disinfectants to reach infections. (Domestos, for instance, has added detergent.) Detergents are thus sometimes called 'wetting agents' or 'surface active agents' – 'surfactants' for short. They have no disinfectant properties of their own. Some detergents actually attract soiling, then disperse it. They act on the surface of water, making the water spread out, rather than remain as 'blobs'. Washing powders and soaps are detergents, some of which contain alkalis to assist the removal of soiling; some contain water softeners, so that they can be used in hard or soft water; and some contain disinfectants, which are normally only bactericidal. Perfume or deordorant may be added to both detergents and disinfectants.

Disinfection and sterilization are, of course, not the only precautions which should be taken against infections. If a cat is obviously suffering from a disease, whether infectious or non-infectious, he should be isolated immediately from all other cats in the same house and in the neighbourhood. But it is not always possible to recognize the presence of an infection because cats can become infected and acquire immunity without showing any symptoms at all. This type of infection is called sub-clinical. Such 'carrier' cats can infect other, high-risk, susceptible cats if in close contact. The infection may remain inactivated until a cat enters, say, a cattery and becomes stressed, when immunity is impaired. Once an infection becomes symptomatic (a clinical infection) the cat suffering from it is an even greater risk to susceptible cats.

A domestic cat can be closely observed by his owner, who can note any slight change of behaviour which may indicate that her animal is unwell. But a cattery owner, or anyone caring for a neighbour's feline, must assume that all cats are a potential risk to others and keep them separate. The aim should be to minimize the risk of infection transfer from cat to cat (cross-infection).

The cattery owner particularly, faced with the awesome responsibility of keeping beloved domestic cats fit, occupied and happy, eating well and infection-free for a fortnight or so, must assume that all cats are a potential risk to others and keep them as far apart as facilities permit. High summer is an especially risky season, when hot, damp conditions are conducive to the survival of infections for longer periods. As well as battling with viruses and bacteria, a cattery owner ceaselessly wages war against fleas, flies, mites, ticks and wasps – just as the one-cat owner does but on a larger scale.

THE USE OF DISINFECTANT/STERILIZER IN CAT ACCOMMODATION

All surfaces and equipment used by cats should be regularly disinfected, both in houses, if practicable, and catteries, thus safeguarding humans as well as cats and maintaining hygiene.

The effectiveness of any chemical sterilizer depends on: (a) using the correct concentration for the task; (b) the amount of soiling present, which must be removed by water and detergent before disinfection or sterilization; (c) the amount of time a surface can be kept wet with the disinfecting solution – that is, whether a wet contact time of ten minutes can be maintained or total immersion carried out; (d) how smooth and impervious the surface is; and (e) whether it is safe to leave without rinsing, thus leaving a residual disinfectancy on the surface and saving time.

Other considerations relate to the detergency of the product –

whether it contains a detergent to 'lift out' dirt; whether it is safe to use in the presence of cats when dilute, and in the vicinity of cats (but not in contact with them) when concentrated; if it is to be used in a cattery, whether it is cheap enough to use in the large volumes required; and above all whether it is virucidal, destroying not only labile (unstable) viruses which are surrounded by an 'envelope' (for example, feline leukaemia, feline rhinotracheitis, rabies), but also the so-called 'non-enveloped' viruses which are highly resistant to disinfectants (for example, feline caliciviris, feline panleucopaenia, feline infectious peritonitis).

The only disinfectants/sterilizers which meet these conditions are those which contain chlorine in solution (that is, dissolved in water), which is slowly liberated. The amount of chlorine in solution is called 'available' chlorine, and is the disinfectant. Liberated chlorine disinfects and then escapes into the atmosphere. Once all the chlorine has disappeared, the solution ceases to be disinfectant.

The two main sources of chlorine for disinfection/sterilization are sodium hypochlorite solution (domestic bleach), such as Domestos, and organo-chlorine compounds like Lever Industrial's Titan Sanitizer SU 357 and VetHealth's VH7. These organo-chlorine compounds are supplied as powders. They are slightly more effective than solutions because they are less likely to decompose on storage. They also have excellent wetting and detergency properties and, being powders, they can be applied neat on a sponge cloth for sterilization.

In fact research workers at the Cornell Feline Health Center, Cornell University, Ithaca, NY 14853, USA, concluded that the most effective, inexpensive, readily available, pleasant and safe-to-use disinfectant (in dilute form) in the presence of cats is a solution of sodium hypochlorite. They discovered that nearly all commonly used disinfectants are ineffectual in destroying even 'weak' feline viruses. In *dilute* solution sodium hypochlorite may be used as a disinfectant; and as a sterilizer if an object can be immersed in it for (preferably) twenty-four hours; in *concentrated* solution (when it is equally dangerous to human skin, cats' skin and infections) it will sterilize high-risk items with a wet contact time of ten minutes.

And yet it is so safe when dilute that we and our cats drink the solution every day, for it is used to disinfect drinking water. It is so safe that it is used to sterilize babies' feeding equipment and the skins of vegetables and fruit fed to babies. Most cats find sodium hypochlorite attractive, and often lick and roll on disinfected surfaces, presumably to acquire the scent! Some cats may prefer their drinking water from a tap left running for a few minutes.

For disinfection of accommodation, it is necessary for a solution to provide 880 parts per million (ppm) of available chlorine (that is, chlorine in solution in water). For sterilization of surfaces 20,000 ppm available chlorine is necessary – this is normally used for toilet trays, with a wet contact time of ten minutes. For sterilization by total immersion, preferably for twenty-four hours but not less than two hours, 220 ppm are necessary: this is used for grooming equipment, feeding dishes and so on.

The so-called 'one-stage' disinfection procedure can be used only on clean, smooth surfaces and is therefore not generally useful for catteries on vacation. One-stage disinfection involves wiping, brushing or spraying a surface with dilute sodium hypochlorite (1 per cent solution or less if Domestos is used) and allowing it to dry. If the surface is uneven, pitted or includes crevices, the amount of added detergent will have to be increased and rinsing will be necessary, thus making disinfection a two-stage process. In the presence of heavy soiling on uneven or very porous surfaces, as would be found in outdoor catteries, disinfection should always be a three-stage process: washing, rinsing, disinfection. Some disinfectants used in catteries (for example, the phenol-based and formalin-based ones) require rinsing *after* disinfection, making a time-consuming four-stage process.

If you wish to use a product other than the three discussed here be sure to get full details of it beforehand from the manufacturer (see the list of questions to ask on page 130).

USE OF DOMESTOS

Domestos is widely available from supermarkets and is inexpensive. If large quantities are used, it is more economic to purchase in bulk direct from the manufacturer. (See Appendix I.)

Domestos solution, as purchased, contains 8–10 per cent sodium hypochlorite in water. At this concentration it is corrosive to cloths, overalls and skin. Great care must therefore be taken when making dilutions to avoid splashing, particularly near the eyes. Make dilutions in a room out of bounds to cats. Concentrated Domestos will also attack painted wood and metals. It can be used for only five minutes on soiled metal surfaces like drains and waste pipes, but does not harm PVC waste pipes. It can be used, if necessary, on plastics, PVC, concrete, vinyl, Formica, polythene and bare (unpainted) wood.

Although Domestos contains a detergent to assist spreading and penetration of uneven surfaces, such as wood or concrete hardstandings, a few extra drops of detergent (for example, washing-up liquid) can be added if needed. Dirt, dust and infections are reached, killed and literally 'lifted out', and can be rinsed or hosed away into the foul-water drainage system.

Domestos can be applied with a soft brush or a hand spray. Hand sprays may result in too-rapid drying for high-risk areas but are useful for low-risk areas such as roofs and ventilators. When using sprays or brushes in a cattery, great care must be taken not to spray or splash any soiling into nearby occupied units. Remember that a warm solution is best for disinfection: cold solutions do not penetrate so well, while hot solutions decompose too fast.

Domestos is pleasantly perfumed and alters the chemical composition of urine and faecal matter, thus removing odour – even that of tomcat urine! It has many other uses, which are dealt with later.

A dilute Domestos solution slowly decomposes, liberating its 'free' or 'available' chlorine into the atmosphere in minute, immeasurable and completely harmless amounts. This occurs rapidly in a warm solution (the most effective temperature for disinfectancy) in the light. For maximum disinfectancy a solution should be made up daily and preferably used at once. A dilute solution can be stored in a dark cupboard, but not for longer than twenty-four hours. Concentrated solutions (as purchased) are more stable, but to reduce the speed of chlorine release, Domestos is supplied in light-proof containers, and should be kept in a dark, cool cupboard. Because of the slow release of the chlorine gas, the cap should be slightly loosened during storage.

Dilutions and Their Application

The dilution required depends on the disinfection/sterilization task. Exact weight or volume measurements are unnecessary. Experience will tell you how much disinfectant solution you need to make up each day. A 10-litre graduated, lidded, polythene bucket may hold a convenient amount, and the calculations given below are based on this quantity. Larger polythene containers can be purchased in the beer-making departments of chemists' shops. For measuring concentrated Domestos, a glass or polythene measuring jug can be used, graduated in litres. Shampoo or small disinfectant bottles (of, say, 100 millilitres) are useful for measuring smaller volumes.

The following is an example of how to calculate the amount of Domestos needed for a solution of a given strength – for instance ¼ per cent:

100 millilitres warm water must contain ¼ millilitre Domestos.

Therefore 10 litres (10,000 millilitres) must contain

$$\frac{10,000}{100} \times ¼ \text{ Domestos} = 25 \text{ millilitres Domestos}$$

Pour the Domestos into a 10-litre bucket and make up to the 10-litre graduation mark with warm water. Use immediately, or store in a cool, dark place for no longer than twenty-four hours.

To make a ¼ per cent solution of Domestos, equivalent to a solution containing 220 ppm available chlorine: 25 millilitres of Domestos are made up to 10 litres as described above. Use for sterilizing feeding equipment, combs and toilet trays by total immersion for at least two hours, or overnight.

To make a ½ per cent solution of Domestos, equivalent to a solution containing 440 ppm available chlorine: 50 millilitres of Domestos are made up to 10 litres as described above. Use for daily damp dusting of occupied premises, allow to dry; no rinsing necessary. Suitable for low-risk areas not in direct contact with cats, or in accommodation used for healthy domestic cats.

To make a 1 per cent solution of Domestos, equivalent to a solution containing 880 ppm available chlorine: 100 millilitres of Domestos are made up to 10 litres as described above. Use in all high-risk areas: isolation rooms, all types of cattery, stray cat sanctuaries, quarantine catteries, and so on. Use also for equipment such as carry baskets, sleeping baskets, grooming equipment (all of which must be washable), claw-maintenance posts, toilet trays.

To make a 20 per cent solution of Domestos, equivalent to a solution containing 20,000 ppm available chlorine: 2 litres of Domestos are made up to 10 litres as described above. Use in very high-risk boarding or breeding catteries to sterilize surfaces of toilet trays with a wet contact time of ten minutes, then rinse.

To compare the disinfection of clean water, it is interesting to know that our drinking water is chlorinated to 1 ppm available chlorine, with a contact time of one to two hours. It is then partially dechlorinated. This can be compared with a smooth working surface, contaminated with a few bacteria or viruses, which requires 440 ppm available chlorine for ten minutes.

USE OF TITAN SANITIZER SU 357
Titan Sanitizer SU 357 is not available from shops but is obtainable by application to the manufacturer, Lever Industrial (see Appendix I). It is more expensive than Domestos, but has many advantages. It is a non-abrasive powder – more stable than liquid sodium hypochlorite and less corrosive to aluminium and can be used, dilute, for washing metal equipment and cutlery as well as dishes. In dilute solution it is bactericidal; it can be used in a 1 per cent solution as a one-stage bactericide for washing utensils, such as those used with

raw meat. In a 4 per cent solution it is a bactericide/virucide. It can also be used as a wet paste to provide 20,000 ppm available chlorine on a surface and can be applied in this form as a sterilizer to toilet trays and worktops, where it should be left for five minutes and then rinsed off.

Chlorine is released more slowly from Titan Sanitizer SU 357 in a dilute solution, so it remains effective longer than a Domestos solution; it incorporates not only a detergent but also a mild alkali which improves soil removal and wetting of surfaces; it contains a water softener, so that even in hard water a good lather is maintained throughout the cleaning process. Even as a powder it does not harm most skins, but people with sensitive skins should wear rubber gloves when handling it. Like Domestos it kills moulds and fungi. It does not smear when rinsed; it can be used hot or cold, but best results are obtained with a hand-hot solution at 104°–122°F (40°–50°C). It has no perfume, so cannot taint containers; it can be bought in shaker dispenser packs; it can be applied as a powder, or as a solution with a cloth, brush or hand spray.

Every 100 grams of powder provides 2.2 grams of available chlorine (that is, 2.2 per cent). Kitchen scales calibrated in grams are accurate enough for measuring organo-chlorine powders.

To make a 1 per cent solution (weight/volume), equivalent to 220 ppm available chlorine: Use 10 grams per litre or 100 grams per 10-litre bucket. Use as a bactericide and labile (enveloped) virucide for washing up, or for low-risk surfaces. Allow five minutes' wet contact time, then rinse.

To make a 4 per cent solution (weight/volume) equivalent to 880 ppm available chlorine: Use 40 grams per litre or 400 grams per 10-litre bucket to obtain a disinfectant which should be applied in exactly the same way as a 1 per cent Domestos solution, allowing a wet contact time of ten minutes. Rinsing is necessary in this case.

To make a wet paste equivalent to 20,000 ppm available chlorine: Add sufficient water to the powder to make a wet paste and use for sterilization with a wet contact time of five minutes, then rinse.

USE OF VH7

To make a solution equivalent to 220 ppm available chlorine: Use 1 gram per litre or 10 grams per 10–litre bucket. Use to sterilize by total immersion.

To make a solution equivalent to 880 ppm available chlorine: Use 3.5 grams per litre or 35 grams per 10-litre bucket to make a disinfectant effective with a wet contact time of 10 minutes.

To make a wet paste equivalent to 20,000 ppm available chlorine: Add sufficient water to the powder to make a wet paste and use for sterilization with a wet contact time of five minutes, then rinse.

USING DISINFECTANTS NOT DESCRIBED IN THIS BOOK

If you are planning to use disinfectants which are not covered in this book, ensure that you ask the manufacturers the following questions first:

(1) If your product is based on chlorine disinfectancy, how can I make up a solution containing 880 parts per million (ppm) available chlorine for routine disinfection, 220 ppm available chlorine for total immersion and sterilization of items such as feeding dishes, and 20,000 ppm available chlorine for sterilization of surfaces?

(2) Does your product include a detergent? If not, which detergent should I use and how much can I add?

(3) If your disinfectant is not based on free chlorine, what is the pH? Is it neutral (pH7 or less), acid (pH6 or less), alkaline (pH8 or more)? Is it buffered – that is, does it contain a chemical which ensures it will remain at the same pH, whatever it is used on? (For example, cat urine is strongly acid.)

Note: Many disinfectants are acid-based, but the parvoviruses, notably the feline panleucopaenia virus, are not destroyed by acids alone, nor by phenolics. The more *acid* a disinfectant is, the more potentially corrosive it will be to metals, causing rusting, pitting and, in the case of steel, stress corrosion. PVC door and window furniture, earthenware feeding bowls, plastic or wooden utensils, plastic combs, PVC toilet trays, buckets, waste bins, and so on, are recommended where practicable. Prolonged contact with water and steam is also corrosive to metals.

(4) Is your product virucidal in a safe dilution, safe to use in the presence of cats, or, at least, not harmful to cats if used 4 feet (120 centimetres) away from them? Will it destroy 'non-enveloped' or 'naked' viruses? If no information is available for animal parvoviruses, will it destroy the equivalent *human* virus – hepatitis B?

Note: If a disinfectant has to be used in a concentrated solution to be virucidal (say, over 1 per cent w/v or v/v – that is, 1 gram made up to 100 millilitres or 1 millilitre made up to 100 millilitres) it will probably be unsafe to use in the presence or vicinity of cats, will need rinsing and will almost certainly be uneconomic. Rinsing will mean more work and may mean that the unit cannot be reoccupied for about twelve hours. Such a disinfectant (for example, formalin) may prove impractical for catteries. Although a 4 per cent formalin solution normally used for disinfection is irritant to small animals by skin contact and inhalation, a very dilute aerosol spray is extremely effective for air disinfection, since air contains very little 'soiling'. Air disinfection works only in air, and surface disinfection is still necessary – for instance, damp dusting of cleaned surfaces with ¼ per cent Domestos solution.

(5) Is your disinfectant a QUAT (quaternary ammonium compound)? These are bactericides only, antiseptics (safe to use *on* cats in dilute solution), or weak virucides, with no activity against parvoviruses. Their chief use is to protect *humans* from the effects of certain bacteria, notably *Salmonella* and *E. coli*, associated with raw meat, and they are used for washing cutlery and crockery.

BACTERICIDES AND ANTISEPTICS

An *antiseptic*, usually a reliable bactericide but in some cases also weakly virucidal, is a liquid or ointment safe to use on a cat's skin. Since cats' claws and teeth harbour potentially pathogenic bacteria, it is important that all cats arriving home with torn ears, bleeding temples, tufts of loose fur, raised hackles and puffed tails, be examined for wounds. Wounds should be dabbed with, preferably, liquid antiseptic, and allowed to dry, if possible, before allowing the cat to lick his coat.

Phenolics are compounds related to phenol (carbolic acid), a white, crystalline solid obtained when coal is heated. Phenol is widely used in soaps, disinfectants, wood preservatives and insecticidal shampoos, some of which smell of coal tar. Disinfectants containing a high concentration of phenol, or a phenolic, turn milky when added to water – a familiar example is Dettol, which is a solution of a phenolic called chloroxylenol. Hibitane is a trade name for chlorhexidine gluconate, a phenolic used in Savlon – a very popular antiseptic used on cats. Phenol is used in TCP. Other phenolics are the antibiotics erythromycin and terramycin and the fungistatic griseofulvin, given internally in some cases of ringworm.

Phenol is the only disinfectant which is absorbed by the skin and this makes it a most efficient antiseptic for use on mangled cats. But, like all concentrated disinfectants, it is poisonous. Cats are less able to cope with phenol in their bodies than are dogs and humans, and for this reason great care must be taken to use only weak solutions when absolutely necessary.

There is no danger from phenol if it is used in the correct concentration. It is weakly virucidal, but ineffective against feline panleuco-paenia, and has only a low activity against feline infectious peritonitis virus.

Iodine-based disinfectants, for example Iodophor, are used for the disinfection of walls, pens, floors, baskets, beds, and so on, in confirmed cases of ringworm. Iodophor is used to dab on ringworm lesions (sore places) on the cat's skin. The iodine-based disinfectants are not effective against the feline panleucopaenia or feline calicivirus at manufacturers' recommended dilutions.

Formaldehyde, known commercially as formalin, is a quick-acting (ten minutes' wet contact time), wide-spectrum virucide, used for damp dusting and spray application (for airborne infections) in high-risk areas like vets' surgeries. Formalin is so effective against feline panleucopaenia that it is used to inactivate the virus in some vaccines! Unfortunately, to be an effective wide-spectrum virucide it has to be used in a 4 per cent solution, and at this concentration its vapour is irritant to cats and humans. It can only be used in vacated units, well separated from neighbouring cats, and very thorough rinsing must be followed by at least twelve hours of airing before reoccu-pation. This is too time-consuming for most cattery owners.

Two recommended products are: VH Formalin Plus, available from VetHealth at the address given in Appendix I; and Floral Disinfectant Air Spray (lavender), available in concentrated form from Cromessol Co. Ltd at the address given in Appendix II.

Soaps are detergents used for penetrating and lifting out dirt (and infections) from furrowed human hands. Some soaps (for instance, coal tar and carbolic) are bactericidal and weakly virucidal. Solid soaps must be kept dry as, when they are wet and exposed to air, bacteria and algae grow on them. This can be avoided by using liquid soaps from dispensers (for example, Sumasept bactericidal soap cream from Lever Industrial). Hands are very high-risk infection transmission agents in catteries. As already pointed out, bacteria associated with raw meat are dangerous to humans. On both counts, clean hands are essential. Never use *any* soap on a cat.

Floor cleaners used domestically may contain a bactericide. As well as detergent, they may contain an alkali, like washing soda (sodium carbonate), which is a degreasing/wetting agent and a water softener. Floor cleaners are safe to use in the presence of cats if diluted strictly according to manufacturers' instructions and allowed to dry. Rinsing is not necessary. When non-abrasive powders or creams are used neat, for baths and basins, thorough rinsing is necessary: many cats will climb into them to drink from running taps, or even to use them as toilets!

Quaternary ammonium compounds (QUATS) are sometimes referred to as cationic detergents. Like many detergents, QUATS do not by themselves work well in hard water, but with added non-ionic detergent, a water softener and an alkali 'buffer' which keeps them alkaline they are non-corrosive to metals. They are bactericidal and *not* useful in cattery accommodation. They are, however, safe to use in the form of antiseptics for cats. Titan Quatdet SU 321 is a blue, liquid, pleasantly perfumed bactericide/detergent, used for washing up and damp dusting in kitchens. It is obtainable direct from the manufacturer, Lever Industrial, who will also supply, on receipt of a large stamped addressed envelope, a helpful booklet entitled *The Role of Chemical Disinfectants in the Food Industry*.

ANTISEPTICS SAFE FOR USE ON CATS
TCP: A solution of chlorine (0.4 per cent), iodine (0.055 per cent) and phenol (0.63 per cent) all weight/volume (w/v) – that is 0.4 grams of chlorine per 100 millilitres and so on. TCP is diluted to half-strength, and used only when necessary – never as a routine antiseptic on cats, say, prior to showing. It is weakly virucidal, absorbed through the skin and the only analgesic (pain-reducing) antiseptic.

Savlon: A solution containing chlorhexidine gluconate (a phenolic) 0.3 per cent w/v and cetrimide (a QUAT) 3 per cent w/v. The 250-millilitre-sized bottle of concentrate should be diluted using ½ capful of concentrate per ¼ pint (150 millilitres) of warm water.

Salt solution kills bacteria by extracting water from them. Use ¼ teaspoonful of salt per ¼ pint (150 millilitres) of warm water.

Hydrogen peroxide: Low virucidal activity, use at half-strength.

Saniphor is an antiseptic spray sold by VetHealth.

Fucidin H and Dermobion are antiseptic ointments, obtainable from vets.

DISINFECTION PROCEDURES ON VACATION OF A CATTERY UNIT OR ROOM

When a boarder leaves for home, or a sick cat is cured and reinstated into the community, vacated premises must be disinfected and equipment, if feasible, sterilized.

Efficient disinfection depends on the construction of the accommodation: construction materials should be as smooth and impervious as possible and there should be no cracks or crevices to harbour dirt which can protect infections. The best cat accommodation is that which can be completely dismantled for cleaning purposes, or that in which every part can easily be reached with a brush, hose and vacuum cleaner. Premises and staffing levels will, of course, be determined by the capital available. The easier the accommodation is to disinfect, the less likelihood there is of an outbreak of an infection, such as cat flu, and any infections that do occur will be easier to contain.

Total disinfection of the environment (surfaces and air) is impossible in the outdoor cattery, however. Outdoor accommodation is exposed to airborne infections, those carried by all flying insects and those transmitted by travelling parasites like fleas, biting lice and mites. To help avoid cross-infection, cats should be housed at least 4 feet (120 centimetres) apart. For economic reasons some chalets and runs have to be much closer, even connected, and in these cases cats are separated by wood or PVC partitions (sneeze barriers).

A far higher degree of disinfection is possible in indoor accommodation as bactericidal/virucidal sprays, or electric volatilizers, can be used. Indoors insecticidal sprays for the environment (for instance, Staykil) are effective far longer. In all accommodation good ventilation is essential to prevent pockets of high-concentration infections which could waft to neighbouring units, particularly those occupied by high-risk cats.

Each unit of accommodation should be disinfected as soon as possible after the departure of the cat, and ideally twenty-four hours should elapse before reoccupation. Since in catteries neighbouring units will be in occupation, it is essential that some form of partitioning (made, for example of wood, hardboard, or thick' polythene sheeting) is used round the vacated unit to avoid any contamination of occupied units. Remember, when cleaning, that vacuum cleaners can blow out dust as well as suck it in; pressure hosing or hand spraying can splash or spray neighbouring units; dusting, brushing and sweeping can all raise dust and fur, together with any infections – large or small.

Abrasives should never be used on *any* surface because they can cause scratches which can harbour infections. This is particularly important high-risk items like feeding dishes and toilet trays.

The aims of disinfection are to:
(1) Kill any mature skin parasites: for example, fleas, ear mites.
(2) Clean all surfaces by (a) removing dirt, dust and debris, and (b) washing with detergent.

(3) Disinfect all surfaces.

(4) Sterilize all high-risk items such as toilet trays, feeding bowls, areas soiled by faeces or vomit.

(5) Burn all disposable items such as cardboard beds and bedding.

(6) Safely dispose of the entire contents of the toilet tray and soiled litter waste bucket (see 'Waste Disposal and Odour Prevention' on page 170).

On vacation, place an 'Empty' sign on the outer door of the unit. Keep the door closed. No item should be removed until it has passed through the disinfection procedure. Some accommodation may be clean enough for one-stage disinfection to be sufficient – that is, by the use of a combined liquid detergent/disinfectant solution.

STEP-BY-STEP DISINFECTION OF ACCOMMODATION

The following procedure is recommended for successful disinfection of cat accommodation as soon as it has been vacated.

(1) Spray Staykil, or a similar insecticide, and leave for two hours.

(2) Using a hand spray and warm water, lightly spray the entire unit and its contents to settle dust and fur.

(3) Remove debris (contents of toilet tray, bedding, straw, grass, catmint, toys, newspaper) in a plastic, lidded bucket kept specifically for the individual unit. This waste material should be set aside ready for incineration.

(4) Using a dustpan and brush, or a vacuum cleaner with a crevice brush, carefully remove dirt and dust from other items.

(5) If the unit is now almost clean, and particularly if all surfaces are smooth, the following washing stage can be omitted. The desirability of having any cracks or crevices sealed with a waterproof sealant will be obvious!

(6) *Washing stage*: Using a bucket of hot water, to which a few drops of liquid detergent (such as Fairy Liquid) have been added, brush the whole area with a soft brush, paying particular attention to scored or uneven areas, wire netting and so on. Brush all fixtures, claw-maintenance posts and toilet trays. Pressure-hose down, or sponge-rinse, to the foul-water drain. The unit is now clean, but not disinfected.

(7) Make up an appropriate Domestos solution (usually 1 per cent; see page 128 for how to make this) plus two drops of liquid detergent for extra penetration and apply to all rough, scored or porous surfaces. Brush, sponge or hand-spray all other surfaces, fixtures, loose items, wire netting, plastic netting and so on. Keep all areas wet for ten minutes, rewetting if necessary, particularly in the case

of absorbent surfaces such as unpainted wood and concrete hardstandings. Cold rinse or hose down to the foul-water drain.

If all surfaces are smooth – say, in a room with smooth, emulsioned walls – a ½ per cent Domestos solution is adequate, with no extra detergent, and rinsing is not necessary.

(8) Allow to dry, preferably in sunlight, and leave empty for twenty-four hours.

(9) Incinerate all waste material, not forgetting the vacuum bag, which may contain parasite eggs and fleas. Incineration is dealt with on page 171.

If you have to remove caked vomit or faeces from floors, use neat Domestos, which is thick and will not spread. Remember that it is highly dangerous to cats and thorough rinsing is necessary. Because it dissolves and disperses organic material, neat Domestos can be used to clean drains, foul-water gulleys, sink wastepipes and toilets. Leave for as long as possible before rinsing, except in the case of metal pipes when you should leave it for five minutes only, then rinse.

A 20 per cent Domestos solution will remove stains from crockery by bleaching. The same concentration is useful for loosening algae and moss growths on damp, concrete walkways, concrete hardstandings and patios. These trap moisture and make a path slippery; and in winter trapped moisture freezes and breaks up concrete and cement pointing. Always rinse after treatment.

Possibly the most important use of Domestos is in removing the odour of cat urine – even tomcat's! Simply wash the affected area in a little warm water mixed with a few drops of Domestos.

USE OF AN ELECTRIC VOLATILIZER

Indoor accommodation such as closed chalets, isolation rooms and cat rooms in houses can be disinfected of airborne infections by means of an electric volatilizer (available from VetHealth – see Appendix I). This consists of a silently operated heating mantle containing an aluminium cup. A few drops of the relevant oil (containing the active ingredient) are poured into the cup. Gentle heat ensures a gradual release of the vapour, which can reach every part of a room, or a house, including underneath the floorboards.

Several types of oil are available for use in a volatilizer. *Bactericidal/ virucidal oil*, in which the active ingredient is triethylene glycol (not to be confused with ethylene glycol, which is used as an antifreeze and is highly poisonous to cats by paw contact), will only reduce airborne infections. It must be used in conjunction with surface

FIGURE 28 An electric wall-mounted volatilizer.

disinfection. It can be used for two hours daily, in the presence of cats if required. Remove food and water bowls to the run if applicable, or to another room in the house. *Deodorizing fragrances* are also available for use in indoor catteries; these are also necessary in some multicat domestic houses! *Menthol/eucalyptus* oil may help some cats with nasal/sinus infections. *Insecticidal/fly repellant oil*, containing Dichlorvos, kills *all* insects. Minute droplets fall on to surfaces, which remain toxic to insects for several days, until, eventually, the Dichlorvos biodegrades (that is, decomposes). As long-term exposure to Dichlorvos can be harmful, the room to be treated should be vacated by cats and humans, and, of course, food and water bowls must be removed. The unit is switched on for about two hours per week only, and the room must be aired before reoccupation.

DISINFECTING EQUIPMENT

All equipment must be capable of withstanding total immersion in ¼ per cent Domestos solution, or wetting by up to a 20 per cent Domestos solution. In some cases – for example, heavily soiled toilet trays and hardstandings – neat Domestos should be used.

Toilet trays are high-risk items, likely to be contaminated with all infections, particularly those associated with faeces. Toilet trays should be sterilized with Domestos, Titan Sanitizer SU 357 or VH7 by any of the methods described on pages 126–30, according to the type of accommodation used and level of risk. Rinse in hot running water and dry in sunlight. Since abrasive powders must not be used, dry faecal matter must first be removed by pouring on neat Domestos. (This method should also be used on floors so soiled.) These procedures must, of course, be carried out in cat-proof premises. A scullery-type utility room, with a quarry-tiled floor and central floor drain is ideal. For further information see page 168.

Brushes, mops, scoops, buckets, dustpans, refuse bins and so on should have plastic or plain wood handles: metal will corrode. Sterilize after washing by immersion in ½ per cent Domestos solution.

Washable clothing – head coverings, overalls, stockings, rubber or canvas shoes – towels, tea clothes, sponge cloths and bedding should be washed and then sterilized by soaking in ½ per cent Domestos solution. Never leave any linen dirty and damp in a warm place for it will become a breeding ground for bacteria.

Grooming brushes tend to trap dust, fur and parasites. Most cannot be sterilized and in the case of boarded cats are best supplied by the owner for her particular feline, kept in the unit and returned to the owner when the cat goes home. Combs, with coarse and fine teeth, more hygienic for grooming, are sterilized by total immersion.

Carry baskets, sleeping baskets, indoor cattery cages, maternity cages and so on should be immersed in a ½ per cent Domestos solution, if practicable; dipped in the solution and kept wet for ten minutes; or 'watered' with Domestos solution from a watering can. Dry in sunlight. Some of these items would be supplied for a boarded cat by the owner and taken away at the end of the cat's stay, thus avoiding the extra work of sterilizing them.

Any items used from the first-aid tin, such as Brunswick syringes, dropper bottles and plastic measuring cups, must be completely dismantled and washed, using, if necessary, cotton buds to remove any debris. They should then be rinsed, sterilized by total immersion and dried with sterile cotton buds.

FIGURE 29   Disinfection/sterilizing equipment: hand spray for damp dusting, Milton sterilizing fluid, Domestos, measuring jug for large volumes of liquids and measuring bottles for smaller volumes, variously shaped crevice brushes, sponge cloths, rubber gloves, 10-litre lidded bucket for dilutions.

8 Setting up a Cattery

Many one-cat owners add to their feline families over the years. Some may become so interested in cats that they decide to run a foster home for a local cat rescue organization, or a rescue sanctuary of their own. There is always a great demand for a good boarding cattery, where owners can confidently leave their cats while on holiday. Some may be willing to travel hundreds of miles in order to place their pets in an establishment which receives high personal recommendations from friends or local vets.

To cope with cats in large numbers you have to love them and accept their eccentricities with patience, if not understanding. For example, an owner can provide a boarding cattery proprietor with full details of her cat's diet but, presented with such food at a cattery, the cat may refuse it yet partake greedily of an alternative! The multicat carer, having acquired cats over several years, will be armed with several years' experience in coping with different felines, many of whom may be vicious, aggressive, powerful, dangerous or at best uncooperative.

A cattery owner needs infinite patience not only with cats, but also with people, both those who are desperately worried about leaving their animals in boarding catteries and those who wish to offload unwanted cats for a variety of ingenious reasons! She will spend much time conversing with anxious cat owners who expect such a person to have confidence in handling unfamiliar cats and be knowledgeable about infections, vaccination, nutrition and so on. Most cats will bring with them a few fleas, many will have ear mites and worms. Great care and tact will be needed to break the news to an owner that her cat has fleas, ear mites and intestinal worms! Proprietors of catteries must have the ability to give straightforward follow-up instructions regarding care of such a cat on returning him to his owner. They should try to have available a stock of simple information leaflets on common cat problems – these can be obtained from vets and the animal rescue organizations listed in Appendix I.

A cattery owner could sport a notice reading 'All infections end here'! This may be an idyllic hope, for in practice money, time and staffing levels will determine the standard of care and disinfection. It should be remembered, however, that boarding catteries obtain most clients by recommendation. A cat arriving home with a circus of fleas or cat flu will not be boarded at the same cattery again, nor will his neighbours!

Those running cat rescue sanctuaries require even more expertise in coping with stray cats, not the least of which is trying to decide whether an alleged 'stray' is simply a lost cat, or a greedy local domestic. Many people feed strange cats, assuming them to be strays. The genuine stray will be thin, dirty and heavily parasitized, although some strays who are able to hunt can keep themselves in fairly good condition during the summer. Strays will need to be nursed back to health before neutering or spaying and, because of enormous infection risks (for instance, most will have contracted feline leukaemia, but may never have *active* leukaemia), they will have to be kept in strict isolation for weeks or months.

The rescue sanctuary owner will face additional problems in the form of fund raising; dealing with people who have lost cats (these may well be 'strays' at other rescue centres in the area!); providing transport to vets; vaccination and de-sexing costs; organizing advertising; rehoming strays and the incessant ringing of the telephone.

All this calls for stamina. A cattery owner must be fit and strong and, if the cattery is outdoors, must enjoy working in the open air – summer and winter. Cat rescue work is demanding, time-consuming and often undertaken in appalling weather. A single-handed proprietor will have no holidays, no free time and no social life. Caring for cats will be a seven-day-a-week, twelve-hour-a-day job.

An outdoor cattery can never be left unattended as the risks of vandalism are enormous. A friend or part-time employee may be available to guard the cattery whilst the owner shops. The dangers threatening outdoor catteries cannot be overestimated: cats may escape, perhaps during a temporary lack of concentration on the proprietor's part – a telephone rings and a safety door is left open; fires can occur as a result of electrical faults or matches cast away carelessly by visitors; vandals can release cats for fun, or steal them; an outbreak of ringworm, cat flu or feline panleucopaenia can close a cattery for months, sometimes forever because of the loss of goodwill and hence of trade. A moment's carelessness can cost the life of a treasured cat, when years of grief for the owner and remorse for the proprietor will surely follow.

Some of the above dangers also exist, of course, in the case of indoor accommodation. In spite of an awareness of the possibility of tragedy, the proprietor must remain cheerful, outward-going and optimistic – not over-anxious, always anticipating problems and fearing to make decisions, but aware of the fact that, when tending cats, very unlikely things can happen.

Unless a holiday relief worker can be engaged, it may be impossible to take a holiday. Nevertheless, a cattery owner must have the strength of mind to take care of her health, for much depends on her fitness. Regular hours for lunch and tea breaks must be set aside, whatever the work load, and time for some relaxation. Finishing work by dusk is a good maxim. A proprietor will be unable to afford the luxury of taking to her bed when ill! Humans, like cats, are more likely to catch infections if stressed. Fatigue is the enemy of efficiency and concentration.

Each day will present totally unexpected problems, but running through each day must be the continuous thread of rigid routine, with work carried out in the right order no matter how many interruptions intervene; otherwise vital steps in disinfection schedules may be missed. Caring for cats in large numbers is not for the squeamish! The daily routine will involve cleaning toilet trays, waste disposal, mopping up vomit and sponging cats' 'trousers' because of diarrhoea.

The financial reward is low, but for those who love cats and enjoy giving a service to their owners and, occasionally, receiving their gratitude, there is no job so worthwhile and personally fulfilling.

FINANCE

Boarding catteries are not highly profitable means of earning a living. Charges must not be too high, thus pricing oneself out of business. Animal rescue organizations rely very much on public generosity. There may be difficult times financially due to economic recession, temporary closure of the cattery because of an infection risk, incapacity of the owner or periods during the winter when accommodation is not fully booked. Insurance premiums to cover these contingencies may be far too high to contemplate.

Most cattery owners – commercial and non-commercial – have an alternative source of income. A married couple may run a cattery, the husband following an outside occupation until redundancy or early retirement. A single person may, on retirement, decide to run a cattery. Most catteries and rescue organizations are privately owned.

Some are owned, maintained, and, if necessary, financed by registered charities and managed by an appointed warden.

The initial capital outlay is high, particularly for an outdoor cattery. The owner of a large cattery, which will probably be sited in a rural area, will have to own her own form of transport. There will be builders' costs, surveyors' and/or architects' fees, planning application fees, possibly appeal fees and insurance premiums. For commercial catteries of more than twelve units, paid staff may need to be employed. Animal rescue sanctuaries, run by charities, are always grateful for voluntary help. A bank loan to help establish the cattery may be feasible, if sufficient collateral is available – for example, the title deeds of a dwellinghouse. Cost, then, is the limiting factor: proposals, suggestions, procedures and equipment referred to in this book will all need to be modified with reference to available resources.

Everyone is allowed to earn a tax-free personal allowance, fixed annually in the Budget. Any net profit above this figure is subject to tax, including any income from investments. The financial year runs from 1 April to 31 March, and for those considering setting up a business it will simplify accounting if their financial year coincides with these dates. Failure to disclose the correct net profit to the Inland Revenue, or failure to keep proper books of accounts, with a view to tax evasion, can result in a demand for tax arrears which may lead to bankruptcy.

Running costs (revenue expenditure) where they relate to business activities (as distinct from the running costs of a private dwelling) are not taxed. Examples of such costs are: an apportionment of rates applicable to the business premises, likewise for water rates, gas, electricity, insurance, petrol, telephone charges and postal charges; staff wages; minor repairs; all items used up during the course of running the business, such as litter, disinfectant, overalls; depreciation (or loss of value due to age) of capital assets.

Capital expenditure on, for example, units, incinerator, waste-disposal unit, kitchen furniture; on a car or van; and on any major repairs to capital items is also tax allowable, but if the business is sold, any *gain* made on the sale of capital assets is liable to tax. All receipts for capital expenditure should be kept.

All receipts, and all account books, must be available for inspection, at all times, by an inspector of the Inland Revenue. Your local branch of the Inland Revenue will provide leaflets and verbal information, and advise on the format in which required information should be presented at the close of the financial year.

Non-retired, self-employed people are advised to pay National Insurance contributions, in order to claim sickness benefit and a state pension. Self-employed persons are not covered for unemployment benefit under the state system, however. Your local Department of Health and Social Security office will provide information on these matters, and supply a National Insurance stamp card.

A cattery owner, whether running a business or a voluntary rescue sanctuary, must insure herself and her staff against accidents, damage to her property by fire, flood, tempest and vandals, and against liability for damage to third parties (for example, an escaped cat killing a valuable racing pigeon!)

If a partnership is considered, both partners contributing to the initial capital outlay, it is advisable to consult a solicitor so that a legal document can be drawn up, and signed, with appropriate release clauses should the partnership dissolve or be declared bankrupt.

The employment of full-time – and some part-time – staff will necessitate deduction of income tax and National Insurance contributions from wages or salaries. Explanatory leaflets and advice should be sought of the relevant government offices.

THE ANIMAL BOARDING ESTABLISHMENTS ACT 1963

When cats are boarded and a fee charged, it is necessary under the Animal Boarding Establishments Act 1963 to obtain a Licence to Board from the local authority, renewable annually. The Act was passed in order to regularize conditions in which animals were kept and it is worthwhile, at this stage, to summarize the Schedule of Conditions (obtainable in full from the local authority) where it relates to boarding catteries, and then consider how these conditions can be met.

Accommodation: This must provide protection from adverse weather and provide an adequate exercising area. It must be sited in a dry, well-lit position and be regularly maintained.

Construction: A draughtproof (but well-ventilated) compartment, heated when necessary, must be provided, containing a bed and toilet tray. The flooring of the entire unit, solid walls, partitions and wired runs must be constructed of impervious materials unaffected by water and disinfectants, so that it can be cleaned, disinfected, hosed down and so on. This precludes grass runs and carpeted areas, of course.

Waste disposal: Excreta must be removed from toilet trays regularly. Additional soiling (for example, vomit or uncontrollable diarrhoea) must be removed and the soiled area disinfected. All waste materials must be disposed of safely and hygienically to the approval of the licensing authority.

Disinfection: All surfaces in contact with cats must be readily accessible, washable and easily disinfected. Units must be kept clean throughout a cat's boarding period. On vacation all toilet tray filler, bedding, straw and so on must be destroyed and the unit cleaned and disinfected before reoccupation.

Safety precautions: Each unit must be totally enclosed and double doors provided to prevent escape. Any electrical installations (for heating or lighting) must be safely installed to lessen fire risk. All exits must be kept clear, water must be accessible for fire hoses, a pressure hose should be located in a central position and buckets of sand and fire extinguishers must be prominently placed and staff instructed in their use. The licensee, or other responsible person, should be on call at all times.

Feeding: A kitchen, impenetrable to vermin, must be available for food preparation, together with a refrigerator and fly-proof larder for defrosting, storage and so on. The food provided must be suitable for cats and water available at all times in each unit.

Health: All cats must be inspected regularly for symptoms of disease. Every care must be taken to prevent transmission of infections and any suspect cat must be placed in an isolation unit.

Records: A record must be kept in respect of every cat boarded. Records must be available for inspection by the licensing authority.

PLANNING CONSIDERATIONS

People who love cats often like to combine two kinds of cattery – one for commercial boarding and one for rescued strays. Finance from boarders can be used for rescuing, rehabilitating and rehoming stray cats.

Often there is no choice of location. If there is, it is wise to study the locations of other boarding establishments in an area, to avoid competition where possible. Addresses of local establishments can be obtained from vets. Most are listed in the Yellow Pages telephone directory under 'Boarding Kennels'.

If a cattery is purchased as a going concern, planning permission and a Licence to Board will have been obtained. If, however, a prospective proprietor owns land on which she wishes to build a purpose-built cattery, or if she is contemplating purchasing a suitable site on which to erect, possibly, both a dwellinghouse and an outdoor cattery, or even if she wishes to erect an advertising board, planning permission must be obtained before commencement of building. A profit-making venture must always have a Licence to Board. Additionally, buildings will be subject to Building Regulation Approval, also obtained from the local authority. Before purchasing land, or erecting external buildings for use as a *business*, a prospective proprietor must consult the local authority planning department and obtain up-to-date advice and the necessary application forms. This will avoid the disappointment of finding out, too late, that planning consent for a cattery would never, under *any* circumstances, be forthcoming. Sketch (rough) details of any proposed building(s) and landscaping must be submitted; and, if outline planning permission is granted, this will be conditional upon the submission of working drawings and full details of the proposal. This work and the completion of application forms, together with their submission to the local authority, is usually undertaken by a qualified architect or surveyor. If planning consent is refused, the applicant has the right of appeal to the Department of the Environment.

Planning permission is most likely to be granted in respect of land which has an established use as a business (not necessarily a cattery) in a rural area, – for example, a smallholding or stable. It is very unlikely that planning permission would be granted for an outdoor cattery in an established residential area, whether rural or urban, but operation of an *indoor* cattery as a business may be acceptable. No planning permission, or Licence to Board, would be required in the case of an indoor cattery *not* run for profit. Where no established use as a business venture exists, the most likely settings in which planning permission for an outdoor cattery would be granted are rural areas with large, isolated, residential properties set in large grounds.

Certain buildings can be erected outside without the need for planning permission, providing they are used to pursue a hobby (that is, a non-profit-making activity), although permission would still not be required if friends' cats were occasionally boarded for a small fee. In the case of tenanted accommodation, a landlord's permission would be needed. Title deeds to the property should be checked for restrictive covenants, prohibiting the erection of any buildings in the grounds. A building or enclosure (but not a dwellinghouse) in which pets or livestock may be kept may be erected in grounds if the following conditions are met:

(1) The building must not extend beyond the front wall of the dwellinghouse. This means that it cannot be erected in the front garden, nor project into it.

(2) The building must not occupy more than half the total garden area.

(3) If the building has a ridged or sloping roof, it must not be higher than 4 metres. If it has a flat roof, it must not be higher than 3 metres.

(4) In some areas, small lean-to buildings using a side or back wall of a dwellinghouse may be permitted, but this must be checked with the local authority.

(5) Special conditions apply if a dwellinghouse is a Listed Building or situated in a Conservation Area.

Any conversions to the *inside* of a house, for whatever use, do not require planning permission, but, again, if a cattery is run as a business, as opposed to a non-profit-making rescue sanctuary, permission to run a business will be required, as well as a Licence to Board. Permission for a Change of Use, from a private dwelling to a business, is very difficult to obtain.

Details of Planning Applications must be published in local newspapers, and displayed on prominent notice boards on the proposed site. This gives neighbours, or any other interested parties, the opportunity to make 'written representations' to the local authority, supporting or opposing the proposals, before the authority makes a decision.

To be forewarned is to be forearmed! A prospective cattery owner should consider all likely objections and try to overcome them. A common objection is that a proposed cattery is 'visually detrimental'. It may be ugly, obtrusive, or spoil a neighbour's view. Appearance is most important. There is much to be said for a 'broken-up' cattery, in which the units are separated by low shrubbery or landscaped areas, as opposed to one long multi-unit concrete building with a corrugated-iron roof! The units could be arranged attractively: perhaps in a circle or semi-circle, with shrubs sited on the perimeter. If one multi-unit is proposed, such a building should blend with the existing dwellinghouse and with the environment – for example, cedar-boarded walls with roofs covered in green felt, or red brick walls with tiled roofs, might be appropriate.

Another possible objection neighbours could raise to the presence of a cattery is the likelihood of large numbers of callers, trade deliveries, noise and nuisance from increased traffic, parking problems and vehicles reversing into neighbours' driveways. A cattery should have private parking, with space for reversing. Opening hours should be restricted to, say, weekday mornings only.

Hygienic waste disposal is essential for health reasons from the point of view of odour objectionable to neighbours (see page 170).

Cats are quiet animals, with the exception of entire toms and queens during the breeding season. If these are boarded, or if the cattery is a breeding cattery, special indoor facilities may be needed. Noise must be minimal.

A local vet may consent to inspect a proposed site and make a favourable written representation to the local authority.

PLANNING OUTDOOR PREMISES

The following information is intended to guide the would-be cattery owner in meeting the licensing authority's conditions. Siting, construction, fittings, equipment, management, disinfection, nutrition and so on will vary considerably according to individual resources.

Outdoor catteries used for breeding or boarding usually consist of weatherproof chalets in which cats can be shut in at night or during bad weather, and exercise runs, which should be exposed to direct sunlight at some time during the day but be capable of covering to protect against intense summer sun. Chalet and run are referred to as a 'unit'.

Rescue sanctuaries may have some individual units for isolation and observation of new arrivals, for aggressive cats or for queens with kittens, and a large, weatherproof, communal chalet surrounded by large, enclosed grounds, where cats roam free.

Cat accommodation must be purpose-built, and is very expensive. Much consideration is necessary before asking a building contractor to construct a cattery according to your own design, or purchasing a ready-made unit. Thinking time is always well spent. Never leap into purchasing what appears, at first sight, to be a bargain.

Apart from the cost, the following points may help the prospective proprietor to make decisions:
(1) Boarded or rescued cats will be stressed – among unknown humans and potentially hostile cats and in unknown territory. Such cats may refuse to use toilet trays, suffer vomiting and diarrhoea, or spray. All chalet floors must be leak-proof. All flooring and walls

must be easily washable or hoseable. Runs must have solid floors capable of being hosed down and sloped towards a rear or side foul-water drain, and so arranged that they can be cleaned and disinfected without contaminating neighbouring units.

(2) All building materials must be chosen bearing in mind that cats are destructive, particularly when bored and confined. All materials must be easily obtainable and easily repaired. Water, steam and most disinfectants (particularly acidic ones) are corrosive to metals (particularly aluminium) if contact is prolonged. Plastic or wood are therefore preferable. PVC door and window furniture are available, and a good substitute for metal.

(3) Disinfection is the key to success. It must be made as easy as possible. Questions to ask when purchasing anything used by cats are:

(a) 'Can I reach all parts of the unit easily, without much bending down? Can I use brushes, brooms, vacuum cleaner, hose, sponge cloths and so on to reach all parts? Are there any crevices or cracks which I cannot reach (or fill) which will trap dirt and infections?'

(b) 'Can the whole unit be dismantled for spring cleaning, or because of serious infections? Can I dismantle it myself; are the bolts easy to undo, but secure? Are the sections light to carry, easy to handle? How easy is it to expose all parts of the unit to direct sunlight, for drying and disinfectancy?'

(c) 'Is the unit escape-proof? Is it difficult for vandals to reach the cats?'

(d) 'Are all the accessories easily washed or removed from the unit? Are all fittings corrosion-free or rust-proof?'

(4) The best type of unit is one which can be moved to an alternative site if necessary. To avoid the ever-present risk of cross-infection in occupied units and contamination of nearby units when disinfecting on vacation, units should be spaced as far away from each other as possible. The recommended minimum distance apart is about 3 feet (90 centimetres). There may be occasions when a unit once occupied by a highly infectious cat will need to be moved well away from the other units pending disinfection. Good ventilation at high level is essential to avoid high infection concentrations.

(5) Fire risk, dangerous fittings within reach of cats, dangers of heat stress, problems like waste disposal: all must be resolved before choosing accommodation.

THE SITE

A single-handed proprietor could expect to provide a high standard of care for twelve units, housing, if sharing is practised, up to sixteen cats. If positioned closer to each other than 3 feet (90 centimetres), units must be separated by an impervious, but not necessarily opaque, partition. Too much land will involve the expense of upkeep: ¼ acre (0.1 hectare) is about right.

The site must be well-drained, the units positioned away from trees or buildings which cast deep shade all day, causing dampness and growth of moss, algae and bacteria. Fresh air and direct sunlight are essential. Black polythene covers over runs will provide shade in conditions of intense sun. Cats suffer far more from heat stress than from the cold, dry temperatures of winter.

Layout should minimize the walking distance between units. For security reasons units should be clearly visible from the house and as near as possible to it. The office, kitchen, storeroom, special cat accommodation and isolation units should preferably be sited in the house.

The easiest way to decide on a suitable layout (which is, ideally, one that can be altered in the light of experience after, say, a year or two) is to make a scale plan of the land available and arrange units to scale on it, taking into account the position and movement of the sun, wind protection, existing trees and shrubs, access from the house, neighbours' views and so on.

CONSTRUCTION

Once a suitable design, or designs, have been decided upon, a chartered surveyor should be engaged to prepare the working drawings (from which a builder will work), and which must accompany the planning application. Few surveyors or builders are likely to be knowledgeable about the construction of cat accommodation. They should thus be provided with the following information in writing:

Cats' ability to escape: Cats can escape through the smallest holes (barely 2 inches/5 centimetres wide) by flattening their bodies and using their heads as wedges to open up gaps. In panic they may attempt to jump from high windows or scramble up wire netting. Thus all accommodation must be completely enclosed. Strong, small-mesh wire or plastic netting should be used. Kittens are very high-risk escapees! Constant checks for gaps in accommodation will be necessary and plenty of spare wire should be kept in readiness for repairs. A double-door extry/exit system is essential, so that an outer door can be closed before an inner one is opened.

Vandalism is an increasingly nightmarish problem for outdoor cattery owners. Vandals may steal cats, damage property, set fire to premises or, at best, let cats out. Shutting cats in locked chalets offers little extra protection against determined vandals and, during hot summer nights, heat stress is an ever-present danger. Some cats, particularly long-hairs, will need access to runs at night – as will all cats when at any time temperatures reach 90°F (32°C). Siting the accommodation near the house, perhaps where it is clearly visible from the owner's bedroom, fitting a night light, providing a house switch to control full illumination, or even installing a burglar alarm may have to be considered. Make sure lights do not shine directly into chalet windows. If the site is small, the erection of a 10-foot- (3-metre)-high chainlink outer fence may exclude free-roaming animals, including man!

Fire risk: Smoke detectors and alarms can be fitted. The materials commonly used in catteries, such as wood, baskets, cardboard boxes, newspaper, straw, wood shavings and bedding, are highly inflammable. Fires have been caused by vandals, faulty refrigerators, electrical wiring faults, sparks from bonfires or visitors' cigarettes (it is advisable to erect 'No smoking' signs).

Fire risk is reduced if light fitments are attached to a brick wall, perhaps an outside wall of the house, so that no electrical wiring is used in the cattery itself. Any multiple accommodation must have at least two exits. A hosepipe must be connected to the water main in a central position. Fire extinguishers and sand buckets must be placed strategically, and staff taught fire drill.

All cats should have carry baskets in their chalets, ready for instant evacuation or for use in deliberate or accidental release. The basket can double as a bed, or a shelf.

Electrical installation: Always hazardous where there is constant use of water and switches operated by wet hands. Most work will be in daylight, cats requiring constant attention being in the isolation unit(s). It may be considered that rechargeable storm lanterns, kept charged from electric power points in the house, are safer than electrical installations, particularly in wooden buildings. Extension leads can be used from the house sockets for vacuum cleaners, fans and Vortex volatilizers. Regular inspection should be undertaken by a qualified electrician and his advice acted upon.

Heating: Cats have their own built-in heating systems – provided they are not in a draught. The pockets of air trapped in their fur act as insulators, keeping body heat in. When chilly, cats curl up, thus enclosing their abdomens, which are supplied with ample blood vessels and therefore body heat. Draught is the chief danger to cats when they are confined.

Where power points are available, as for example in garages housing rescued cats temporarily, heating pads can be used. Various designs are on the market, but it is vitally important that all cables are *metal*-covered and not even remotely chewable! Stone hot water bottles are preferred by some cattery owners. Any heated beds are dangerous to pregnant cats and can cause stillbirths or congenital deformities. Direct-contact heat (for example, radiators, open fires) has been implicated in some forms of eczema and coat damage. An all-round, even form of heating is preferable.

Danger of fittings: No part of a 6-foot- (180-centimetre)-high building can be assumed inaccessible to cats! Claws can become embedded in virtually any fittings – infra-red heaters, thermometers, fixed electric cables, light switches, power points or light fittings. It must be assumed, when constructing cat accommodation, that if cats can reach a fitting they can destroy it and, in so doing, injure themselves. All fittings should be outside the units, or totally enclosed within by securely bolted access hatches.

CONSTRUCTION OF THE UNIT

Once planning permission has been granted, estimates based on the working drawings should be obtained from local builders. This may be cheaper than buying units ready-made, though secondhand units may be worth considering – carefully. The construction details below are intended only as a guide. Infinite variation is possible within the terms of reference laid down in the Animal Boarding Establishments Act 1963.

Dogs are not normally boarded or bred for sale or showing at a cattery, unless the size of the site is at least 1 acre (0.4 hectare) and cat and dog accommodation can be well separated. Cats unfamiliar with dogs are stressed by their barking and odour. Staff in a mixed establishment should be employed to care exclusively for dogs or cats.

Breeding and/or showing of cats is not normally undertaken at boarding catteries, nor rescued cats boarded, unless sufficient staff are available and the various functions can be well separated.

Many boarding catteries do not accept full toms because of their caterwauling, spraying and the infection risk to other cats posed by a full tom's lifestyle. Breeding catteries, however, may provide boarding facilities for full toms. Some boarding catteries are reluctant to take pregnant queens, nursing queens with kittens, or young kittens, because they are high-risk where infections are concerned, but again a breeding cattery may help.

DRAINAGE

Drains are required in a cattery to convey rainwater and foul water to the main drains and hence into the public sewage system. Roofs and concrete hardstandings are usually sloped towards drains at the back of units, but units can be arranged in pairs side by side, with a shared gulley and drain in between. PVC guttering, downpipes and drains are maintenance-free. A pressure hose can be tapped off the water main, and for this a licence is required from the local water authority.

CHALETS

Ideally these should measure 4 feet × 4 feet × 6 feet high (120 centimetres × 120 centimetres × 180 centimetres high). If constructed in 25-millimetre hardwood, insulation will not be necessary, but joints must be draughtproof. Should plywood be used, an insulator, such as bituminous felt or fibreglass quilting, will be needed between the outer and inner (impervious) walls. If any wood used in the construction of the unit is freshly treated against wood-worm, or weatherproofed with creosote, the unit must not be occupied for at least three months.

A chalet should be raised on 15-centimetre brickwork to keep the floor above the soil or concrete base. It is easier to clean if a human can stand up in it; but, for economy, chalets may be made half-height, standing on stout wooden feet, raised on bricks. Any arrangement must provide for the easy removal of debris which inevitably collects beneath the chalet. A half-height chalet may have a small door opening into the run, or the rear wall constructed as a hinged door (which should be kept padlocked) to facilitate cleaning.

A window should be provided in the chalet, preferably incorporating a wire mesh frame, so that it can be opened up in hot or wet weather. It is also useful for a quick check at bedtime, or to check toilet trays, without entering the unit. A shelf is often fitted below the window, but this can be a nuisance when cleaning, unless detachable. A carry basket may serve as a shelf when closed, or a bed when opened.

The carry basket, incidentally, is essential for use in an emergency. If not used as a bed during the cat's stay, it can be used for spare bedding provided by an owner, clean litter, toys or grooming equipment. A stout cardboard box with high sides, lined with newspaper

FIGURE 30 Types of cat bed for domestic or cattery use: traditional wicker basket, cardboard box, bean bag.

topped with old blanket or sheeting, also makes an excellent bed which can be incinerated on the cat's departure. Alternatively owners may provide beds. Bean bags are much favoured by cats, but many assume them to be toilet trays (they *do* have that feel about them!) and washing and disinfection are extremely difficult and time-consuming.

Surfaces in direct contact with cats – that is, the chalet floor and the wall up to about half its height – should be lined with a smooth, impervious material such as Formica, vinyl or ceramic tiles. All joints between wall and floor must be filled with waterproof sealant. A good *temporary* sealant is masking tape. It is inadvisable to line the whole of the internal wall surface with impervious material, since condensation will occur in very cold weather from water vapour breathed out by cats, and in humid weather as a result of water vapour making contact with a cold, smooth surface. Gloss-painted surfaces are unsuitable, as cat urine is an excellent paint stripper! Wallpapers, even washable ones, are stripped off by bored cats.

Open/shut louvred ventilators should be fixed at a high level, designed so that they do not attract condensation and/or corrosion.

The chalet roof should be sloped towards its rainwater guttering and be weatherproofed with bituminous felt with mineral chippings, or other weatherproof material advised by the builder.

A cat door giving access to the run is essential, bearing in mind that there will be occasions when chalet cleaning will necessitate cats being shut in the run, and vice versa. The door must be lockable and draughtproof. The best kind is a sliding wooden door (non-corrosive) which can be removed from the slider bars for easy cleaning. Some means of opening the cat door without entering the unit is useful for letting cats out quickly in the morning – for instance, an 'eye' on the door, operated by a long-handled hook.

If the whole unit, or the run only, is designed to be dismantled, the bolts must be well greased and regularly tested to guard against seizing up. The run can be secured to the chalet by hooks to allow ease of resiting, if necessary. Alternatively, the run can be hinged to the chalet to allow opening. If the units are completely movable, the building materials should be as light as is feasible. Screws are always preferable to nails and should be rustproof – brass or stainless steel.

RUNS

Each run should be a minimum of 4 feet wide × 6 feet long × 6 feet high (120 centimetres wide × 180 centimetres long × 180 centimetres high), so that humans can stand up in it. The run, and preferably

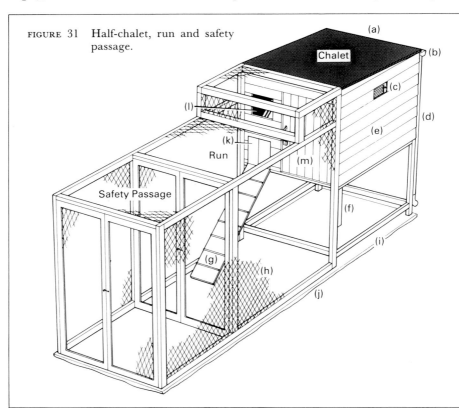

FIGURE 31   Half-chalet, run and safety passage.

the whole unit, should rest on, and be bolted on to, a concrete base (hardstanding) to prevent rising damp and enable disinfection. It should be tamped to as smooth a finish as possible. If sloped towards

KEY AND NOTES TO FIGURES 31 and 32

(a) Roof, sloping towards gutter (b).
(b) Gutter.
(c) Open/shut ventilator (one on each side of chalet).
(d) Downpipe to foul-water drain.
(e) 25-millimetre weatherproofed boarding.
(f) Legs of chalet, standing on bricks.
(g) Climbing board (half-chalet only).
(h) Smooth concrete base sloped

towards foul-water drain (or gulley).
(i) Damp-proof membrane (for example, felt) attached to horizontal timbers in contact with concrete base – to prevent rising damp.
(j) Ground level.
(k) Sliding cat door.
(l) Glazed window.
(m) Door for cleaning.

In individual units (as shown) the individual safety passages, measuring 4 feet × 4 feet × 6 feet high (120 centimetres × 120 centimetres × 180 centimetres high), provide a double-door safety system. In multiple accommodation, when units are joined, the safety passage will have a door at each end.

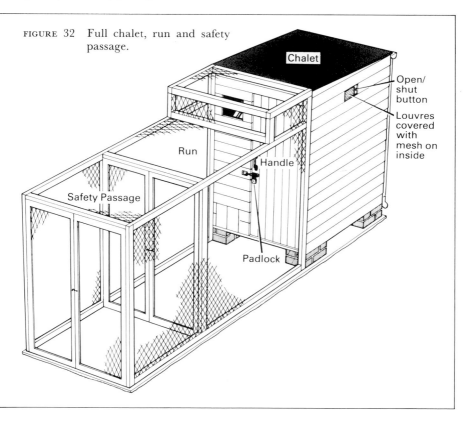

FIGURE 32 Full chalet, run and safety passage.

Chalet

Open/shut button

Louvres covered with mesh on inside

Run

Handle

Safety Passage

Padlock

a gulley, it will dry quickly after rain and growth of algae will be discouraged. It should be free of indentations which can trap water which in winter will freeze and break up the concrete. In multiple units over 12 feet (360 centimetres) long, expansion joints are advisable as concrete expands in hot weather. It must be possible to disinfect individual concrete hardstandings without contaminating neighbouring units. In multiple units each concrete hardstanding should have a raised edge to prevent water running into an adjacent unit, and it should be sloped towards a gulley at the back. Cleaning is far easier if the whole unit (chalet and run) can be removed from its base.

Concrete hardstandings and floors made of concrete in utility rooms, kitchens, outhouses and stores become very cold in winter and tend to powder with age at the surface. It is inadvisable to lay sheet vinyl or Formica directly on concrete for if it is thus laid, condensation will occur underneath, giving rise to algal or fungal growth and odour. Even vinyl adhesives do not work on some concrete floors. If installing a raised, wooden floor above the concrete with an air space below is impractical, the only alternative is quarry or ceramic tiles, fixed by tile cement and with waterproof grouting.

The run should be made of small-mesh wire or plastic netting stapled to horizontal and vertical wooden battens. Some wire meshes turn white and corrode. The units must be inaccessible to free-roaming animals – usually accomplished by a perimeter chainlink fence. This will prevent fighting through the mesh of the runs which could result in injury and, of course, transmission of infections.

The run should contain a claw-maintenance post of rough wood. A tree trunk about 3 feet (90 centimetres) long, sawn in half lengthwise, will make two posts. Vertical fixing is unnecessary: cats often choose horizontal posts in gardens.

Cats enjoy dustbathing in dry sand contained in a shallow cardboard or wooden box (disposable on vacation). Toys such as balls, cut-out cardboard boxes and catmint mice provided by owners – and newspaper – will provide entertainment.

Every cattery should have beds of couch grass and catmint (or catnip), separate from the cattery and well covered against free-roamers. These items should be provided fresh each day to confined cats.

Figures 31 and 32 show a half-chalet and a full chalet respectively. If units are joined, the safety passage will be continuous along the length of the multiple unit, with outer doors at each end. Ventilators should be at the front and back of chalets, to minimize cross-infection risks.

Larger units, for sharing by cats in the same family, rescued strays (who tolerate each other), studs who accept visiting queens, and pregnant or nursing queens with kittens, can be built on the same lines. Each unit must be clearly numbered.

ALTERNATIVE CAT ACCOMMODATION

THE INDOOR CATTERY

A large house, providing a domestic dwelling on the ground floor with its upper floor(s) specially adapted provides ideal cat accommodation, offering enormous advantages over the outdoor cattery. Planning consent will not be required for internal alterations – say, converting three small rooms into one large room for the cattery. If the concern is run as a business, a Licence to Board and permission to operate as a commercial enterprise will be needed (see page 143).

Long-term indoor residence is not advised for most cats, as they tend to suffer stress if not allowed access to a garden (preferably enclosed or, at least, dog- and human-proof). However, some cosy domestics are quite happy to remain indoors.

An indoor cattery has the following advantages over an outdoor cattery: it can be locked up securely and the cats left for brief periods if necessary; there is less risk of fire or damage by thieves or vandals; the distances the owner is required to walk are dramatically shorter; loss of time spent donning weatherproof clothing is eliminated; heating costs may be reduced for ambient heating is provided by domestic central heating, if installed; the lighting is better; there is easier access to power points for vacuum cleaners and other electric appliances; fire and burglar alarms are more easily fitted; and supervision, observation and late-night checking are much facilitated. In the indoor cattery wire-mesh-covered windows can be opened to provide ample fresh air and direct sunlight by day. Louvred night ventilaters, if fitted, must be burglar-proof.

Units can be very simple, perhaps PVC-coated steel-mesh cages, positioned away from the walls and bolted to vinyl floors 4 feet (120 centimetres) apart. The walls of the room should be emulsioned and there should be waterproof sealant between floor and skirting boards. Carpets, curtains and upholstered furniture are inappropriate. Under the conditions described, disinfection of air and surfaces in the indoor cattery is easy and very efficient; flying insects and flea control are

FIGURE 33 Equipment for domestic or cattery use: cat litter, toilet tray with litter, carry basket, sleeping basket, blankets, lidded storage bucket (with scoop) for soiled litter, dustpan and brush, water bowl, grooming combs, claw-maintenance log, toys, fresh grass, catmint, catnip.

far easier. Many essential household tasks, such as ironing, sewing and paperwork, can be done in the cattery, providing entertainment for the cats; the office desk can be in the cattery, but *not* the telephone, unless a flashing light can be used to indicate a telephone call.

Fire fighting equipment and carry baskets must always be kept ready.

THE LEAN-TO CATTERY
A lean-to is an extension to the main house, constructed so that one of its walls is formed by the side or back wall of the house. It may be constructed of wood or brick, with a sloping tiled roof to match the existing house roof. It may be divided into individual units separated by PVC partitions, equivalent to the chalets of outdoor units. It should be possible for these chalets to be securely closed off from the outdoor runs for night-time security.

Alternatively, chalets could be constructed in a room in the main house, with the lean-to used for runs. Runs could have a wire-mesh framed sunroof for use in warm, dry weather.

THE COMMUNAL ANIMAL SANCTUARY
There is an urgent need for more rescue centres for stray, unwanted,

unhomeable, disabled, very old, tameable ferals and cats whose owners have died, or who have had to move to a flat or hospital. Foster homes, where cats can be brought back to health and/or housed temporarily are in far too short supply. These centres, often run by voluntary rescuers and financed by public donations, fund-raising events, members' subscriptions and so on, usually consist of communal and individual housing, with large gardens, preferably enclosed with a 10-foot- (3-metre)-high chainlink fence, where cats can enjoy their freedom. In some cases, cats live in the dwellinghouse.

This type of rescue sanctuary requires no planning permission, and small units can be built in gardens. No multicat establishment should allow large numbers of cats to roam free. Apart from the dangers of road traffic, vandals, hostile humans (particularly gardeners!) and other animals, the public at large (some of whom may detest cats) must be protected from free-roaming cats who worry pigeons, budgerigars, rabbits or guinea pigs, or damage neighbours' plants, or, worse, enter neighbours' houses, terrorizing domiciled cats, appropriating food and spraying. Most people will tolerate a few roaming cats, but if they really become a nuisance an owner faces risk of prosecution under the Public Health Act 1936 under the section dealing with Statutory Nuisances. Complaints are made to the local authority.

Enclosures are very expensive to construct and it may be feasible to make small enclosures in the garden at first, gradually enlarging the enclosures as more money becomes available. Fruit cages are very useful for confining cats, but great care must always be taken to ensure that cats are not left in hot sun with no shade into which to retreat. All cats must wear safety collars for identification should they escape.

The work of an animal sanctuary may consist of some or all of the following: caring for permanent residents, financed by legacies of deceased owners; caring for unhomeable cats who may be financed by 'sponsors' who visit them and contribute to their keep; looking after found cats who may be rehomed if their owners cannot be traced; feeding 'outboarders' consisting of feral colonies who cannot be tamed; trapping feral cats, taking them to the vet for treatment or de-sexing and returning them to the wild; taming ferals who are amenable to it and integrating them with the community; caring for abandoned pregnant cats, and queens with kittens; preparing and serving meals, ensuring fair shares for all; arranging for vaccinations; carrying out routine deparasitization and disinfection; fund raising; publication of news sheets; advertising for new homes; inspecting prospective homes; holding coffee mornings, entertaining patrons and visitors.

All new cats arriving at the sanctuary must be kept in isolation for at least a week, and be vaccinated against feline panleucopaenia before introduction into the community. Some inveterately aggressive cats may have to be housed separately, as well as pregnant cats and nursing cats with kittens.

Animal-control equipment is expensive, but it may be possible for several animal rescue organizations in the area to pool resources as far as traps and crush cages are concerned. Advice and help in the use of traps may be obtained from the RSPCA and PDSA (local branches are listed in the Yellow Pages). Other equipment, such as toilet trays and carry baskets, may represent a source of income for it can be hired out (with a deposit to cover the cost of replacement, but returnable to the borrower on receipt of the undamaged equipment). Such items should, of course, be disinfected before and after hiring. Traps safe for cats, and interlocking crush cages for veterinary injections, are available from M. D. Components at the address given in Appendix II.

Sanctuaries with sufficient land may be able to offer commercial holiday boarding, thus helping to finance the rescue operation.

THE ISOLATION UNIT

Every house with a cat should have a quiet, escape-proof, easily cleaned/washed/disinfected room where an infected cat – or one which is suspected of being infected – can be isolated and monitored. A room with even an average human noise level, perhaps with the television on and the telephone ringing, is *not* the place for an ailing cat.

Every cattery should have a similar room, termed the 'isolation unit', which for convenience should be in the main house, but it must always be quite separate from the main cattery and approached by a separate entrance. It is dangerous for the isolation unit to be entered via the main cattery, as infections can be brought in *and* taken out of a unit via human hands, clothing, hair and feet.

In multicat environments all-rubber shoes (from gardening shops) should be kept in a foot bath containing ¼ per cent Domestos solution, placed at the door of the isolation unit, for use only in the unit. Similarly special overalls may be hung at the door. Hands should be sprayed with ¼ per cent Domestos solution or washed with bactericidal soap on arrival and departure. If possible, a person who tends sick cats should not tend healthy boarders. If this is not feasible, cats in isolation should be tended last. A careful record should be kept in the isolation unit of inmates who have passed through it, their treatments, the administration times, their daily excreta and vomit, and so on. Ideally such notes should be pinned to a notice board where they can easily be referred to.

The isolation unit must be draughtproof, ventilated at high level and a temperature of about 70°–75°F (21°–24°C) maintained. Curtains, upholstered furniture and carpets are inappropriate, but if the room is strongly lit in the daytime, Venetian blinds can be used, which can be disinfected as usual. Do not allow artificial light to shine directly on to sick cats.

Floors should be of sheet vinyl, vinyl tiles or ceramic tiles, and gaps between skirting boards and floor should be sealed with waterproof sealant or with masking tape as a temporary measure. (Polyclens will remove masking tape adhesive from surfaces, if necessary.) Walls should be smooth and emulsioned. If cats are in contact with gloss-painted wood (doors, window frames, skirting boards), these should be wiped frequently to lessen the paint-stripping effects of cat urine. Hardboard doors may need a wooden batten along the bottom as urine collecting at the base of such doors can cause the hardboard to become swollen and spongy.

Sick cats need to eat, sleep and be easily accessible to humans! Small cages about 3 feet (1 metre) square are normally large enough. They should contain disposable or easily washable bedding, a water bowl and toilet tray. Litter must be light in colour for monitoring excreta: possibly sawdust or shredded white kitchen paper. If one or two cats of the same family are free in the room, a washable nylon rug could be placed on the floor, but furniture under which cats can make themselves unavailable for treatment should be avoided. The unit may contain a sink, Formica-topped examination/treatment table and storage space for medicines, sterilized equipment and bedding. Again fire extinguishers and sand buckets must be at hand, and carry baskets for rapid evacuation.

Double sink units are very useful in the isolation unit for washing and sterilizing food dishes and utensils. Food, however, should be prepared in the main kitchen. Food should be high-protein, moist, mashed and easily digestible, served frequently in small portions. Examples of suitable foods for a sick cat are: white fish, rabbit, chicken liver, eggs, tripe, puffed wheat. Suitable liquid foods, given by Brunswick syringe if the vet advises it, are: water, glucose and water, Marmite or Bovril juice, Brands Essences, warm chicken jelly (minus fat), milk, dilute evaporated milk, goat's milk, roast beef jelly (minus fat), fish and rabbit juice, Cimicat (from vets), Ostermilk, Bengers pre-digested milk food, Complan. Remember that some cats cannot digest milk or milk products. Cats with respiratory infections may not eat because they cannot smell, or taste the smell by their Jacobson's gland. See page 28 for how to cope with this problem.

If a cat is too ill to wash, sponge over gently every other day with a sponge dampened with warm water, and dry thoroughly. Discharges from nose, mouth, eyes or anus should be removed frequently with damp tissue or cotton wool. Use white Vaseline for sore areas, such as the nose or anus. Sick cats should be kept as clean and comfortable as possible.

Control of odour is as important in the isolation unit as in the rest of the cattery. Follow the instructions on page 171.

THE KITCHEN

Food preparation, serving, mealtime supervision, washing up, steriliz-ation of food bowls and equipment, purchasing and storage of food, excluding flying insects and daily disinfection of kitchen surfaces will comprise much of a multicat owner's working day.

EQUIPMENT

Catteries will have a kitchen in addition to the house kitchen, used exclusively for boarders or rescued cats. The cattery kitchen should be constructed with a view to easy cleaning, with no gaps, cracks or crevices, or inaccessible places behind cookers and refrigerators where dirt and infections can lurk. Kitchens should contain a refrigerated larder where food can be defrosted in summer, and, if raw, served straight from the larder; a ventilated larder for use in winter to bring refrigerated food up to room temperature; a deep freeze; a cooker, preferably with a fold-down top which is much safer in cat accommo-dation; impervious worktops and ample storage space. A microwave oven will save fuel for small feline families. Other essential equipment may include: a supply of disposable dishes for use in an emergency; plastic cutlery for use when cutlery sterilization is routine; cutting boards; sharp knives; large casserole dishes; cooking foil; roasting bags for meat and for steaming fish and retaining the fish juice; steamer or fish kettle; pressure cooker, can opener, kitchen scissors; and a notice board, to which should be pinned details of any special diets.

Some owners like to serve solid foods, like raw mince, directly on to a work top or large tray. These are easy to sterilize and save time. Bowls should have gently sloping sides (some cats have difficulty getting food out of steep-sided bowls), should be made of china or earthenware and heavy enough not to move along a worktop or shelf as the cat licks the last morsels. Steep-sided bowls may be needed to serve milk or water to those cats which tend to slurp liquids in a 12-inch radius of the dish! Kittens will need shallow, heavy plates which will not tilt if the edges are stepped upon. Polythene or plastic dishes and containers tend to get scratched, and are therefore an infection hazard. Some cats refuse food stored or served in these materials.

FOOD STORAGE AND HYGIENE

If the kitchen is part of an outdoor cattery complex, it is very important that it is inaccessible to free-roaming cats, dogs and rodents. All flying insects are potential carriers of infections and the use of fly sprays or an electric volatilizer (see page 136) should be routine. Food should never be left exposed.

All food must be absolutely fresh, or freshly defrosted. Cooked food can be kept for up to two days in a refrigerated larder, raw food for one day. Cooked foods should preferably be stored in a separate refrigerated larder from raw, defrosted foods; if kept in the same larder, they should always be placed *above* raw foods.

As fresh food ages, it loses vitamins. This applies to unopened canned food which, on canning, may even contain too high a vitamin

FIGURE 34 Cat feeding from bowl with gently sloping sides.

content (see page 19). The vitamin content of canned food is guaranteed for only one year, so expiry dates should be checked and cans used in strict order of purchase. Never store leftovers in which raw and cooked food have been mixed. Leftovers in households of more than one cat should be covered, identified with the cat's initial and stored for the next meal; then, if not consumed, they should be thrown away if raw or kept refrigerated for one more day only and re-served if cooked. Food sharing among domestic cats is unwise, for there is always the risk that one cat has an infection.

Before opening any canned food, put a drop of liquid detergent on the top and scrub with hot water. Any unused food should be immediately transferred to a glass or earthenware dish and covered since, once opened, food reacts with the can, in the presence of air. If possible, empty cans should be crushed before safe disposal.

In domestic households a liquid detergent such as Fairy Liquid is adequate for washing up, and rinsing is unnecessary. Some people prefer to keep all the cats' dishes separate from humans' – for no good reason! If one cat in a multicat household shows any symptoms of an infection, it is a wise precaution to sterilize all the *cats'* dishes. A bactericidal QUAT can be used, for extra safety, in households where there is raw meat preparation (see page 131).

To avoid wasted food, and disposal problems, some multicat owners prefer to serve food, a tablespoonful at a time, from a large serving bowl. This may be useful in hot weather, when appetites are variable. Beware, however, of the greedy cat.

Most indoor accidents happen to cats allowed in the kitchen when food preparation or cooking is in progress – the commonest type of burn treated by vets is caused by hot fat. The safest course, therefore, is to exclude cats from the kitchen at this time.

In catteries cats are usually fed in their chalets, after which all food bowls should be promptly removed and sterilized: it is usually impractical to keep a separate set of bowls for each cat. Use a sterilizing fluid sold for babies' equipment – such as Milton or Boots – or a ¼ per cent Domestos solution (see page 128 for how to make this up), which is just as effective for cats' bowls and far cheaper. Sterilizers corrode metal in time, so wood or plastic utensils should be used where feasible.

For the routine sterilization of all bowls and equipment used in catteries, a large PVC container or dustbin is recommended. This should be kept solely for the purpose of sterilizing such equipment. Drainage racks inside the container are preferable to outside ones, which need separate sterilization before use.

STEP-BY-STEP STERILIZATION OF FEEDING BOWLS

(1) Remove waste food by scraping the bowls and rinsing into a waste disposal unit if possible.

(2) Wash the bowls in hot water and detergent. Rinse in warm water.

(3) Immediately submerge the bowls in the sterilizer, ensuring that no air bubbles are trapped and that all parts of each bowl are submerged.

(4) Leave the bowls until needed, preferably overnight, but for at least two hours.

(5) When the bowls are required, wash your hands and remove the drainage rack to the drainer. *Do not rinse the bowls, or wipe dry.*

All equipment should be sterilized in the same way. All kitchen surfaces should be washed in 1 per cent Domestos solution with a wet contact time of ten minutes. No rinsing is necessary.

When feeding individually housed cats, do not touch any cat. In catteries, high-risk cats are fed first and those in isolation units last.

TOILET TRAYS AND LITTERS

The provision of toilet trays for adult cats, and their rejection by a great many, cause endless problems in households and catteries. This is an additional reason for chalets and runs in catteries to be easily cleanable. Domestic cats may have to be kept out of carpeted rooms. Many adults refuse to use garden soil which is wet or frozen, and many are reluctant to go outside in the winter. Most adult cats prefer to use the garden, and both sexes may spray-urinate rather than dig a toilet hole. Kittens readily use a toilet tray until they reach about a year old when many will change to spray-urination, and a toilet tray may then be unacceptable or missed altogether!

It is interesting to study your cat's toilet behaviour out of doors. Most will choose an open site so that they can see clearly in all directions, if they dig holes, or they will spray-urinate against a wall or bush. Cats who dig holes do so with immense vigour, throwing earth in all directions, always choosing dry, freshly dug soil. If they cover up their holes, they begin to cover up a yard or so away from the hole. This is why so many cats try to cover up their excreta in toilet trays by scratching at nearby walls! Some cats refuse to use the same toilet tray twice, some will only use a tray if it smells like a toilet. A study of a cat's toilet behaviour outdoors may give an owner some clues as to why a particular toilet tray is rejected.

Toilet trays seem, on the whole, to be necessary evils. The dangers of letting cats stay out all night are immense, particularly in areas heavily populated with felines where fights with full toms are likely. Car drivers cannot see cats at night to take avoiding action. Cat thieves, foxes, wandering dogs, low night temperatures, full toms entering a house and spraying their pungent urine around and various prey brought in by your cats are some of the hazards more prevalent at night-time, when humans are not around to supervise!

The cat who refuses to use a toilet tray is a problem not only when shut in for the night, but also when ill. He also deprives his owner of the other advantages offered by the toilet tray: for example, an inspection may give warning of illness because symptoms of diarrhoea, constipation, kidney failure or bladder disease can be spotted, and an early diagnosis made. Some cats vomit in their trays. A vet may require samples of urine or faeces. An owner may be asked to observe the presence, absence, appearance and approximate volume of urine, and the ease of passing it, or otherwise. Copious, dilute urine may indicate chronic kidney failure in an old cat. Small quantities of urine passed, or none, may indicate a blockage of the urethra (or passage to the outside) in male cats. Pink urine or the passing of blood clots may indicate cystitis. Bright orange urine may indicate liver disease. Faeces may be hard, black, sparse and difficult to expel, indicating constipation; or they may be liquid and odorous, indicating diarrhoea. Vomit may contain prey remains, or food *you* did not give your cat. Any straining to pass excreta, or constant hole digging, are danger signals.

Cats who totally reject a toilet tray will, however, have to have access to the garden at all times, or a suitably adapted room (see page 160). Adult cats are very continent and, if shut in for up to about twelve hours, may not need a toilet tray, particularly if attractive meat and fish juices are served at midday and only plain water for the rest of the day! A toilet tray must always be provided, however, in case it is needed.

The following points are for guidance only. Owners are advised to experiment with the many toilet products on the market, and try to make arrangements acceptable both to their cats and to themselves.

TOILET TRAYS
These should be not less than 2 feet (60 centimetres) square for adult cats, placed centrally in the chalet/cage/room. The sides should be about 3 inches (8 centimetres) high, and the tray heavy enough not to tilt if a cat steps on the side. Smooth-surfaced, thick-walled, pliable, polythene trays with reinforced edges are the most durable: some

trays are brittle and soon crack; metal is unsuitable because of corrosion problems. A good tray currently on the market is the 'Multi Tray' by Sankey, obtainable from garden centres, priced at about £3.50. In a multicat household one tray per two cats is the advisable minimum.

Some cats may try to spray-urinate and miss the tray. Old cats cannot squat easily. Some cats fling litter everywhere. It is inadvisable to stand a tray on carpet, except for very young kittens who are generally the most reliable toiletwise! Some owners stand trays in kitchens on several sheets of newspaper, but this presents disposal problems. Polythene sheeting is unsuitable as it soon leaks after claw damage. Perhaps the best base for a toilet tray is a large sheet of vinyl flooring. If strips of wood are stuck round the edges and the tray placed in the centre, any spilled urine will fall towards the tray. If only litter is scattered, the tray can be placed in a very large, high-sided cardboard box, but this may deter some cats from using the tray.

Some cats instinctively urinate down plug holes in baths or hand-basins, or even human toilets! Some are happy to use a toilet tray minus litter. In this case, one end of the tray should be slightly raised with rubber feet or a bar of wood to prevent a cat getting his feet wet!

FIGURE 35 Some cats instinctively urinate over a bath plug hole – very convenient for cat and owner!

TOILET-TRAY HYGIENE

Low-risk domestic trays will only need sterilizing when cats are infected. Any methods given on pages 128–30 are suitable, namely sterilization by total immersion or by five to ten minutes' wet contact time. Boarding catteries should always sterilize toilet trays on departure of boarders.

The owner of a boarded cat may prefer to supply the tray and filler to which her cat is accustomed.

A lidded, 10-litre, PVC bucket with scoop should be provided for each unit of a cattery, and kept outside the unit, for storage of soiled litter. Bucket and scoop should be sterilized on departure in the same way as toilet trays.

If faeces are removed promptly, auto-infection (self-reinfection) cannot occur from parasite eggs. At frequent intervals toilet trays should be gently shaken to loosen unsoiled litter from wet areas and these urine-soaked patches, together with faeces, should be placed in the waste bucket. The remaining litter is then stirred. Alternatively, after shaking the tray, remaining clean litter can be transferred to dry newspaper, solids removed to the bucket and the reserved clean litter replaced in the tray and topped up with more if necessary.

Waste disposal, without risk to free-roamers and humans, is dealt with on page 170.

LITTERS

Many proprietary litters are available, as well as far cheaper substitutes such as peat, wood shavings, sawdust and sand (see the next section for the merits of the various types). The following points are for guidance on methods of testing and individual choice. A litter acceptable to one cat may be anathema to another.

(1) The practice of renewing litter completely every day is unnecessary, unless diarrhoea has occurred. Some cats are more likely to use a tray if it smells like one; others may refuse to use a tray if it is not fresh.

(2) Litter must be cheap, light to carry, acceptable to cats and, for catteries, available in bulk.

(3) Litter must clump together when urinated upon, so that wet patches can easily be removed with a scoop and thus an estimation made of the volume of urine passed if required. But it must not set hard on the base of the toilet tray, leading to scoring on removal.

(4) For cats showing clinical symptoms of infection who have been isolated, shredded white kitchen paper should be supplied and replaced after every use. Urine samples can be expressed into a glass

bottle. (It is difficult to collect urine by holding a bottle under a cat, in the right place and at the right time!) Faecal samples will be clean – that is, not contaminated with litter. It is helpful, though not obligatory, if the litter usually used is close in texture to that of kitchen paper (for example, wood shavings or sawdust) as this will ensure a cat's acceptance of kitchen paper should he fall ill.

(5) Litter should be light in colour, for easy diagnosis of unusual signs and easy location of faeces.

(6) Toilet trays are very high-risk areas for they may contain viruses, bacteria, protozoa oocysts, and roundworm and tapeworm eggs which may infect a cat. Humans, particularly if pregnant, should *never* handle used cat litter with bare hands: wear rubber gloves or use a plastic scoop. Excreta must be removed promptly and kept as dry as possible pending hygienic disposal. Toilet trays must be kept dry at all times, for any damp, warm medium will prolong the survival time of infections if present, accelerate maturation of parasite eggs, encourage the growth of bacteria and fungi, become odorous, encourage flies and become an infection risk.

(7) If litter is reusable or continually usable (for example, pea gravel, tiny pebbles or wood-based hardened granules), it is vital that sterilization is possible. All reusable litter should be sterilized after use by soaking in a 1 per cent Domestos solution overnight (see page 128), rinsed and dried in an oven or in sunlight where it is inaccessible to animals. This involves far too much work for the average cattery.

(8) Cat litter must be easily disposable, in view of the infection hazards. Many councils refuse to remove cat litter because of the dangers of infection, odour and spillage. Therefore soiled litter must be flushable down lavatories or biodegradable on compost heaps or when buried in gardens, or it must be possible to burn it (after drying if necessary) or at least to sterilize it by exposure to dry heat of about 176°F (80°C) for forty-five minutes (for example, on a garden bonfire). A litter can be tested by leaving an unused sample of it in the garden or on the compost heap, to see if it decomposes. Any litters that will not biodegrade cannot be used as soil conditioners, and valuable cat manure is lost. No litter can be used directly on garden plants, as cat urine will 'burn' leaves.

(9) Floors of cat accommodation may need to be washed before spilled cat litter is swept up. Litter must not become too soggy to sweep up under these circumstances.

(10) Litter should not be so hard that it damages vacuum cleaners, carpets, litter trays, vinyl floors and so on. It must not stain floors or upholstery when wet, nor stick to cats' 'trousers' excessively, nor

should it be trailed round the house. It should be dust-free.

(11) Litter must have a pleasant odour, deodorize excreta (if the cat makes a good job of covering up) and be guaranteed free from pesticides – that is, safe for use in the presence of animals.

TYPES OF CAT LITTER

These are briefly examined in the context of points 1–11 above. The depth of litter in a toilet tray should be about 2 inches (5 centimetres).

Garden soil: Always an infection risk, even if taken from the bottom of a deep hole. It must be dried before use and preferably sterilized in an oven: a time-consuming process for more than one cat!

Newspaper: Very cheap, but it soon becomes soggy and needs constant replacement. It is unsuitable for damp outdoor conditions, is not deodorizing and ink may come off on the cat. It can, however, be composted.

Shredded kitchen paper: Very absorbent, used for the isolation unit.

Sand: If clean, dry and stored in a place inaccessible to animals, this is suitable. Can be reused after rinsing and sterilization.

Peat: Close in texture and colour to garden soil, this is useful as a transition litter for rescued strays. It can be gradually mixed with more acceptable litters (to humans!) as it has many disadvantages shown up by a consideration of points 1–11 above.

Proprietary cat litters: Many are very heavy to carry, expensive, do not biodegrade and are damaging to carpets and vacuum cleaners. Experimentation with various types is essential.

Wood shavings: Do not clump noticeably, but are otherwise a good buy.

Sawdust: This, and wood shavings, can often be obtained very cheaply in bulk from sawmills, but must be pesticide-free and from untreated wood. It may stick to some cats' coats and does tend to trail round the house, but not too noticeably. Sawdust clumps easily and is very useful for soaking up urine, liquid faeces or vomit prior to sweeping floors. It is probably the 'best buy' for cat litter.

WASTE DISPOSAL AND ODOUR PREVENTION

Waste disposal and odour prevention are contentious issues, particularly in the case of catteries. Their effective solution will overcome neighbours' objections to planning applications, objections from refuse collectors and infection risks to boarders and free-roamers. It will also create a favourable impression with clients!

From the points of view of economy, disposal and odour, it is essential to avoid meat waste. Each cat should be served food he will eat in the correct amount, since no leftovers should ever be used. Food should never be left down for a cat to finish later. Cans are dangerous and odorous when empty, and should be washed and crushed before being placed in dustbins. Fresh food can, with good management, be used entirely, with only perhaps bone remaining to be disposed of in dustbins. The wrappings of fresh meat and fish, and meat string, should be burnt. Sink waste disposal units (available in various sizes) can be fitted to waste pipes and will hygienically dispose of nearly all kitchen waste except empty cans and large bones.

Meat odour will attract flies. Even regular use of a Vortex volatilizer or fly spray in a kitchen will not prevent flies laying eggs on exposed meat before they die. All refuse bins should have fly-proof, close-fitting, clipped-on lids. A fly repellant/deodorizing powder is obtainable for refuse bins.

Faeces in toilet trays will also attract flies. In catteries an observation window at the back of each chalet is useful to check whether toilet trays need attention, thus removing the necessity to enter each unit to carry out an inspection. Faeces are best flushed down a lavatory, but can be disposed of by being placed in the *centre* of a compost heap, along with urine-soaked litter. Here, temperatures reach 140°F (60°C) which, over several months, will destroy parasite eggs, viruses and bacteria. Valuable cat manure is thus available for the garden.

Incineration is the best method of disposal of all waste material, however, unless the property is in a smokeless zone. A brick incinerator with a secure cover, situated well away from the cattery and neighbours' houses, is used to burn waste or expose it to a dry heat of about 176°F (80°C) for a minimum of forty-five minutes. Such sterilized material can then be composted or buried.

The odour of cat urine can be deodorized with ¼ per cent Domestos solution.

Drains, waste pipes, gulleys, paths and so on should be disinfected and deodorized as described on page 136.

THE OFFICE

Basic equipment in the cattery office or office area will include: a desk with drawers, a filing cabinet, a typewriter or word processor (with printer), a telephone, calculator, notice board, brochures describing the cattery, headed notepaper. All licensed premises must display a Licence to Board and Schedule of Conditions supplied by the licensing authority.

Records must be completed daily: paperwork should not be allowed to mount up. Record everything – when you are caring for a number of cats, your memory cannot be relied upon. Catteries should keep records of clients in alphabetical order according to surname, and records of all cats taken into care and rehomed. Examples of the type of records used in catteries are given in Appendix III.

In the case of a business enterprise, account books and other financial records must be available for inspection by the Inland Revenue.

All insurance policies must be filed in a safe place. Some large catteries may require a safe.

THE CATTERY BROCHURE

The cattery brochure will vary according to the type of cattery – boarding, breeding, quarantine, indoor. The following information will be required by prospective clients and should be clearly set out in the brochure:

Name of proprietor, address and telephone number.
Fee per cat per week. The minimum fee if a cat is boarded for less than a week.
Deposit required on arrival, or deposit on written confirmation of booking, or payment on collection of cat.
Cancellation fee.
Brief description of premises, viewing hours, whether units can be shared, extra charges (for example, heating costs, special diets).
Hours of business. Collection times.
Details of vaccination certificates required.
Supply and labelling of carry baskets/bedding/toys.
Location map.
Details of any types of cat *not* accepted, or special facilities provided, such as stud houses, nursery pens.

The initial booking will probably be by telephone. Clients will normally wish to view the cattery before using its services. A brochure can be sent by post in advance of such a visit, or handed to a client when viewing the cattery.

CATTERY RECEPTION AND DEPARTURE PROCEDURES

It may be convenient for receptions and departures to take place during mornings only. Once vacated, a unit can be cleaned and disinfected in the early afternoon and dried, if possible, in sunlight. Reoccupation should ideally be delayed for twenty-four hours.

A reception room in the main house, usually the office, can be kept disinfected with an electric volatilizer using a virucide/bactericide (see page 136). On reception cats can be taken out of their baskets and examined briefly in the presence of their owners and all necessary forms filled in. The cat's ears should be inspected for brown wax, his coat for flea excreta or sore, bald patches, his 'trousers' and anus for any signs of diarrhoea and his mouth for any odour or gingivitis indicative of bad teeth or a respiratory infection. As much medical information as possible should be obtained in case of emergency. On departure the owner should be asked to sign the Release Form (see Appendix III) and be presented with the final account, for which a receipt should be given on payment.

Once a cat has arrived at the cattery, it is unwise for a proprietor to refuse admission for any reason as this may present serious inconvenience to a client. If the vaccination certificate has been forgotten, or if the cat appears to be suffering from an infectious or non-infectious disease, he can be placed in isolation and veterinary treatment sought at the owner's expense.

Any items brought with the cat, kept in the unit and removed on departure by the owner will need no disinfection.

After being taken to his chalet and being fondled by his owner and the cattery proprietor, a bowl of water and perhaps some food should be placed in the unit and the cat left alone to explore his new surroundings. If the cat does not eat, on this occasion it may be decided to leave food in the chalet overnight, although food should usually not be left in this way.

New arrivals should always be observed closely for a few days for any symptoms of infection which, as previously explained, may be present in an inactive form, likely to reactivate under stress, or, in any event, likely to infect other susceptible cats. Newcomers should be fed last for the first few days, but *before* cats in isolation.

DAILY CATTERY ROUTINE

Variations in cattery routine will be necessary at times. For example, some form of heating will be required in the chalets of an outdoor cattery and there will be an earlier lock-up as the days shorten. Any outbreak of infection will mean extra sampling of secretions, excretions or fur brushings for veterinary examination, closer monitoring of cats' behaviour, resiting of infected units, the preparation of extra isolation rooms and so on. However, taking into account the variations mentioned above, once a routine is decided upon, it must be rigidly followed, no matter how many interruptions or telephone calls intervene. A stage missed in a disinfection schedule could result in an outbreak of infection. A suggested routine may sound complicated on paper, but once a proprietor, and her staff, grow used to it, it becomes second nature and they can take small variations in their stride.

When a routine has been decided upon, put it in writing for staff/ relief help/weekend help and ensure that it is followed to the letter. While planning a routine, a cat's usual daily routine should be considered, although, as stated, there is no such animal as an average cat – all are individualists. All that may be said is that most domestic cats spend a leisurely morning, cat napping in patches of sunshine, anticipating lunch and watching humans at work. So humans can do the bulk of cattery work in the morning without disturbing the cats, and even providing them with entertainment. In summer, the morning is the cooler part of the working day; and any necessary medical treatment can be carried out in good light, particularly as cats are more amenable before lunch. Since most cats are moderately active in the mornings, their behaviour can be studied while you are working and any abnormalities noted (for example, a cat remaining in his chalet). Cats spend their afternoons in deep sleep, indoors in cool weather, outdoors in summer. Afternoons can be used for disinfecting vacated units, tending cats in isolation and office work.

Activity time for cats is from dusk to dawn, but most domestics will settle for human bedtime! During activity times free-roamers hunt, scavenge, play, fight, eat grass, vomit it, spray, seek catmint or catnip and draw their claws over wood to blunt them and remove old claw sheaths. If confined at this time, they may embark on an orgy of destruction centring on carpets, upholstered chairs and wallpaper. When they are confined in a unit, 'hunting' will consist of leaping after and sometimes eating flies, moths and beetles, which are natural prey items. Cats will chase balls, burrow under newspaper, throw up and catch catnip mice, leap into litter trays, scatter litter and dart in and out of cardboard boxes turned upside down and with holes cut in the sides. Every effort must be made to interest

FIGURE 36   When cats are confined, every effort must be made to interest them and encourage them to exercise. Throw a ball – most cats will play with it.

confined cats and encourage them to exercise. If security permits, cats should be allowed the freedom of the run in warm weather during the night. Some insist upon sitting out in all weathers, and if a run cannot be covered to protect against summer downpours, such cats may have to be shut in chalets during bad weather.

Cats dislike sudden movements and noise. Noise interferes with their hearing and therefore their recognition of danger. Avoid noisy visitors, smoking, children running around a cattery, the presence of dogs, dogs barking, continuous noise from vacuum cleaners, ringing telephones, blaring radios and banging doors. Cats need a quiet environment, where essential cleaning and disinfection is carried out in a peaceful, unhurried manner.

Once occupied, a unit does not need to be disinfected daily, but damp dusting of areas (preferably smooth) in contact with cats with ¼ per cent Domestos solution (see page 128) will minimize infection risk and keep the unit odour-free. Some cats are frankly messy. They hook food out of dishes, particularly when not hungry; spread it on the floor; splash milk on the walls; knock over water bowls or dip paws in them, plus dirt; and spread litter or refuse to use litter trays.

The units of such cats will often need cleaning several times a day, but do not require disinfection daily.

In view of the widespread milk allergy among cats, causing vomiting and/or diarrhoea, some cattery owners withhold milk. If it is served, early-morning milk can be placed just inside the run to avoid the infection risk consequent upon entry.

SUGGESTED DAILY ROUTINE

(1) Release cats from chalets, preferably from *outside* each unit, to avoid entry and need to disinfect hands.

(2) If applicable, serve milk just inside run, without touching cats.

(3) Carry out main cleaning, handling, fondling cats: disinfect hands before entering *each* unit. Empty toilet trays, replenish. Note urination, defecation, vomit, diarrhoea, for recording on daily record sheet (see Appendix III).

(4) Examine bedding/shelf/resting places for evidence of parasitic infections – tapeworm segments, flea dirts and so on. Treat cat/unit/bed as appropriate.

(5) Carry out medical treatment/grooming of each cat.

(6) Deal with reception/departure/bookings. If there is a break in routine whilst attending to an occupied unit, disinfect hands before resuming work. Deal with cats in order of infection risk – kittens, pregnant cats, indoor domestics, old domestics, adolescents, healthy adults, studs, isolated cats.

(7) Serve lunch/milk/water, placing bowls inside run without entering, as in point (1). Avoid touching *rims* of bowls, or cats. Remove bowls and sterilize as soon as possible. This procedure avoids the necessity of disinfecting hands for each unit.

(8) Afternoon work: disinfection of vacated units, care of cats in isolation, waste disposal, office work, shopping, maintenance of property.

(9) Serve evening meal, as for lunch.

(10) Ventilate chalets at maximum if cats are shut in on hot nights.

9 Sex

Determining the sex of a cat or kitten is often very difficult. Rescue organizations are constantly faced with the problem of deciding whether an adult cat is a queen, spayed female or neutered male. Even deciding whether a cat is a full tom or not is by no means easy in long-hairs, particularly if the cat in question is an aggressive stray!

It is impossible to know, even on close examination under anaesthetic, whether a cat is a queen or spayed female. In the latter case, once the fur has grown over the operation scar (usually situated on the flank, near the back legs, or sometimes, in the case of pedigree cats, on the abdomen) the scar is virtually invisible. Only subsequent behaviour will clinch the issue!

In the case of rescued cats, it is very important to know whether a cat has been neutered or spayed because, if so, he or she probably has a grieving owner somewhere in a 50-mile (80-kilometre) radius. An adult stray tom in poor condition is unlikely to show sexual behaviour until his health improves. Even behaviour after puberty varies from cat to cat. Some, about 5 per cent, do not need de-sexing. Multicat owners have the advantage of being able to compare the hindquarters of a cat of unknown sex with the hindquarters of a cat of known sex.

All cats resent an examination of their hindparts and the best time to do so is when the cat is receptive to human attention. If another human is available to pat the rump, the cat will raise his tail. Timid rescued cats have to be examined on the move.

Figure 37 will help you determine the sex of a cat. The anus, directly below the tail, is easy to see, but the male penis is kept inside the body (ensheathed) and only the tiny, pink tip can be seen within another circle called the sheath. The penis, about ½ inch (15 millimetres) long, protrudes only for cleaning purposes in the neutered male, but if the male was neutered too early (under one year) this ability to protrude the penis is lost. Such a male may not have the wide, flat head, thick scruff and broad shoulders of the late-neutered or full tomcat. Late-neutered males, when sexually aroused and

(a)   (b)   (c)   (d)

FIGURE 37   A comparison of hindquarters.

KEY

In all diagrams the 'daisy' under the tail represents the anus.

(a)   The hindquarters of a female kitten, a queen or a spayed female. The slit below the anus is the vulva. The duct from the bladder (called the urethra) drains into this slit. Note that the vulva is closer to the anus than is the tip of the penis in the tomcat in (b), (c) and (d).

(b)   The hindquarters of a tom kitten. The raised areas are the scrotal sacs, into which the testicles descend. In the centre is the pink tip of the penis, surrounded by a circle representing the sheath.

(c)   The hindquarters of a full (or entire) tomcat. The two raised areas are the scrotal sacs which contain the testicles.

(d)   The hindquarters of a neutered male. The raised areas are the scrotal sacs from which the testicles have been rèmoved.

padding clothing, cushions and so on in a mating posture will also extrude the penis. (Females also exhibit this mating posture.) The tip of the ensheathed penis is round, compared with the slit of the female vulva, which is nearer the anus. A full tom, if fit, will of course attempt to mate other cats – not necessarily females! By the time a kitten is six months old, the growing testicles in the male should be large enough to identify his sex, but paradoxically the better fed and cared for a kitten is, the less developed he may be physically. Kittens are easy to sex when about three weeks old, if both sexes are in a litter, by the small protuberances beneath the anus of the toms.

The tragedy of the cat world is over-population, but the domestic feline is the only member of the cat family not faced with extinction. Domestic cats can be kept indoors because they are the only good-smelling carnivores! They breed rapidly under the protective cloak of domesticity. Feral cats may only have one litter of two kittens a year, and those may not survive infections and predators, compared with the domestic cat's two litters per season of three to six kittens. There are never enough good homes to go round and every year thousands of unwanted cats and kittens are euthanased by vets, or dumped to fend for themselves. The only way to ensure a better deal for our cats is to limit the numbers of kittens born, and this end is best achieved by spaying the females. As far as toms are concerned, so many people keep full toms that, if one is neutered, there is always another to take over his territory and his queens.

BEHAVIOUR OF THE SEXUALLY MATURING TOMCAT

Most tomcats begin to mature around one year old. Although not physically mature nor able to act as studs until about two years old, most toms will begin to exhibit sexual behaviour from one year and their development will determine the age at which they should be neutered, unless required for stud purposes.

A maturing tom will begin to caterwaul (utter a coarse yowl or mating call). This he uses to threaten potential rivals. Having accepted the nightly lock-up, he will now be active and demand to go out, or miss meals and refuse to come in at night. From about six months old, a tom begins to spray-urinate in the garden, as opposed to squat-urinating (digging toilet holes). On maturity he will begin to 'mark' his territory with a few drops of urine every few metres,

FIGURE 38   A short-haired full tom can be easily recognized, without too close an inspection of his hindparts. The two scrotal sacs contain the testicles.

and the urine will develop a pungent odour which is designed to warn off males rather than appeal to humans. The odd night out is insignificant, but if he spends less and less time at home, is seen in distant gardens and begins to show aggression, the decision should be made to neuter him for his own personal safety. If he is not neutered too early, the presence of his sex hormones will have ensured that his body is mature and he will be able to defend himself. The neutering operation involves the removal of the two testicles from the scrotal sacs (which then shrivel) under general anaesthetic.

If a tom is not neutered before complete maturity, he will extend his territory and fight to establish his right to sire all the kittens in a 5–10-mile (8–16-kilometre) radius. He will be at risk from traffic. He will arrive home with tatty ears and serious wounds. He may leave home altogether. He will become the terror of the neighbourhood, threatening quiet domestics, entering houses and spraying and keeping neighbours awake with his caterwauling.

Exposure and unsuitable food will lower his resistance to all infections. His coat will become flea-ridden. If unable to hunt, he will lose weight. At this stage the lucky cats are recognized as strays, taken into care, neutered and rehomed. For information on rehoming, see page 185.

It cannot be assumed that roaming, fighting neighbours' cats, aggressive behaviour to domiciled neuters or spraying in the house are attributable entirely to the sex hormones, which cease production on neutering. Fully mature, sexually active toms may not totally abandon full tomcat behaviour on neutering, and certainly not under a week following neutering. Such cats will need further confinement for at least two weeks. Some neutered cats cannot be homed because they roam, spray or fight, and the only options are to keep them permanently confined in separate accommodation, which is unacceptable to a born-free cat, or return them to the wild, but arrange for feeding and, if possible, veterinary treatment when necessary.

If not neutered, tomcats cease sexual activity around twelve years old.

BEHAVIOUR OF THE SEXUALLY MATURING QUEEN

A queen matures far earlier than a tom, usually between eight and ten months. She is then capable of having kittens of her own, but breeders do not allow kittening until a queen is at least one and a half to two years old. Pedigree cats can be bred most of the year, but mongrel cats normally commence their breeding season in late January, continuing until about October. Female kittens born in the spring may well have their own kittens by autumn, but autumn-born females may not mature for a year or eighteen months.

A queen approaching puberty will begin to 'call'. This new sound has been mistaken for a crying baby! Females may spray-urinate, the odour of which will attract all full toms in a 5-mile (8-kilometre) radius. These toms will congregate outside the house, enter it if they can, and 'mark' it with their own unwelcome, odorous urine.

A queen will indicate the onset of her first heat, or oestrus, by belly-shuffling along the floor, crooning, holding her tail high or to one side thus exposing her genital area, waving her tail and stamping or treading with her back legs. (Some of this behaviour may persist in spayed females.) Her appetite may increase, she may be unusually affectionate and possessive towards her owner, or aggressive towards other cats. She may shred newspaper and select a quiet, dark place, suitable for the birth of kittens. The first oestrus is usually a short affair, lasting a few days. Queens not required for breeding should be spayed after this first indication of sexual maturity. If a queen is not mated, the oestrus will occur with ever-increasing frequency and last longer and longer. An unmated queen will lose weight and become bad-tempered, even vicious. It is cruel to keep an unmated queen in captivity. If she is free-roaming, she may leave home to have kittens in the wild. It is possible to prevent heats by using Ovarid (synthetic progesterone) but this can have dangerous side effects if taken for longer than two months. However, the use of a vasectomized tom to suppress oestrus in a queen is an option for a breeding cattery.

Where rescue resources are limited, it is obviously prudent to give spaying of queens top priority. This operation, carried out under a general anaesthetic, involves the removal of the ovaries and uterus. Spaying is a major operation compared with neutering, but nearly all queens are back to normal within two days. The operation scar, usually on the flank, will soon become invisible as the fur grows over it in about two to three months.

The gestation period for kittens (the period from conception to birth) is sixty-three to sixty-five days. Queens in kitten often leave home to have their kittens in the wild, and it is prudent to confine pregnant queens for a week prior to kittening. The birth of kittens in the wild results in the establishment of a feral colony. Many kittens born thus are destined to die of infections, starvation or attack by predators: wild or farm dogs, foxes, owls, stoats and so on.

Kittens born in domesticity are weaned from about three weeks, and are ready to go to new homes at six to eight weeks old, depending on their progress. Pedigree kittens are usually homed later, around ten to twelve weeks. Until the kittens are weaned, the queen should be confined or she may leave home in search of a sire for her next litter. Queens can become pregnant again within three weeks of giving birth! Breeding continues until the age of twelve years, but an ageing queen normally aborts before full term.

Rescue organizations are faced with an ever-rising tide of kittens during the peak months of July and August, and it is heart-rending to have to make a decision to rescue an obviously pregnant stray and have her aborted and spayed simultaneously. This can be done by a vet up to thirty days after conception.

To help limit the numbers of unwanted cats, some rescue centres allow only one male kitten per litter, asking a vet to enthanase all the others – male and female – at birth. Black and black and white females are highest on the 'unwanted' list. It may, therefore, be prudent to keep only male kittens – and then perhaps only gingers, tabbies, greys and whites. Tortoiseshell males are almost invariably sterile. If all kittens are removed, the queen should have a veterinary check-up to ensure that her milk is dispersing naturally.

THE SEX HORMONES

Hormones are protein particles produced by various glands in the cat's body, and carried round the body by the blood. Some are dissolved in the plasma (blood water), others are fat-soluble. They act as chemical messengers, 'instructing' organs what to do.

Anabolic steroids are the fat-soluble, body-building hormones produced by the sex organs (ovaries and testicles). The female hormones are oestrogen and progesterone, the latter secreted by the ovaries only when maintaining pregnancy. The male hormone is called testosterone. Contrary to common belief, all cats produce both oestrogen and testosterone, but females have more oestrogen and males more testosterone. Both these hormones are secreted, in minute amounts, by the adrenal glands just above the kidneys, so, even in de-sexed cats, *some* sex hormones are produced. Testosterone is sometimes referred to as an androgen. The adrenal cortex (or outer part of the gland) secretes corticosteroids (for example, cortisone).

It cannot be denied that a de-sexed cat of either sex is likely to suffer hormone deficiency diseases, but some so-called hormone deficiency diseases, although treated with sex hormones, have not been proved to be caused by sex hormone imbalances. Certainly the sex hormones are body-building, and too early neutering accounts for the lack of physique in some castrated males. Castration alopecia in male neuters, in which the back legs and abdomen go bald, is treated with testosterone, but many other so-called non-specific eczemas (skin diseases), whose causes are unknown, are treated with oestrogen or testosterone on a trial-and-error basis.

Progesterone in the form of Ovarid can, as has already been explained, have side effects if given for longer than two months, but it is used for eczema, as a short-term contraceptive and even to control spraying in male neuters!

Cortisone is fat-soluble and widely used to control inflammation but has its dangers, like *all* drugs, and can cause further damage in already failing kidneys.

De-sexed cats of both sexes may benefit from about half a Sesoral tablet (a mixture of male and female hormones) twice a week, sometimes more, to offset any possible hormone deficiency diseases.

THE ETHICS OF DE-SEXING

Some cat owners are understandably afraid of having their cats de-sexed, or they disagree in principle. Others object to spaying and neutering because, they say, de-sexed cats are fat, lazy, uninteresting and short-lived. The owner is to blame for this: do not overfeed!

One argument against neutering toms is the loss of condition some suffer following neutering. The best solution here is a compromise. Watch your tom for impending signs of sexual maturity, then have him neutered to prevent him roaming and becoming involved in serious fights. He will be physically or almost physically mature. Then give him Sesoral tablets as hormone replacement therapy.

Some owners believe that a tom is entitled to his sex life. If you live in the country, well away from through roads, where there are few other toms for yours to fight with, and he does not spray in the house, then, to try to limit the numbers of unwanted kittens, consider vasectomy as an alternative to neutering.

Females have to be spayed when sexually mature (see page 180). There is no acceptable alternative, if endless litters of unwanted kittens are to be avoided. Females seem to suffer far less from sex-hormone-deficiency diseases. However, like males they too benefit from Sesoral tablets. Remember that *both* sexes produce oestrogen and testosterone in varying proportions.

One reason for not spaying or neutering is a fear of the effects of anaesthetic. It cannot be denied that an anaesthetic can trigger dormant, deadly viruses, such as feline leukaemia. It cannot be over-stressed that rescued strays must be brought back to health before de-sexing. After effects from an anaesthetic are very, very rare in healthy cats, however, and veterinary techniques in anaesthesia are improving all the time.

The pro-de-sexing lobby, vets among them, suggest that de-sexed cats make better 'pets'. This term is anathema to a true cat lover: cats are individuals, not 'pets'. Another supposed recommendation is that early de-sexing improves the appearance of the cat, ensuring a more rounded head and body. This is merely a manipulation to please humans. It should be borne in mind that a physically mature, powerful cat is able to defend himself or herself – a very important consideration in artificially high cat populations. Most breeders would totally reject the 'good appearance' argument, and a visit to the National Cat Show at Olympia proves them right – for most exhibited pedigree cats are entire.

10 Cats on the Move

THE PROBLEMS OF REHOMING

When a cat is introduced into a strange environment occupied by potentially hostile humans, cats, dogs, babies or other animals, his first instinct is to flee from these unknowns, back to his well-loved territory. (Few cats are attached to owners more than territory, although we like to think so!) Cats in this frame of mind can escape through a 1½-inch (4-centimetre) gap in an open window from which they may fall to their death, or they may be killed on the road, or at best get lost and become heavily parasitized, hungry strays.

Time, patience and de-sexing solve most integration problems. Most kittens are happy anywhere and resident adults rarely show hostility towards them for more than a week. Some cats are extrovert, friendly animals, used to other cats and dogs; these integrate well and are soon indicating a desire to play by tum presentation (rolling on their back). A stray cat out of human contact for months or years may take two months to integrate. A newcomer may remain permanently aggressive to other cats, or just to one cat in a domiciled feline family, and may have to be kept permanently separated, or possibly rehomed in a one-cat household. Some cats are terrified of dogs. Most cats, on being introduced to a new environment, will probably disappear under the nearest settee for a few hours.

THE PERSONAL ROOM

All new introductions must have an escape-proof room with a double-door safety system along the lines set out on page 149, but furniture can remain (providing it is not too valuable!). The rest of the house should be escape-proof – block up chimneys, shut off any rooms with open fires, close all windows and shut off access to cat doors. Kittens do not usually try to escape but they are very fragile, with easily broken bones, and very sharp claws which can so easily be caught up in upholstery or curtains. They should be shut in the personal room, checked frequently, and not let out into a busy house until humans have finished work and are able to sit down and entertain them. Kittens are easily kicked, sat upon or trodden on. It is good practice for humans in their presence to adopt the slow shuffle-walk – never lift feet from the floor. Be aware also that they may swarm up your legs! Kittens should never be lifted more than 2 feet (60 centimetres) from the floor as they will very likely be injured if dropped; and they should be discouraged from climbing on to indoor windowsills as they can so easily fall.

Introductions to a new environment and a new family must be made methodically, leisurely, tactfully, patiently and with understanding, in a series of steps. No step should be hurried; each must be mastered before proceeding to the next.

Adult cats adopted from rescue organizations are usually visited several times by a prospective owner, so that they can grow used to the owner's appearance, odour and sound. The home will be vetted, a trial period arranged with the proviso that the cat be returned immediately if the homing does not work out, and access to the cat at any time will be required. A rehoming form will be signed (see Appendix III). From this point on the rule for the new owner is: 'Proceed from the known to the unknown.'

INTEGRATION OF A NEWCOMER INTO THE HOUSEHOLD

Step 1: Talk softly to your new cat whilst carrying him home in his basket. Place the basket in his personal room, open it and leave him alone for about an hour to explore the room thoroughly. Provide a bowl of water. Do not allow other animals to gather at his door, making hostile noises and unfamiliar odour.

Step 2: Enter quietly, using his name as much as possible. Do not place yourself *above* a newcomer as this indicates dominance and threat. Kneel down, extend your hand, call him and invite *him* to approach *you*. Never attempt to touch or lift him, or to prize him out from any hideaway. He may growl or scratch you, in fear. If he approaches you, he will probably present his head, for you to scratch. Do not stroke him unless he presents his whole body, or rubs your body. If he appears receptive, sit down and invite him on to your lap. If he disappears under the furniture, just sit with him, saying his name, for as long as possible.

Make sure that any other animals in the house do not have to wait for their meal, or have their routine disturbed, for this may result in resentment of the newcomer.

Step 3: Offer him a meal to which he is accustomed. If he eats in your presence he has accepted you. If not, leave the meal and with-

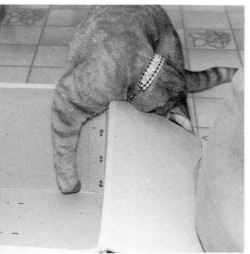

FIGURE 39 Provide plenty of entertainment for domiciled domestics and newcomers. Shared games assist integration. Toys will provide hours of fun for cats – and humans!

draw. Never fondle a cat whilst he is eating. (For advice on feeding see Chapter 2). Always move quietly and slowly: sudden movements frighten most cats.

Step 4: After a meal, cats usually use their toilet trays, wash and sleep. There should be no external noise, such as the barking of dogs or the roar of a vacuum cleaner: for all cats these mask sounds of possible danger and are annoying or alarming. After about two hours, present the new cat with a little milk. He may purr for you, or raise his rump to allow rump pats or stroking. Try placing your hands under his tum and raising him a few inches from the floor. Try placing him on your lap, but never hold him there. If he appears tense and uneasy, withdraw.

Step 5: Lift him into your arms by curling his tail over his bottom, and sitting his bottom on one hand, resting his forepaws on your forearm. Later, rest his forepaws on your shoulder. Never hold an unknown cat near your face until you have his confidence – and he has yours!

Step 6: Try a little grooming, inspect for fleas (see page 208).

Step 7: Begin training in restraining techniques (see page 39).

Step 8: It is now time to introduce the cat to the rest of the *human* family. Allow domiciled humans to introduce themselves as you did, in steps. Never allow children to pick up a new cat or kitten. Children under five should never be left alone with a cat or kitten. Older children should be taught the correct way to lift and hold a cat. Once all humans have been introduced and accepted, then, in the absence of other animals, the door of his personal room can be left open. He will now gradually widen his 'territory', bolting back into his room whenever he feels at risk. Shut him in his personal room at night, or when outer doors are likely to be opened. Remember that some cats are active from dusk to dawn – they do not respect, or conform to, humans' sleeping hours, nor should they be under any obligation to do so.

Step 9: If there are other domiciled animals, keep the door of the newcomer's personal room shut, but allow other animals to approach the door. Both parties will receive information about each other by sound and odour. Most dogs are terrified of kittens and are usually dominated by adult cats. Many dogs are far too trusting for their own good! Hold dogs by the collar and let the animals see each other. Remove a dog who appears about to have his nose scratched.

Resident cats will not rush straight into alien territory. Most will 'freeze' – that is, raise the fur along their spines (hackles), puff their tails and present themselves sideways on in order to convey the impression that they are larger, powerful and more dangerous than they actually are! They may paw the floor, growl or hiss at each other, but differences are usually settled by confrontation (a kind of eyeball-to-eyeball psychological clawfare). Confrontations involve staring each other out, until one cat concedes inferiority and withdraws. It is advisable, however, to have a cup of water or an old coat handy so that if the two cats should hurl themselves at each other, they can be separated. Never intervene with hands in a cat fight: cats know what they are doing and fight each other with equal weaponry – teeth and claws! A good fight usually clears the air.

FIGURE 40   Occasional aggression among members of a feline family can be regarded as normal.

Active combat is a sign that cats are equals, and they are unlikely to fight again.

Step 10: Never leave animals alone together, without supervision, until you are sure they are on good terms. Cats have killed and eaten small dogs – dogs have killed cats. Shut a new cat in his room at mealtimes and allow plenty of privacy for toilet, washing and sleeping.

Step 11: Mealtimes are great levellers of rank! Even warring factions call a truce on these occasions. If a new arrival can be persuaded to eat with the rabble, complete integration and harmony are just around the corner. Confident newcomers will quickly locate the communal eating place. If a newcomer is reluctant, try moving his feeding dish nearer and nearer the usual feeding place. Soon a new cat's personal room becomes a novelty and existing incumbents of the household begin to savour the delights of a new cat's bed, toys and toilet tray!

Step 12: Allowing a cat to go out in the garden is the most dangerous time. If he is still afraid of domiciled animals, he will flee. He might accept a harness for the first few days (see page 197). Leave the back door open, allow him to find his own way out and always accompany him. Bear in mind that a safe direction at his old house may be a patently dangerous one at another. Encourage him to follow you in a safe direction. He will now probably prefer to use the garden for toilet, and the tray should be removed during the day and replaced after lock-up. If this is not done, some cats will use the tray all the time.

INTRODUCTION OF A NEW BABY

The cats of a household will regard a baby as just another new animal, with the advantage that there is no hostility from the baby! The baby should be introduced to other residents in *his* personal room – that is, the nursery. Protect cots and prams with safety nets, and only allow animals into the nursery under supervision. Cats and other animals love to share such cosy places!

ADOPTING THE LOCAL STRAY

Homeless cats who are able to hunt can keep themselves in good condition, at least for the summer months. So it is not always easy to know whether a cat visiting you regularly for a meal is a genuine stray or just a greedy domestic. In doubtful cases, once the cat is presenting himself for food regularly and can be inspected, a quick-release safety collar can be slipped on (though it must be inspected daily for any signs of chafing). The collar should bear the words: 'Is this cat a stray? Please telephone me on . . . [give number].'

The non-hunting stray can be easily recognized by his thin body, poor coat, battle scars and protruding spine and hipbones. He will be very timid and may take weeks of feeding in the garden before he can be enticed into the house. He will probably appear about once a day, be entire and will spray. A small, thin female with bulging tum will probably be pregnant. Most strays seem to be entire toms, however, and it has to be said that they may harbour many potentially dangerous infections and may not make old bones.

FIGURE 41   A typical stray tomcat. The haw partially covers the right eye and the ear flaps are damaged. These injuries are the result of serious cat fights between rival full (unneutered) toms.

Other cats may have to be shut in the house, while you are feeding and fondling the stray. Once a stray is in the house, he can be isolated from domiciled cats and built up before de-sexing or vaccination. Underlying vir-aemia or septicaemia may be present, and, because of the unavoidable change of diet, diarrhoea or vomiting may occur. It is important not to overfeed a rescued stray.

Integration through Steps 1–12 given on pages 186–9 can take months, but the work is very worthwhile and rescued strays often show appreciation – a rare quality in cats!

MOVING HOUSE

His owner's move to a new house is usually a traumatic experience for a cat. Many are lost forever when allowed out into a new, potentially hostile environment.

Moving house should be regarded as a rehoming, and the same step-by-step process of integration followed as given earlier in this section for newcomers to a household.

During the move it is essential to lock a cat in a room, or he may bolt in terror as a result of the noise, confusion and the presence of strangers. He may be confined to his usual sleeping quarters, with familiar possessions, and transferred to his basket for transportation at the last moment. Alternatively, a friend of the owner may be prepared to keep him in a room at another house. Some people prefer to board a cat in a cattery close to the new home until the move is complete and the new house tidy. Then the cat should be placed in his new room, with his familiar possessions and furniture.

The most dangerous time is when he is allowed out into the garden. Exercise on a harness and lead will accustom him to new surroundings. He should, of course, bear his new address and telephone number in the event of his escaping and becoming lost.

TRAVELLING WITH FELINES

Consider the following two cases.

An adult cat was being carried home from the vet's after an anaesthetic in what had, hitherto, been considered a strong wicker basket, with a lid secured additionally with strong elasticated straps. Within seconds the cat had used his head as a wedge to open up a gap between lid and basket, and, by flattening his body, managed to squeeze out.

A newly spayed female cat, also still under an anaesthetic, with recently weaned kittens at home, was being transported free in the family car. The driver momentarily lost his concentration and opened his window about 4 inches to give a traffic signal. In a flash, the cat had leapt from the window. Two months later she was found in an appalling condition and, because of an intestinal blockage, had to be euthanased.

Cats are born escapologists. Even young kittens can be unbelievably powerful and dangerous when being placed and carried in baskets, travelling in cars, carried in human arms in unknown areas or when confined in catteries. Only those cats trained from kittenhood to travel in a harness, with lead, can be safely carried to a strange place. The danger here is that the cat may escape with harness and lead attached.

If a car is not available at all times, it is essential to have the means at hand to transport your cat, unaided, to the vet, since every second may count in saving a cat's life. An adult cat is too heavy to carry far. A carry basket can conveniently be strapped to a two-wheeled shopper, or the carrier of a bicycle.

What is the safest type of carry basket? Wicker baskets are clearly unsafe for nervous cats or rescued strays, even with additional straps. Probably the most secure carry basket is one made of steel-wire mesh coated in white plastic (see Figure 42). This allows all-round vision for the cat, whereas vision is limited in a wicker or fibreglass basket. Some cats are more tranquil if they can see all around them; others travel best if completely covered with a dark cloth. In hot weather the dangers of heat stress are, of course, far greater in covered or non-mesh baskets. If the carry basket is side-loading, the cat should be placed in tail first. If the cat has to be lowered into the top, hold his legs close to his body with your forearms to avoid him latching on to the sides of the basket. Kittens can travel together in one basket but adults, even from the same family, may fight if so confined.

Steel-mesh baskets, available from pet shops and mail order firms (see Appendix II) are expensive, but will give a (human) lifetime's use and serve many generations of cats. Neighbours are often grateful to hire such a basket for a small fee.

FIGURE 42   Carry basket of steel-wire mesh.

Cardboard pet carriers are sold for use in emergencies. They should never be used routinely. An adult cat can bite and claw his way out in fifteen minutes. Additionally, cats under stress are likely to urinate, vomit or suffer diarrhoea. Once wet, cardboard disintegrates and the cat will fall out of the bottom.

Because of the effects of stress on a long journey, all carry baskets should be lined first with a sheet of heavy-duty polythene, then with a thick layer of newspaper and finally with disposable old sheets or blankets. On a long journey of, say, more than three or four hours, it is advisable to carry replacement bedding, a box of tissues and some bin liners for temporary storage of soiled items. A separate toilet tray will be needed and the cat should be allowed out of his basket to use it – after you have ensured that all car windows and doors are closed. To reduce the risk of soiling bedding, it is advisable to provide a slightly-larger-than-usual meal in the afternoon prior to the journey and withhold food until the journey's end.

Some cats may need tranquillizers during transportation. These must be obtained from your vet and be of the right kind for cats. Tranquillizers may calm a cat and reduce the likelihood of vomiting, but they will not necessarily induce sleep. On the other hand, they may excite the cat! It is, therefore, advisable to try out an intended tranquillizer a week in advance, to test the cat's reaction. A tranquillizer becomes effective in about an hour, so can, if necessary, be given to a cat when the journey is under way. (See page 41 for how to give a pill.)

For all travelling cats there is the ever-present possibility of escape, so all cats should wear a collar bearing relevant addresses and telephone numbers. Quick-release safety collars are available from the Cats Protection League at Horsham (see Appendix I). Boarded cats should bear the details of their cattery. Baskets left at catteries should be clearly labelled.

Soiling, odour, noise and annoyance to passengers on public transport, and the danger of soiling in taxis, mean that permission to carry the cat by these means must be sought in advance.

Cats should never be left in an unventilated car – car ventilators for pets are available from car accessory stores. Nor should they ever be left in cars parked in sunlight. Finally, remember that theft from cars is always likely: the best course is not to leave your cat alone in the car if you can avoid it.

HOLIDAY BOARDING FOR YOUR CAT

Preparations must be made well in advance for the welfare of your cat during the family holiday.

Most cats are best left in their home environment provided that a reliable human, experienced in cat care and known to the cat, will visit him at least twice a day, feed him, fondle him and monitor his health. Some cats are very miserable without human company, however, and have been known to take up residence in an alternative, receptive home offering human companionship – never to return. This is a particular danger in the case of 'only' cats. For those owners who feel that they must take their cats with them, some hotels offer boarding facilities for cats, as well as humans. Hotel guide books will identify these. Some people take their cats with them on caravanning holidays, or to country or coastal cottages, but this arrangement is not without risk.

If a boarding cattery is to be chosen, bear in mind that these vary enormously in size, standards of care, hygiene, disinfection and food, type of accommodation and degree of human contact. The best person to advise on local catteries is your vet, who will have visited many during the course of his work. If your cat is to be boarded in a new neighbourhood, for instance, during the course of moving house, prospective neighbours, local vets or friends may be able to recommend a boarding cattery. If not, two organizations will help (their addresses are given in Appendix I):

The Cats Protection League. This registered charity offers boarding facilities at shelters. Some local branches offer boarding facilities.

The Feline Advisory Bureau. A list of approved catteries will be sent on receipt of a stamped, self-addressed envelope.

During the peak holiday months of July and August, at Christmas, Easter and the Spring Bank Holiday, reputable boarding catteries will be fully booked up several months in advance. Reputable catteries will require up-to-date vaccination certificates for feline panleucopaenia (feline infectious enteritis) and cat flu. Once addresses of prospective catteries have been obtained, telephone for a brochure and make an appointment to view.

Always view a cattery before leaving a cat. A glance through Chapter 8 will give ample guidance as to how a good cattery should be run. Points to look out for which should ring warning bells are summarized below:

(1) Overcrowding: cats sharing units; units closer than 2 feet (60 centimetres) and not separated by solid partitions; cats housed one above the other.

(2) Grass runs, carpeted floors, dingy corners, inaccessible places where disinfection would be impossible.

(3) Noise: some catteries actually advertise the fact that they play continuous music, under the impression that cats like it! Non-stop radios, barking dogs, traffic noise, constant ringing of outside tele-

phone bells, use of drills, electric saws, incessant use of lawn mowers – all are disturbing to cats.

(4) Toilet-tray odour or other odours. Toilet trays containing faeces or soiled areas, indicating lack of care or insufficient staffing levels. Heavy infestation by flies. Food left-overs remaining in the units.

(5) Premises sited in damp, shady areas, near claustrophobic high walls or fences. Overhanging trees. Proximity to compost heaps, bonfires or incinerators. General untidiness, accumulation of dirt and debris under units.

(6) Other activities being carried out close to boarding cattery units – for example, cat breeding, dog boarding or breeding. Rescued strays or domestics allowed access to boarders' runs.

(7) Isolation units close to boarding units, or reached by passing through the boarding section. All isolation units should be well separated and brick-built, or preferably in the main house.

(8) Unsupervised visitors, particularly children. Visitors or staff smoking.

(9) Exhorbitant charges. £2 per cat per day is reasonable at the time of writing.

(10) An unfriendly proprietor, who does not seem to possess a wide knowledge and understanding of the needs of cats. A brief chat will soon reveal all!

(11) Assistants who fondle separately housed cats without disinfecting their hands after touching each animal.

Generally speaking, the best-run, most homely catteries are small ones (taking around twelve to fifteen cats) run by one person, perhaps with her husband or relief staff helping out on a part-time basis. They are well-spaced, airy, well-ventilated, with plenty of sunlight, and situated (preferably) indoors, boarding only domestic cats.

The local authority will have inspected the property and issued a Licence to Board. Ask to see this. Any complaints about the cattery should be made, in writing, to the licensing authority. The public can help maintain standards, since the licence can be revoked if a complaint is justified.

When taking a cat to a cattery for boarding, always arrive in plenty of time to provide full information and fill in forms. Take vaccination certificates, familiar possessions – bed, toilet tray and filler, blankets, toys.

It is always heartbreaking to leave a cat for the first time, because he cannot know you are coming back. But cats have excellent memories. If he has been happy at a cattery, he will accept boarding again, hardly giving a departing owner a second glance!

COLLAR, HARNESS AND LEAD

CAT COLLARS

Most cats hunt in dense undergrowth, climb trees, play, fight and scratch their necks. By these means a collar can become trapped in the mouth or under a front leg; impale a cat on a branch or even hang him from a tree; or become enmeshed in his claws. All-leather or plastic flea collars, without any elastic insert, are patently dangerous. Other commercially produced collars do release under certain circumstances, unless the collar is caught at the back of the cat's neck. If a collar is fitted too loose, it can get caught up easily; if fitted too tight, the cat cannot release himself. Therefore, to be safe, a collar must come straight off when caught up, by both ends breaking apart.

Even a safe collar treated with an anti-flea preparation can cause hypersensitivity reactions in some cats, resulting in baldness and chafing round the neck, discoloration of fur, or lethargy.

Many cat owners find that a cat's ability to catch birds is unacceptable, and try to interfere with this natural hunting by attaching a bell to his collar. However, some vets have reported that a bell causes the cat to shake his head, scratch excessively in an effort to remove the bell or even to develop stomach ulcers! If you still wish your cat to wear a bell, be sure to attach it to a quick-release safety collar, which will flick apart if a claw catches in the bell. Likewise, any device for opening a cat flap can be attached, but, of course, if the collar is lost, the cat will be shut out!

The fact remains that a collar, bearing the cat's address and telephone number, is the owner's only link with her cat. It is her only hope of learning the whereabouts or fate of a missing cat.

Quick-release safety collars are approved by the Cats Protection League and are obtainable from the headquarters office at the address given in Appendix I. They cost £1.20 for two. Please send a stamped, self-addressed envelope with your request. These collars are instantly releasable, bear nothing metallic to catch in claws, are light and undetectable by most adult cats and are available in a wide range of bright colours. They can be adapted for use as a flea collar, and can be worn in addition to a harness and lead for extra protection. The collars are safe only for adult cats. Kitten trainer collars are available for use on *supervised* kittens over three months old.

FIGURE 43   A quick-release safety collar.

FIGURE 44 A cat modelling a quick-release safety collar, inscribed with his address and telephone number.

HARNESS AND LEAD

A lead should never be attached to a cat collar, as the collar may come off and the cat be lost.

Cats prefer to take their own exercise, but there are some instances when this is inadvisable:

(1) If home is a flat, without a garden or means of access by a cat flap.

(2) If home is a house near to a very dangerous road.

(3) When allowing rehomed strays out for the first time; when you allow your cats out for the first time after moving house.

(4) When exercising pedigree cats who are entire and may roam.

(5) During early days in the garden for kittens who have reached the adventurous stage – around four to six months.

(6) In the case of elderly cats with failing hearing, eyesight and sense of smell.

(7) In the case of blind, disabled or convalescent cats.

(8) In the case of those with feline leukaemia or other immunosuppressive virus, who must not come into contact with other cats.

There are adult ex-strays who take to a harness and lead immediately, but most cats, from about six months old, need a period of introduction. Start with a safety collar, followed by the harness worn for a short time, then the lead; follow this with exercise indoors, then outdoors away from traffic, and finally on the pavement of a busy road.

A harness must be soft and bear no stitching or staples which may

FIGURE 45   Cat wearing a collar, harness and lead.

come undone. It should be strong (toothproof), seamless, washable, quick-drying and fitted to allow ease of movement coupled with safety. The Hagen 'H' harness, shown in Figure 46, has all these advantages. It is very simple to fit, consisting of two buckled straps: a short one fitted round the neck and a longer one fitted round the tum, just behind the front legs. It is made of strong nylon, with all seams heat-bonded and therefore safe and smooth. The material is open-weave, so that no eyelets are necessary – the prongs of the buckle slip into the strap at any point, thus ensuring an exact fit. The lead has a strong trigger hook and wrist strap. Available in

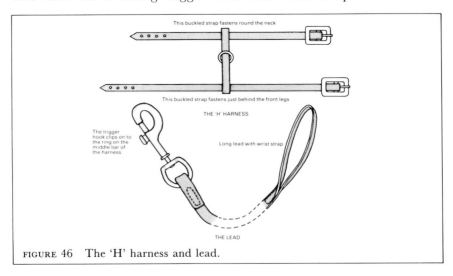

FIGURE 46   The 'H' harness and lead.

several colours from pet shops, the harness costs £2.75 and the lead £1.75.

Although it may be necessary to change wrists while using the lead, it must be borne in mind that the greatest danger is that the cat will escape wearing harness and lead, which could then get caught up in some way and injure or even strangle him. Always use the wrist strap when leading your cat, and hold the lead additionally with your fingers. The cat should also wear a quick-release safety collar bearing his address and telephone number).

MISSING FROM HOME — THE CAT OWNER'S NIGHTMARE

One of the greatest tragedies that can befall a cat owner is a missing cat. Cats will not respond to frantic human calls unless they want to, so tramping the streets, plate-tapping and calling your cat's name may prove ineffective.

Every year thousands of cats disappear. Where do they all go? The possibilities are endless: they may be 'rescued' by a well-meaning neighbour, and decide to live with her instead; they may enter a parked car and be transported hundreds of miles from home; cats approaching sexual maturity may leave home; many escape from cat baskets or new homes; some decide to take a few weeks' holiday in the woods during high summer, living off the land; many, probably young cats who have not acquired road sense, or old cats whose hearing and sight have deteriorated, are victims of road accidents; and moving house is always a dangerous time.

The worst heartbreak is not knowing the fate of your cat. A quick-release safety collar bearing the cat's address and telephone number will ensure he is returned home if he makes contact with humans, but not always. Cases have been reported of lonely people who deliberately 'adopt' an attractive, personable cat, knowing him to be owned.

Most de-sexed cats remain within a radius of 200–300 yards of home. Once lost, they may stay in an area for a few weeks and then move further from home. For this reason, search procedures should be instigated at once.

SEARCH PROCEDURES
(1) Search your own premises thoroughly: cupboards, deep freeze, washing machine, refrigerator, car, garage, garden shed.

(2) Prepare circulars giving details of your cat. While delivering these, search by torchlight all hedgerows and front gardens bordering roads. Cats struck by cars crawl away to hide, if able. Where time is limited, or in a very densely populated area, place circulars in the letterboxes of Number 1 house in a road (the odd-number side) and Number 2 house (the even-number side) requesting that notes be passed on to the next house on the same side of the road. These two simple measures will often locate kittens and adolescents found by concerned neighbours.

(3) Cats resent uprooting from their beloved territories and may head back to an old home, however long they are kept in at a new one. Exercise on a harness and lead at the new home may help prevent this as the cat becomes accustomed to new sights, scents, sounds and neighbouring people, cats and dogs whilst under control and in the company of his owner. If your cat disappears shortly after moving house, it is always wise to alert the new occupants of your old home and your former neighbours. The so-called 'homing' instinct of cats is over-rated; admittedly some find their way back to their old home, but most become lost, hungry strays, or victims of traffic accidents.

(4) Caring people, on finding a cat injured, may take him to their own vet, not necessarily the nearest one. Telephone all vets in a 10-mile (16-kilometre) radius. At the same time request details of any local animal rescue centres they may know, where an injured cat might have been taken. Look up other addresses under 'Animal Welfare Societies' in the Yellow Pages. These, again, may be able to give you details of other unlisted welfare societies. There may be delay before a found cat is taken into care. Rescue societies are very busy, too busy to telephone the numerous frantic owners of lost cats, so keep telephoning them each day. Descriptions of lost cats can be very deceptive, so go round all the rescue societies, and look at all cats recently taken in. Addresses and telephone numbers of branches of the Cats Protection League are obtainable by ringing the headquarters at Horsham (see Appendix I).

(5) Cats found wandering or injured may be reported to the police who regard them as 'lost property'. Some constabularies show concern and interest, and will know if any cat thieves have been reported operating in their area. Stolen cats have been abandoned many miles away from home. Telephone all police stations in a 20-mile (32-kilometre) radius.

(6) Wide publicity is important. Arrange for eye-catching notices to be displayed in as many shops as possible, on local notice boards, in vets' surgeries, post offices and so on. Stick notices on gates, trees,

fences – ensure that the public know your cat is missing. Leaflets can be distributed by post offices with the morning mail, or by newsagents with the daily national or local papers. Local children can be paid to deliver notices or form search parties, but they must be warned never to search in lonely woods or fields unless accompanied by an adult. Local schools may be prepared to give out details at morning assembly, or display notices. If you obtain a positive 'siting', intensify the search in that area. Always offer a reward, as much as you can afford, and state the amount. Use as many colour photographs in key positions as you can. Many cats 'found' will prove to belong to a neighbour, so ensure that, if brought to your door, they are returned whence they came.

(7) Friendly, fearless cats sometimes follow people who stop to stroke them. Cats have been enticed away from the front garden wall of their home by children – to meet their deaths on distant roads. Question regular passers-by who may have noticed this happening. A home-loving but aggressive cat may follow a would-be feline tres-passer out of his area and become lost: try to locate the homes of strange cats visiting your garden and search the area around them.

(8) Insert advertisements in the classified colums of all local papers under, for example, 'Cats' and 'Lost and Found'. Search these columns for 'found' cats. Offer a reward.

(9) Contact your local council to enquire whether ferals, strays or colonies attached to hospitals, warehouses, and so on, are being trapped. Contact refuse departments to ask if any dead cats have been removed from roadsides.

(10) Contact local farmers for permission to check rabbit traps. Cats are often shot accidentally (sometimes deliberately) by shotguns or airguns. Ask of farmers whether there are shooting rights on their land, or if they have seen poachers. Ask to check any cat colonies on farms.

(11) Contact a national charity called Petwatch. They have a network of Missing Pets' Bureaux. For details write to PO Box 16, Brighouse, W. Yorks, HD6 1DS, enclosing a stamped, self-addressed envelope.

(12) Your cat may have entered a parked vehicle and been driven away. Contact drivers of any vehicles who may have visited your road that day – Gas, Electricity or Water Boards, British Telecom, removal vans, grocers' vans – and ask the name of the road where they made their next stop.

(13) Ask for an appeal to be sent out by your local radio station. Ask owners of Citizens' Band radios for help.

11 A Cat About the Home

CAT DOORS

Many owners are forced to leave their cats for long periods and a cat door (or cat flap), fitted into the back door of the house, allows a cat to come and go at will. If the home is left for short periods, it is reasonably safe to shut cats out in the garden as long as it is dog-proof and has trees for extra protection and some cover in the event of sudden storms. Alternatively, for short periods cats may be shut in the house, with toilet trays, but the risk of fire must be taken into account.

Cat doors have their disadvantages. They are bolt holes for escape from 'enemies', so entry must be rapid and easy for the cat. If opened by a device attached to a collar, this must ensure rapid entry. It must be borne in mind that a *safe* collar must release, and if the collar is lost, the cat will be shut out.

Ordinary cat flaps may allow in not only your own cat but also most other cats in the neighbourhood, including, almost certainly, a full tom who finds it necessary to spray in your house! Your own cat too, if a hunter, will bring in prey, alive or dead, mouldy bread, old bones, and mud from the garden will be trailed all over the house. On wet days it may be preferable to restrict entry to a kitchen or back hall, and blot paws on tissue before allowing access to the main house.

There are many types of ready-made cat flap on the market, or they can be home-made by sawing out a panel about 7½ × 9½ inches (20 × 25 centimetres) from a back door and refitting the panel on hinges. This can be constructed so that the cat enters and leaves by the same method – that is, by pushing it open with his head. Alternatively, a sliding panel may be preferred. This is made slightly larger than the actual sawn-out panel to prevent draughts, and slides open or closed on grooved battens. It can remain open during the day for quick entry.

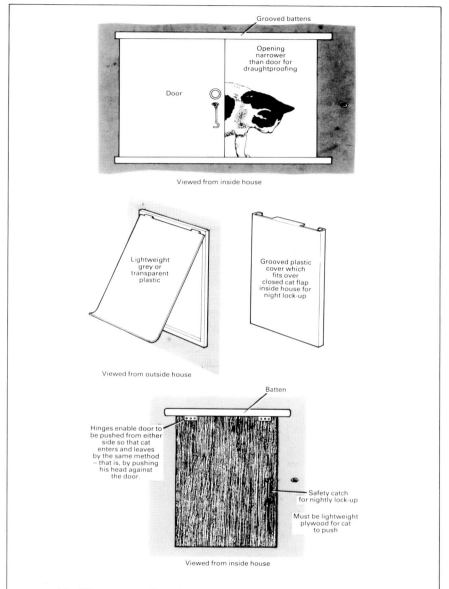

FIGURE 47   Three types of cat door, made by cutting a panel out of a door –
usually a back door leading to the garden.

CLEANING THE HOUSE

Upholstery, bedding, curtains, carpets and clothing will inevitably
collect fur, however much a cat is groomed. A powerful suction

vacuum cleaner will be needed – at least 1000 watts. Fur can also be removed with a damp sponge cloth or one of the patent fabric brushes.

If there is a choice, carpets should be washable, shrinkproof and not tacked down around the edges. Such a carpet, if soiled, can be washed by placing a bowl beneath the soiled area, and pouring through the carpet, into the bowl, warm water to which a few drops of liquid detergent have been added. After rinsing, excess water is removed with a towel and the carpet allowed to dry.

THE MULTICAT GARDEN

About half the population of the UK are cat lovers – the other half are not! Non-cat lovers justifiably resent cats killing birds, scratching up their seedlings and worrying their pigeons and pet rabbits. It is always best to discuss a cat problem with new neighbours, and encourage them to spray visiting cats with a jet of water from a washing-up liquid bottle, reinforced by hand-clapping and shouting. This way, it is to be hoped, cats will remain in your garden, on commonland or in woodland, and neighbours will not find it necessary to resort to more extreme tactics to get rid of cats – like brick-throwing!

In the cat domestication is merely a veneer. Cats stay with us because of what we have to offer; if they do not like what is on offer, they 'vote with their feet', leave home, and often find another offering more acceptable food or company. This somewhat cavalier attitude of cats towards owners is reinforced by the well-meaning neighbour who insists that any cat traversing her garden is a 'stray' and rewards him with food whenever he pays a visit. Cats are essentially creatures of the wild woods and should be allowed as much freedom as possible. If your house borders a busy road, your cats may have to be confined and exercised on a harness and lead (see page 197).

An ideal cat garden is ¼ acre (0.1 hectare) upwards, completely enclosed with a 10-foot- (3-metre)-high chainlink fence, with metal posts. This will confine most cats. Even a 3-foot- (1-metre)-high wire-mesh fence will contain kittens and non-agile, lazy, stay-at-home and old cats. Above all, an ordinary fence will exclude dogs. Some breeds of dogs, like lurchers and fox hounds, are bred to kill and cannot be expected to distinguish between a rabbit, fox or cat. Now that the RSPCA openly opposes foxhunting, it is to be hoped that such horrifying incidents as foxhounds tearing cats and dogs to pieces in private gardens may be events of the past.

If cats are very young, very old or unable to climb, they should be confined. Enclosing a whole garden is very expensive, but small areas could be enclosed, or a large fruit cage used. For the average cat, trees provide a means of escape from hostile animals, even other cats, and at least two standard-sized trees (possibly fruit trees) should be planted.

A garden should be made interesting for cats, particularly from March to November, when most cats like to spend whole days sleeping or playing outdoors. However, some cats, even de-sexed ones, will never stay in a garden, and continue to roam.

Cats like to sleep in deep shade in hot weather and in dappled shade in warm weather, and they like the shelter of huge-leaved plants like rhubarb during summer showers. Tall, bushy perennials will provide dense cover and 'jungle' conditions. Other plants of use to cats are:

Catnip, catnep or European catmint (*Nepeta cataria*): Cats love to roll in this plant, and sometimes eat it. When dried and crushed it is used to make catnip mice. (Fun fur and cotton corduroy are strong cat-proof materials which are ideal for these toys.) Although a perennial, it is not hardy in a severe winter, and some plants must be well protected from cats and allowed to seed. Young plants will need protection from cats with wire.

Catmint (*Nepeta mussini*): This is not quite so attractive to cats as catnip, but its beautiful lavender flowers are far more attractive to humans! Again, it can be used to stuff cat toys. Most at home in dry, chalky soil, it is hardy and can be increased by cuttings. It is not known why cats find this plant, and others, so attractive but, like all plants, it contains an insecticide (in this case, nepetalactone).

Great valerian or cat's valerian (*Valeriana officinalis*): This spectacular perennial with pink or white flowers grows to 4 feet (120 centimetres)

FIGURE 48 A mouse made of strong fabric, stuffed with dried catmint or catnip, is greatly enjoyed by cats.

in height. Cats drool over it; according to some writers the base of the plant smells like leather to felines.

Micromeria corsica, sage, rosemary and *thyme* are attractive to some cats.

Actinidia kolomikta is a very attractive climbing shrub with green leaves splashed with pink and white. Cats love to rub this, and it may need some protection when young. If the leaves are tossed on a garden bonfire, cats savour the vapour and drool and roll on the ground.

Abbotswood rose (*Lychnis coronaria*) and *lamb's ears* (*Stachys lanata*) have soft woolly leaves which make ideal cat beds (and probably a local flea exchange!).

Fennel and *gypsophila* are well frequented by cats because of their dappled shade.

Seedlings and newly planted stock will need protection from cats with pea guards of small wire mesh. Wire can be fastened round tree trunks to avoid damage by cats. For the rest of the garden, cat manure is excellent!

Rough fencing posts or tree trunks laid horizontally throughout the garden will provide ample claw-maintenance posts.

Couch grass usually grows in abundance in the garden, whether wanted or not, especially in rockeries. If introduced into a garden, it is wise to confine it with a metal or wood square, sunk into the ground around the roots.

An area covered with peat may encourage cats to dig toilet holes there rather than in the middle of the seed bed. It can be periodically spread over the garden, or dug in, and replaced with new peat.

All cats select dry, sandy, loose earth for dustbathing. If this is not provided cats will make their own dustbaths, bringing death to resident plants. Areas can be kept dry during a period of wet weather by covering with polythene. Cats find cloches attractive to sleep in on cool, rainy days.

Cats dislike getting their feet wet, unless there is a reward like a goldfish from an uncovered garden pond! They enjoy sleeping on paving slabs, which dry rapidly after rain and retain the sun's heat on cooler days.

Cats cannot be expected to do anything useful in the garden but, presented with a cabbage patch attracting hordes of cabbage white butterflies, they may catch and kill many. Their presence in a garden will deter pigeons and other birds from making a meal of vegetables and fruit, at least until the cats fall asleep!

It is true to say that there is no garden pesticide or herbicide which is safe to use near cats, or any other animal, including man, come to that. It is only the *concentration* which makes such products reasonably safe to use, and it cannot be stressed too much that the manufacturers' instructions must always be followed to the letter. As far as cats are concerned, they will lick any contaminant off their fur or pads, however toxic. All weedkillers must be diluted strictly according to instructions, and allowed to dry before cats are allowed out into the garden. Slug killer must be applied at the rate of one pellet every foot (30 centimetres) and preferably covered with wire mesh or a flower pot hung upside down on a stick. Always store unfinished garden poison containers well out of reach of your cats.

Nearly all plants, at some time in their life cycle, contain substances poisonous to insects and therefore often poisonous also to cats and other animals. This is a plant's way of protecting itself. A few plants can be dried and used to repel fleas from a cat's bedding, for example pyrethrum. Most house plants, berries such as holly and ivy, and seeds such as laburnum, are poisonous if eaten by a cat in large quantities. All depends on the amount swallowed. Small amounts of poison are removed by the kidneys without harm to the body.

SPRAYING

Spraying urine is as much part of a cat's body language as the gentle tail-tip twitch of acknowledgment or mild annoyance or the rapid, full-tail swish of anger. Like all body language, urine spraying can express several emotions and varies from cat to cat.

It is, therefore, surprising that very few cats spray regularly in the house, although most adult cats of both sexes spray-urinate in gardens. It is true to say that owners of more than one cat are more likely to encounter the problem of house spraying. Cats in large communities are more likely to behave like wild cats. Spraying may be temporary – perhaps indicating resentment on the introduction of a new adult cat or pleasure at the arrival of a new kitten. There is no cure for the permanent sprayer, who has probably sprayed unrecognized from kittenhood. Unfortunately, he can do irreparable damage to upholstery, curtains and paintwork. The house will have an odour which visitors will find unbearable but which is unnoticed by the occupants because of their familiarity with it!

The cat owner should be aware that inveterate sprayers will not adapt to human needs; we have to adapt to *them*. It is not ethical to expect cats to behave like humans, for cats are another race with another culture and another set of rules.

Many remedies have been suggested for adult cats, usually males, who insist on spraying a few drops of urine here and there in the house. Some may work for some cats. It is not possible to 'train' a cat, least of all train him not to spray, because spraying is, to him, a natural activity. A loud 'No!', a slap on the rump, a clang of a saucepan lid, a tweak of the upturned tail – all may result only in a look of hurt surprise from your cat and a deterioration of your relationship. Other remedies include: dabbing vinegar, oil of citronella or human perfumes on favoured spraying targets; or hanging lemon peel, tinkling bells or shimmering aluminium foil on these sites. Vets may prescribe Ovarid, but in view of the dangers of long-term use, it is not advisable.

It is important to remember that an adult who *suddenly* begins to spray may be suffering from cystitis (see page 114), in which case veterinary treatment is urgently needed.

As night and bad-weather accommodation for the incurable sprayer, the only alternative to an outdoor unit is a modified indoor room similar to that described on page 160. A sprayer can never be allowed in the main house unless to sleep or under strict supervision. Exclusion from carpeted areas is a wise precaution. On fine days he should be shut out in the garden: a tired sprayer is more likely to sleep soundly and not spend the night spraying the walls of his room.

Once a sprayer has been dealt with as described, the house will have to be thoroughly washed and upholstery, carpets and curtains probably replaced. The merest whiff of spray will put ideas into other domiciled cats' heads and they may be encouraged to follow his example.

GROOMING

Some cats enjoy being groomed, most tolerate it for only a few minutes, and one or two fly into an uncontrollable rage at the sight of a comb!

Certain parts of a cat's body are constantly being destroyed and renewed. This applies not only to fur, skin and claws, but to blood and bone as well. All cats constantly shed fur, which will collect in the stomach to some extent, however much grooming is carried out.

Healthy, well-fed, domestic cats should only lose fur in appreciable quantities during the period of maximum moult, coinciding with the

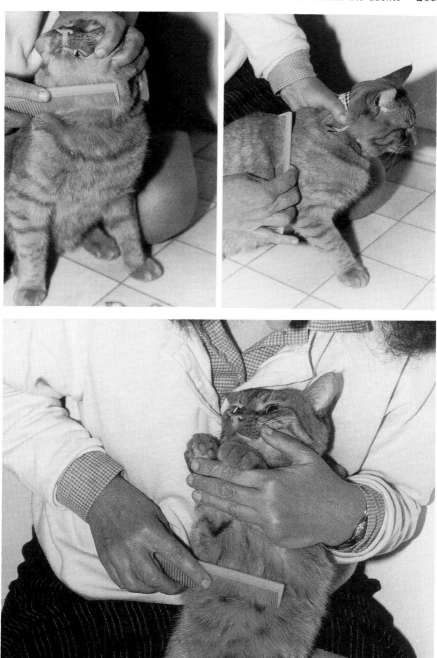

FIGURE 49 Grooming. Start with the chin and neck, move on to the flanks and back legs, and raise the cat on his hind legs to groom his underparts.

advent of warm weather in early summer. This maximum moult seldom takes place until the cat's second summer. It should be a brief affair, not longer than about fourteen days. If moulting occurs at other times, it may be due to an extra hot, humid spell; the incubation of an infection or other illness; or, if following de-sexing, a lack of sex hormones.

The aims of grooming are:
(1) To remove as much loose fur as possible to minimize the amount swallowed by the cat.
(2) To minimize the amount of fur adhering to upholstery, carpets and human clothing.
(3) To improve the appearance of the cat and remove grass seed, burrs, slugs and so on from the fur.
(4) To allow a routine inspection of the skin and fur for parasites.
(5) To locate injuries, inflamed or bald patches, abscesses, tumours and so on. Any area which needs treatment or further investigation should be marked by cutting away the fur.
(6) To prepare a cat for showing.

Grooming should be carried out in strong light, using a large, light-coloured comb with both fine and coarse teeth long enough to reach down to the skin where loose fur collects. Combs are more efficient than brushes, and can be washed and sterilized easily. Raise the fur and examine the skin, backcombing against the lie of the fur (cat permitting). Then finish with the lie of the fur. This can be done in sections, starting with the chin and neck (acceptable areas for most cats), and moving on to the flanks and back legs. Raise the cat on his hind legs to groom his underparts, then his 'trousers' and tail. Some animals may allow only minimal grooming, so a section may have to be done one day, another the next and so on. Some intractable cats may have to be groomed literally 'on the move'. During the period of maximum moult or when grooming has been neglected, felty, matted portions of fur may have to be cut out with scissors: hold the lump to be cut between your fingers so as not to nick the cat's skin.

Perhaps the easiest method of grooming, often undetected by the cat, is to raise the fur with your fingers and tweak out loose fur. This can be done on an unsuspecting cat when he is receptive to human attention. Dampening the hands will make grooming even easier, for the fur will then stick to your hands and is easily removed.

Daily grooming is usual for all cats during the period of maximum moult. At other times, twice a week for long-hairs and once a week for short-hairs is ample.

Sources of Information

Perspectives on Cats. This is a newsletter published four times a year and written by vets and other cat specialists at the Cornell Feline Health Center, College of Veterinary Medicine, Ithaca, NY 14853, USA. The purpose of the Health Center is to improve the health of cats everywhere by developing methods to prevent or cure feline diseases and by providing continuing education to vets and cat owners. Membership is $15 per annum. The Center has published a book entitled *Felis domesticus: A Manual of Feline Health* (about £8 – exact price on application).

The Feline Advisory Bureau (FAB), 350 Upper Richmond Road, Putney, SW15 6TL. Telephone (01) 789 9553. Apply to this address for information on membership. Boarding cattery information is available from: Miss S. M. Hamilton-Moore, 1 Church Close, Orcheston, Salisbury, Wilts. FAB is a registered charity.

The Cats Protection League (CPL), 17 Kings Road, Horsham, West Sussex, RH13 5PP. Telephone Horsham (0403) 65566. A registered charity whose aims are: to rescue stray and unwanted cats and kittens, rehabilitate and rehome them where possible; to inform the public on the care of cats and kittens; to encourage the neutering of all cats not required for breeding. Membership costs £5 per annum (UK), $15 (USA/Canada). The official journal, called *The Cat*, is published six times a year. Numerous pamphlets on cat care are published by the CPL, which will be sent free on receipt of a large, stamped, self-addressed envelope.

The People's Dispensary for Sick Animals (PDSA), a registered charity, has numerous branches throughout the country. Its headquarters are at South Street, Dorking, Surrey. Telephone Dorking 888291.

The Royal Society for the Prevention of Cruelty to Animals (RSPCA), a registered charity, has numerous branches – see your local Yellow Pages under 'Animal Welfare Societies'. The headquarters are at The Causeway, Horsham, West Sussex. Telephone Horsham (0403) 64181.

Cat World is a monthly magazine for all cat lovers – owners of pedigree and mongrel cats, cat breeders and animal rescue organizations. It contains articles by vets, show judges, breeders, cat lovers and fiction writers. The subscription is £6 per half year or £12 per year. The affiliated Cat Association

(CA) holds shows for pedigree and non-pedigree cats. *Cat World Annual* is published in December. Details from: Cat World Ltd, Scan House, Southwick Street, Southwick, Brighton, BN4 4TE. Telephone Brighton (0273) 595944.

Cats, the only weekly publication available, acts as the official journal of the Governing Council of the Cat Fancy (GCCF). As such, it is the only magazine to carry judges' show reports, which makes it essential reading for any real cat-show enthusiast. However, the contents are varied and also cover more general subjects on cats, with regular special features on different breeds and products. There is usually a *Cats* stand at main cat shows, selling a range of books, pedigree forms, *Cats* sweatshirts and back magazine issues. Each December an annual of over 120 pages is produced – copies being available from *Cats*, 5 James Leigh Street, Manchester, M1 6EX. Telephone (061) 236 0577. The GCCF organizes the Supreme Cat Show at Olympia in early December, where many suppliers of cat products and animal charities exhibit. The Supreme Cat Show has classes for pedigree and non-pedigree cats. Exhibitors' advice is very useful for all those involved in the care of cats and those wishing to set up a boarding/breeding/rescue cattery.

VetHealth, The Animal Care Centre, Little Tey Road, Feering, Colchester, Essex. Telephone (0206) 212444. This organization publishes information on disease control and health maintenance for both cats and dogs. It also supplies disinfectants, mineral/vitamin supplements and Vortex vaporizers.

Lever Industrial, PO Box 87, Lever House, Wood Street, Bebington, Wirral, Merseyside, L62 4ZH. Telephone (051) 644 8144. This company publishes pamphlets on the use of disinfectants. It can provide bulk supplies of Domestos, one-stage cleaners/disinfectants, bactericidal soaps, QUATs and other products of use to cattery owners.

ERRATUM

Cat World is a totally independent publication and is not affiliated to the Cat Association (as stated on page 211) or any other body.

Stockists of Cat Equipment and Accommodation

Many of the following firms exhibit and give advice at the many cat shows held throughout the year. Guidance has been given in this book on choosing boarding cat accommodation. As far as equipment is concerned, it is impossible to generalize. Most equipment is excellent, some is useless and some dangerous. Much depends on the individual cat – the only way to find out whether it suits a particular cat is to try it out. Most firms will send a catalogue on application.

Agriframes Cat Runs, Agriframes Ltd, Charlwoods Road, East Grinstead, Sussex, RH19 2HG. Telephone 0342 28644.

Ralph Allen Eng., Forncett-end, Norwich, NR16 1HT. Telephone Bunwell (095389) 420.

Animal Control Equipment, M D Components, 16 Havelock Road, Luton, Beds, LU2 0PE. Telephone (0582) 20428.

Catac Products, Catac House, Bedford. Telephone (0234) 60116.

Challoner Marketing Ltd, Raans Road, Amersham, Bucks, HP6 6HT. Telephone Amersham 21270. (Suppliers of cat beds.)

Cromessol Co. Ltd, 279 Drakemire Drive, Glasgow, G45. Telephone 0416 34 1195. (Suppliers of disinfectant air spray.)

M. A. Drayton Ltd, Laughton, Gainsborough, Lincs. Telephone Laughton (042782) 381.

E. & J. Accessories, 197a Galliard Road, Edmonton, London, N9. Telephone (01) 807 0927.

Ellmere Ltd, 36J Hartlebury Trading Estate, Hartlebury, Kidderminster, Worcs. Telephone (0299) 250033. (Suppliers of heating pads.)

Grange Aviaries & Pet Centre, Dept. CW6, Hillier Garden Centre, Woodhouse Lane, Botley, Southampton. Telephone Botley (04892) 81260. (Suppliers of accommodation.)

Hamster Baskets, Much Marcle, Ledbury, Herefordshire, HR8 2PD. Telephone (053) 183 209.

Harkinee Pet Supplies, 37 Cecil Street, Lytham, FY8 5NN.

Jaybeds, 12 Fernleigh Cottages, Harrop Street, Stockport, Cheshire, SK1 3JP. Telephone (061) 477 1591. (Suppliers of bean bags, etc.)

Jesters, Glebe Road, Dorking, Surrey, RH4 3DS. Telephone (0306) 888132.

Ladymead Pet Supplies Ltd, The Orchard, Grove Road, Little Clacton, Essex. Telephone (0255) 861886.

J. & A. Leonard, Rose Cottage, Quidhamptom, Salisbury, Wilts. Telephone Salisbury (0722) 642112. (Suppliers of white cat blankets.)

Lindee Lu Products, Unit 4, Taveners, Southfield Road, Nailsea, Avon. Telephone (0272) 853800. (Suppliers of accommodation.)

M D Components, 16 Havelock Road, Luton, Beds, LU2 0PE. Telephone (0582) 20428.

Moncaster, Belvoir Way, Fairfield Industrial Estate, Louth, Lincs, LN11 0JG. Telephone (0507) 606724. (Wire-mesh specialists.)

Mortimers, Salters Lane, Lower Moor, Pershore, Worcs, WR10 2PQ. Telephone Evesham (0386) 860677. (Suppliers of pet beds.)

A. Neaverson & Sons, Ltd, Peakirk, Peterborough, PE6 7NN. Telephone Peterborough 252225. (Suppliers of accommodation.)

G. N. Officer, c/o Cats Protection League, 17 Kings Road, Horsham, West Sussex, RH13 5PP. Telephone Horsham (0403) 65566. (Supplier of quick-release safety collars.)

Petdoors Ltd, PO Box 10, Romford, Essex, RM1 4HX.

Petnap, Section L16, Spinkes Works, The Causeway, Chippenham, Wilts. Telephone (0249) 650644. (Suppliers of pet beds.)

Jean Pratt, Cat Books for Cat Lovers, Farnham Common, Bucks, SL2 3QH.

Rayners (Buildings) Ltd, Llanaway Works, Guildford Road, Godalming, Surrey, GU7 3HR. Telephone Godalming 6242.

Scotts of Thrapston, Bridge Street, Thrapston, Northants, NN14 4LR. Telephone (08012) 2366. (Suppliers of accommodation.)

Uropets (Dept. LB 12), 37b Mildway Grove, London, N1. Telephone (01) 226 1734.

Vetbed, Elvan Pet Supplies, 3 Coverfield, Hanley, Swan, Worcester, WR8 0EG. Telephone (0684) 310590.

Westpole Products Ltd, Dept. C, 4 Centre Way, London, N9 0AP. Telephone (01) 807 8978.

SUPPLIERS OF PLANTS FOR CAT GARDENS

Bressingham Gardens, Bressingham, Diss, Norfolk, IP22 2AB. Telephone Bressingham (037 988) 464. Catalogue £1.

The Herb Garden, Cae Rhos Lligwy, Brynteg, Tyn-y-gongl, Anglesey, Gwynedd, North Wales. Telephone Tyn-y-gongl 853407. Catalogue 50p.

Hopleys Plants Ltd, Much Hadham, Herts. Telephone (027 984) 2509. Catalogue 50p.

Examples of Record Sheets

ACCOUNT BOOK

An example of the layout of an account book is given below. As each page is completed, it is totalled and the total is brought forward on to the next page.

At the end of the financial year the total expenditure is subtracted from the total income. The difference will be the net profit.

Bear in mind that *major* repairs to capital expenditure items (such as units) are usually included in the total estimated value of that item at the end of the year, and are recorded separately.

Page 1
April 1987

DATE	INCOME	£	DATE	EXPENDITURE	£
8	Boarding (Smith)	50.00	8	Litter	10.50
				Domestos	5.00
	Boarding (Taylor)	20.00		Milk	4.00
				Mince	20.00
9	Boarding (Johnson)	60.00	9	Rubber shoes	10.00
	Boarding (Dynes)	50.00		Trays (2)	7.00
	Carried forward	180.00		*Carried forward*	56.50

Page 2
April 1987

DATE	INCOME	£	DATE	EXPENDITURE	£
	Brought forward	180.00		*Brought forward*	56.50
12	Boarding (Grimm)	50.00	12	Overalls (2)	10.00
				Stationery	20.00
	Boarding (Jones)	60.00		Postage	6.50
	etc., etc.			etc., etc.	

MONTHLY BOOKING SHEET

April 1987

UNITS	W	T	F	S	S	M	T	W	T	F	S	S	M	T	W	T	F	S	S	M	T	W	T	F	S	S	M	T	W	T	F	S	S	M
	1	2	3	4	5	6	7	8	9	10	11	12	13	14	15	16	17	18	19	20	21	22	23	24	25	26	27	28	29	30				
1						(S O O T Y S M I T H)																												
2	March 1987			(F I O N A J O N E S)———————————→																													
3																																		
4																																		

This form should be kept near the telephone and filled in *in pencil* for provisional bookings. On arrival of boarder, the booking should be inked in. Three or four of these forms may be needed, pinned together, so that any bookings overlapping from the previous month and advance bookings for the next month can be seen. The sheets can be duplicated, and only the month and days need completion by hand.

INFORMATION SHEET ON CURRENT BOARDERS

April 1987

UNITS	M 1	T 2	W 3	T 4	F 5	S 6	S 7	M 8	T 9	W 10	T 11	F 12	S 13	S 14	M 15	T 16	W 17	T 18	F 19	S 20	S 21	M 22	T 23	W 24	T 25	F 26	S 27	S 28	M 29	T 30	W	T	F	S	S	M
1	(SOOTY SMITH)													etc., etc.																						
		F UV	U	F U	F U	D U	U																													
2	March 1987	(FIONA JONES)											etc., etc.																							
		F UV	D U	D U	F U	F U	F U																													
3																																				
4																																				

In this example: F = defecated; D = diarrhoea; U = urinated; V = vomited.

This sheet, which is exactly the same as the Monthly Booking Sheet, can be hung at the entrance to each unit (provided it can be kept dry), or kept on the office notice board. It can be used to record any information the proprietor considers necessary. Entries must be made daily.

RECORD SHEET

Owner

Surname..............................Initials ....

Address ....

....

Tel. no. (Home) ....(Holiday) ....

Holiday address ....

Tel. no. of friend/relative (in case owner cannot be contacted)...........

Name, address and tel. no. of usual vet ....

....

Cat

Name of cat...............................Date of birth ....

Arrival date................................Departure date...........................

Description: Long-/Short-hair   Coat colour...................................

Sex: Male/Female/Neutered/Spayed/Entire tom/Queen

Recent or recurrent infectious or non-infectious diseases (e.g., sinusitis, cystitis, flea bite allergy) ....

Allergies (e.g., allergic to milk, canned catfood, vegetables)...............

Usual diet and approx. quantity of food per meal...............................

....

Special instructions (e.g., 2 tbs milk only per day, ½ tablet Pet Tabs Feline per day)..

Usual toilet-tray filler..

Normal temperament (e.g., unco-operative with strangers, needs human attention) ....

Date of booster vaccination (FP)..

Date of booster vaccination (Cat flu) ....

Notes for cattery use, e.g., details of any medical/deparasitization treatments, can be entered on the back of the form.

Current record sheets should be referred to daily. On departure of cat, these should be filed in alphabetical order under surname of owner.

DISPOSAL FORM

If I fail to collect...[name of cat] within one month of the specified departure date, the...................................

.... [name of cattery] reserves the right to rehome the cat.

Signed ....(Owner)   Date ....

FORM AUTHORIZING VETERINARY TREATMENT

I accept that my cat is boarded at my own risk. Should my cat, in the opinion of the ....

[name of cattery] require veterinary treatment, I hereby authorize this treatment to be carried out, and undertake payment of any fees due, on receipt of the veterinary surgeon's account.

Signed ....(Owner)   Date ....

RELEASE FORM

I hereby certify that I have received my cat from.............................

.... [name of cattery] in a satisfactory condition.

Signed ....(Owner)   Date ....

REHOMING FORM

I undertake to obtain veterinary advice should...................................

[name of cat] appear ill, and undertake to have him/her neutered/ spayed on or about...[date recommended by rescue organization]

Signed ....(New owner)   Date ....

The first two forms are signed by the owner on the cat's arrival. The third is signed by the owner on collection. The fourth form is used by animal rescue organizations. Rehomed cats are usually rehomed on a trial basis for a few weeks.

Index